SILICON LITERACIES

'This wide-ranging discussion of digital literacies in a fast-changing global world is essential for anyone interested in literacy and learning in or out of school.'

James Paul Gee, *University of Wisconsin at Madison*, USA

'An invaluable resource for anyone interested in the development of new literacies and the consequences for education.'

Chip Bruce, *University of Illinois at Urbana-Champaign*, USA

2005

Electronic communication is radically altering literacy practices. With the advent of screen-based technologies, made widely accessible via the Internet and the World Wide Web, written, oral and audiovisual modalities of communication have become integrated. Language now comprises a wider range of semiotic systems that cut across reading, writing, viewing and speaking.

Silicon Literacies unravels the key features of the new communication order to explore the social, cultural and educational impact of electronic literacy practices. Written by leading international scholars from a range of disciplines, the essays in this collection examine the implications of text produced on a keyboard, visible on a screen and transmitted through a global network of computers. The book covers topics as diverse as role-playing in computer games, the use of graphic symbols in onscreen texts and Internet degree programmes, to reveal that being literate is to do with understanding how different modalities combine to create meaning.

Recognising that reading and writing are only part of what people have to learn to be literate, the contributors enhance our understanding of the ways in which the use of new technologies influences, shapes and sometimes transforms literacy practices.

Ilana Snyder is Associate Professor in the Faculty of Education at Monash University, Australia. Her publications include *Hypertext* (Melbourne University Press and New York University Press, 1996), *Page to Screen* (Routledge and Allen & Unwin, 1998) and *Teachers and Technoliteracy: Managing Literacy, Technology and Learning in Schools*, with Colin Lankshear (Allen & Unwin, 2000).

LITERACIES
Series Editor: David Barton
Lancaster University

Literacy practices are changing rapidly in contemporary society in response to broad social, economic and technological changes: in education, the workplace, the media and in everyday life. The *Literacies* series has been developed to reflect the burgeoning research and scholarship in the field of literacy studies and its increasingly interdisciplinary nature. The series aims to situate reading and writing within its broader institutional contexts where literacy is considered as a social practice. Work in this field has been developed and drawn together to provide books which are accessible, interdisciplinary and international in scope, covering a wide range of social and institutional contexts.

CITY LITERACIES
Learning to Read Across Generations and Cultures
Eve Gregory and Ann Williams

LITERACY AND DEVELOPMENT
Ethnographic Perspectives
Edited by Brian V. Street

SITUATED LITERACIES
Theorising Reading and Writing in Context
Edited by David Barton, Mary Hamilton and Roz Ivanic

MULTILITERACIES
Literacy Learning and the Design of Social Futures
Edited by Bill Cope and Mary Kalantzis

GLOBAL LITERACIES AND THE WORLD-WIDE WEB
Edited by Gail E.Hawisher and Cynthia L. Selfe

STUDENT WRITING
Access, Regulation, Desire
Theresa M. Lillis

SILICON LITERACIES
Communication, Innovation and Education in the Electronic Age
Edited by Ilana Snyder

Editorial Board:

SILICON LITERACIES

Communication, innovation and education
in the electronic age

Edited by Ilana Snyder

London and New York

First published 2002
by Routledge
11 New Fetter Lane, London EC4P 4EE

Simultaneously published in the USA and Canada
by Routledge
29 West 35th Street, New York, NY 10001

Routledge is an imprint of the Taylor & Francis Group

© 2002 Ilana Snyder for selection and editorial matter; individual
contributors their contribution

Typeset in Baskerville by Taylor & Francis Books Ltd
Printed and bound in Great Britain by Biddles Ltd, Guildford and King's Lynn

British Library Cataloguing in Publication Data
A catalogue record for this book is available from the British Library

Library of Congress Cataloging in Publication Data
A catalog record for this book has been requested

ISBN 0–415–27667–5 (hbk)
ISBN 0–415–27668–3 (pbk)

FOR JOHN IREMONGER

CONTENTS

CONTENTS

FIGURES

CONTRIBUTORS

Chris Abbott is a Lecturer in ICT Education, the School of Education, King's College, University of London. He has written on issues of youth, identity, ICT and schooling, as well as on symbol use among learners with special needs. His most recent book is *ICT: Changing Education* (RoutledgeFalmer 2000).

Catherine Beavis is a Senior Lecturer in the School of Social and Cultural Studies, Faculty of Education, Deakin University. Her teaching and research focus on literacy, English, popular culture, technology and reading. Catherine's most recent book is *P(ICT)ures of English*, co-edited with Cal Durrant (AATE & Wakefield Press 2001).

Chris Bigum is an Associate Professor in the Faculty of Education and Creative Arts, Central Queensland University. His research and teaching interests include innovations in education, actor-network theory and digital epistemologies. With Leonie Rowan, Colin Lankshear and Michele Knobel, his latest book is *Boys, Literacies and Schooling* (Open University Press 2001).

Nicholas C. Burbules is Professor of Educational Policy Studies, University of Illinois, Urbana/Champaign. He publishes in philosophy of education, technology and education, and critical social and political theory. *Watch IT: The Promises and Risks of New Information Technologies for Education* (Westview Press 2000) was co-authored with Thomas A. Callister, Jr. He is also the editor of *Educational Theory*.

Ron Burnett is President, Emily Carr Institute of Art and Design and one of the founders of Film Studies in Canada. He is a digital videomaker, Web designer and author of *Cultures of Vision: Images, Media and the Imaginary* (Indiana University Press 1995). His forthcoming book is *How Images Think* (MIT Press).

J. Yellowlees Douglas is Associate Professor of English, University of Florida. She is the author of *The End of Books or Books without End? Reading Interactive Narratives* (University of Michigan Press 2000) and of the hypertext fiction *I Have Said Nothing* (Eastgate Systems 1994).

Michael Joyce is Associate Professor of English and Director of the Centre for Electronic Learning and Teaching at Vassar College. His hyperfictions include *Twilight, A Symphony* and *Twelve Blue* (Eastgate 1996). *Of Two Minds* (1995) and *Othermindedness* (2000) were both published by the University of Michigan Press.

Douglas M. Kellner is George Kneller Chair in the Philosophy of Education at UCLA and author of many books on social theory, politics, history, and culture, including *Media Culture* (Routledge 1995), and, with Steven Best, *The Postmodern Turn* (Guilford and Routledge 1997). Forthcoming books include *Grand Theft 2000: Media Spectacle and the Theft of an Election* (Rowman and Littlefield 2001).

Michele Knobel is an Adjunct Associate Professor, Central Queensland University, and a freelance education writer and researcher based in México. Her books include: *Everyday Literacies: Students, Discourse and Social Practice* (Peter Lang 1999) and *El Estudio Crítico-Social del Lenguaje y la Alfabetización* (IMCED 2000) with Colin Lankshear.

George P. Landow is Shaw Professor of English and Digital Culture and Dean, University Scholars Programme, National University of Singapore. His books on hypertext and digital culture include *Hypertext: The Convergence of Contemporary Critical Theory and Technology* (Hopkins University Press 1992, 1997) and *Hyper/Text/Theory* (Hopkins University Press 1994).

Colin Lankshear is a Visiting Researcher, Center for University Studies, National Autonomous University of Mexico, a freelance educational researcher and writer, and an Adjunct Professor, Central Queensland University. Recent books include *Ways of Knowing* with Michele Knobel (Primary English Teaching Association 1999) and *Curriculum in the Postmodern Condition* with Alicia de Alba, Edgar González Gaudiano and Michael Peters (2000).

Ilana Snyder is an Associate Professor in the Faculty of Education, Monash University. *Hypertext* (Melbourne University Press 1996), *Page to Screen* (Routledge 1998), and *Teachers and Technoliteracy*, co-authored with Colin Lankshear (Allen & Unwin 2000), explore changes to cultural practices associated with the use of ICTs.

Mark Warschauer is an Assistant Professor in the Department of Education, University of California, Irvine and editor of *Language Learning & Technology*. He is the author or editor of six books on language, literacy, culture, and technology, including *Electronic Literacies: Language, Culture, and Power in Online Learning* (Lawrence Erlbaum 1999).

ACKNOWLEDGEMENTS

The idea for this book sprang from a conversation with John Iremonger, Publisher at Allen and Unwin. With his characteristic enthusiasm, intellectual engagement and humour, John encouraged me to edit a collection of essays about the changes to communication practices that have emerged since *Page to Screen* was published in 1997. As the project developed, he continued to offer invaluable advice. I am most grateful for his generous involvement.

I thank David Barton, Lancaster University, for including the book in the *Literacies* series. Louisa Semlyen, Commissioning Editor at Routledge for English Language and Linguistics, has been excited by the project since its inception for which I am very appreciative. Christy Kirkpatrick and Lauren Dallinger have provided much help in the preparation of the manuscript. In the revision process, Barbara Kamler's critical reading of my two chapters proved to be most generative.

For permission to reproduce images from their software products and computer games, I thank Widget Software and Virgin Interactive. For permission to reproduce screens from websites, I thank the developers of the Meldreth Manor School website and the Majaky website. For permission to use the Milosz poem, I thank HarperCollins.

Finally, I owe special thanks to the contributors. Editing *Silicon Literacies* offered me a further opportunity to engage with imaginative ways of thinking about the intriguing connections between literacy practices and the use of the new communication media.

July 2001

INTRODUCTION

SILICON LITERACIES

Ilana Snyder

This book moves beyond narrowly defined explanations of literacy to understandings that capture the complexity of contemporary literacy practices within
a broader social order, what Brian Street (1998) and others have called a 'new
communicative order'. In particular, this new communication order takes
account of the literacy practices associated with screen-based technologies. It
recognises that reading and writing, considered traditionally as print-based and
logocentric, are only part of what people have to learn to be literate. Now, for
the first time in history, the written, oral and audiovisual modalities of communication are integrated into multimodal hypertext systems made accessible via
the Internet and the World Wide Web. Silicon literacy practices represent the
ways in which meanings are made within these new communication systems
(Snyder 2001a).

In an electronically mediated world, being literate is to do with understanding
how the different modalities are combined in complex ways to create meaning.
People have to learn to make sense of the iconic systems evident in computer
displays – with all the combinations of signs, symbols, pictures, words and
sounds. Language is no longer just grammar, lexicon and semantics: language
now comprises a wider range of semiotic systems that cut across reading, writing,
viewing and speaking (Snyder 2001b; Street 2001). What looks like the same text
or multimedia genre on paper or on screen is not functionally the same. It
follows different meaning conventions and requires different skills for its
successful use. Further, it operates in different social networks for different
purposes as part of different human activities (Lemke 1997). Understanding
these multimodal texts requires an interdisciplinary range of methods of analysis: linguistic, semiotic, social, cultural, historical and critical. –

The challenge for literacy educators is profound. Information and communication technologies (ICTs) cannot be dismissed merely as tools that prescribe
certain communication styles. As all media now interface in a manner both
complex and perplexing, teachers have to find ways to make sense of the 'information bricolage' (Burnett 1996: 71), to work through the labyrinth of material
with students to interpret its many different meanings and shifts in direction.
However, preparing the current generation of students to become literate is

3

difficult, not only because it is uncertain what the literacies of the future will be, but also because the task falls to educators who are not fully literate themselves in the use of these new technologies.

Silicon Literacies builds on the work begun in *Page to Screen* (Snyder 1997). The list of contributors includes some of the original line-up – Michele Knobel, Colin Lankshear, Jane Yellowlees Douglas, Nicholas Burbules, Michael Joyce and Catherine Beavis. But there are also some new names: George Landow, Chris Bigum, Ron Burnett, Douglas Kellner, Chris Abbott and Mark Warschauer. This new collection is not simply a reworking of its predecessor: none of the essays has been published before; they all offer fresh perspectives on the new communication order; each examines some aspect of the developments that have emerged in the field of literacy and technology studies over the past five years since *Page to Screen* was first published.

As editor, I have invited writers located not only in Education, but also in Composition, Literary, Media, Film and Cultural Studies. This decision reflects a belief in the usefulness of a wide range of theoretical and methodological approaches to research in literacy and technology studies as no one theory or method is adequate to engage the richness, complexity, variety and novelty displayed in contemporary assemblages of emerging silicon literacy practices (Snyder 2000). By attempting to overcome the boundaries of academic divisions, an interdisciplinary approach suggests multiple ways to analyse, evaluate and critique the new spaces, cultural forms and experiences. It also suggests new pedagogies which take account of the forms of knowledge, information, images and spectacles associated with the use of the technologies, or, as Kellner and Durham (2001: 28) describe them: 'the often distorted forms of knowledge, misinformation, deceptive images and seductive spectacles of the media and consumer society'. Individually, the writers endorse the value of engaging in the act of theoretical promiscuity, but never at the risk of sacrificing integrity and coherence. Collectively, their work bears testimony to the reality that literacy and technology studies is essentially an interdisciplinary endeavour.

Integral to *Silicon Literacies* are a number of key understandings about the contexts, both global and local, in which literacy and technology studies are located. First, this new communication order, centred around information technologies, is part of the technological revolution that is reshaping the material bases of society. New technologies have made massive incursions into all facets of life, albeit unevenly in different parts of the world. They have altered everyday modes of communication and are becoming so fundamental to society that most areas of social practice in day-to-day life are affected by the information revolution.

Second, the new communication order is embedded within a dominant political and ideological order that has its own distinctive interests and values. We are moving from the capitalist era which valued individualism, profit, competition and the market into a world of high tech and global capitalism. The prevailing contemporary ideas intrinsic to the new global capitalism are those that promote globalisation, new technologies and an unrestrained market society – ideas that further the interests of the new governing elites in the global economy (Castells 1996, 1997, 1998).

Third, the new communication order is also imbricated with what Gee, Hull and Lankshear (1996) have called 'a new work order'. The dominant features of the new work order include: more stressful and demanding work for those with good jobs; a proliferation of low-paying and temporary jobs and many without jobs; a widening gap between the rich and poor; a world in which national borders matter less. But the world of the new work order also includes the promise of more meaningful work, the valuing of diversity, the dispersal of centralised authority and the wider distribution of knowledge across communities. The sheer challenge of attempting to reconcile these apparently contradictory forces is sobering to say the least.

Even a cursory examination of the principal features of these 'new orders of things' reveals that our whole way of life, from the shape and structure of our communities, to the organisation and content of education, from the structure of the family to the status of art and entertainment, is profoundly affected by the extension and development of new information and communication technologies. Although the focus of this book is the new communication order, its features, manifestations and influences cannot be conceived as separate from the changes which are taking place in the worlds of politics and work. The complex interplay of all three constructs – the new communication order, the new political order and the new work order – shape and circumscribe the lives, identities and possibilities of contemporary students. Indeed, as a sociocultural perspective assumes, the emerging technology-mediated literacy practices – the silicon literacy practices – can be understood only when they are considered within their social, political, economic, cultural and historical contexts. The challenge for the contributors has been to find ways to provoke readers to consider what the use of these technologies means for educational practices. Together, they account for what we already know about the new communication order and what we have yet to discover. They suggest how teachers and their students can use the new technologies effectively, but also critically.

The book is divided into two parts. The first part, 'Online literacy and rhetorical practices', looks at the emergence of new types of text, new language practices, and new social formations as people find different ways of communicating with each other. We are learning to read, write, speak, listen and view in different ways as new forms of communication are made possible by technological development. We send faxes, leave messages on answering machines, use mobile phones, send SMS messages, use scanners, surf the net, use search engines, create websites, e-mail, participate in synchronous online chat and more. When we engage with these technologies, some of us use standard English, some use different varieties of English, some use other languages altogether, and some use combinations of all these possibilities. Literacy practices in the age of the new information and communication technologies are highly complex phenomena: they are not just about deciphering texts; they are also about understanding how culturally significant information is coded. Finding the language to talk about these new practices, discerning how meanings are made with them and explaining them theoretically are some of the issues taken up by the writers in this part of the book.

In the first chapter, Michele Knobel and Colin Lankshear focus on eBay, a person-to-person online auction venue. To achieve their purposes as online buyers and sellers, 'eBayers' need to know how to navigate through the site, read taxonomically, read between the lines, and judge authenticity in a new space. But these new discursive practices also evoke social issues and responsibilities. Drawing on Thomas Friedman's (2000) sociocultural analysis of eBay as a 'shaper' – companies, countries, and institutions that shape up activities within a globalised world of networked coalitions and practices – Knobel and Lankshear examine eBay's feedback system by which users rate each other's reputation, trustworthiness and reliability. However, eBay acts not only as a shaper; it also acts as an 'educator': eBay socialises people about what counts as an exemplary global space, encouraging the 'right' kind of cyber practices that lead to a well-organised and civil World Wide Web. Knobel and Lankshear investigate eBay as a case of new civic and literacy practices at the interstices of globalisation, new technologies and 'shaper' organisations, and explore the role of formal education in relation to these practices.

Also concerned with the production of electronic texts and the social and cultural practices by which they are informed, Chris Abbott identifies signs indicating that the visual will be privileged in the future. Abbott demonstrates ways in which young people make eloquent use of the visual in their online texts, especially those that form representations of themselves, their practices and their aspirations. In particular, he draws attention to the use of symbols by students with special needs. Although text replacement symbols have been around for a long time, their availability through ICTs has provided new opportunities for students with special needs to learn more effectively. Abbott draws connections between two parallel developments: young people publishing visually literate websites and people with special needs communicating through symbols. There appears to be an increasing number of websites using symbols either in addition to or in replacement of written word-based texts. But it is not just sites for people with special needs that are engaging in this practice; symbols are also used more and more in other online environments. Indeed, Abbott believes there is mounting evidence to support the argument that the shift to iconic communication will continue and will be lasting.

The contrast between young people's outside school interests and proficiency with ICTs and what goes on in schools provides the focus of Catherine Beavis's chapter. She asserts that the literacies young people learn through their use of computer games are different from those with which the literacy curriculum has traditionally been concerned. By examining the worlds of several popular games, Beavis argues that the literacies they entail present young people with highly developed mythologies and symbol systems, often more demanding than those chosen for them in school contexts. Game playing involves reading complex combinations of print and iconic representations. It also involves risk taking and social negotiations with peers and older people. Concerned with students' future development in literacies, both print and digital, Beavis identifies the mismatch between school expectations and definitions of literacy and the kinds of knowledge young people bring with them to school. She argues that we need an expanded set of understandings of texts and literacies and also an extended repertoire of how to work with computer games in literacy classrooms.

In a world in which the local and the global are increasingly connected, Mark Warschauer suggests that something apparently contradictory is happening to English. At the same time as it is becoming a world language and the common language of global commerce, media and politics, English is also breaking into increasingly differentiated Englishes, marked by accent, national origin, subcultural style and professional communities. Although the rise of English as a global language can be cast as a threat to language pluralism, Warschauer identifies examples of the emergence of new forms of language, which he depicts as part of a social struggle of individuals and communities to construct and express their identities online. While acknowledging that linguistic diversity is a complex social phenomenon that will not be determined by a single technology, the increasing availability of the Internet could amplify trends. Warschauer points to the false dichotomy between those who advocate standard English as giving power and those who advocate cultural and linguistic diversity. The growth of other languages on the Internet is representative of the importance of multilingualism and while English is spreading as a global language, other languages are also important for media, marketing and communications within countries.

Nicholas Burbules shifts the discussion to the rhetorical spaces of online learning. He focuses on 'hyperlinks', the basic structure of the World Wide Web, which act both as semantic connectives and as actual pathways of navigation. His essay considers this dual character, suggesting that it provides new metaphors for thinking about learning with, through, and about ICTs. Burbules explains two different ways in which rhetorical spaces become rhetorical places: the first is through mapping, a process of representing a space in order to be able to move and work within it; the second is through architectures, the structures that reconfigure spaces. He argues that the webs we encounter and the webs we make are not just navigational conveniences, but real avenues of learning: they are both tools and products. Burbules provides a fresh set of metaphors for thinking about learning as a kind of mobility that has special import for reconceptualising education in an information age.

Also concerned with the new online rhetorical spaces, Michael Joyce considers the implications of silicon literacy practices for writers and for teachers of writing. He asks: How can we find rhetorics to engage restless audiences? How do we write for readers who are looking for an excuse to move on? How do we write for audiences who think words are a waste of time? In response, Joyce proposes a rhetoric for a post-hypertextual age. By post-hypertext, now that everything online actually is hypertext, Joyce means not the end of something but the virtual setting for something new. His call is for a post-hypertextual rhetoric that finds purpose in surface. Joyce argues that surface reading is what we have always done anyway – both with print and digital media. Reading from the surface is a way of valuing something even more than reading at depth: we let things disclose themselves successively. By drawing our attention to his own use of rhetoric and to how rhetoric works, Joyce highlights important character- istics of the Web and of hypertextuality.

Building on the understandings about silicon literacies established in the first part of the book, the second part, 'Teaching, learning, technology and innova- tion', looks at the possibilities for creative changes to pedagogical and institutional practices when ICTs are used. Both directly and indirectly, the writers ask a number of questions about the nature of innovation: What are the optimum conditions under which innovation can thrive? Is conflict between institutional goals and pedagogical objectives inevitable? They raise these ques- tions within the context of a culture that champions 'innovation' at the same time as it honours the value of the traditional. Despite these tensions, several writers point out that 'innovation', often directly connected with the use of ICTs, has emerged as the catch-cry of those involved in marketing education. By commodifying education as product, marketeers have a vested interest in promoting technological innovation as an appealing selling point (Snyder 1999). But it seems that efforts at innovatory practices can have good results even though the best outcomes are often the unexpected ones. There are lessons to be learned: it is essential to keep track of innovations and they need to be evaluated in terms of institutional goals and needs. Further, those in control of institutions need to have an understanding of technological innovations, they need to support the innovations, and they must be prepared to take risks. It is clear that applying paradigms from the world of the book is fatal.

The second part of the book also focuses on the implications of silicon literacy practices for the future of formal institutionalised education. The polit- ical configurations that are engulfing educational policy and practice make familiarity with ICTs essential to effective participation in the emerging global economy. Yet many young people are already *au fait* with technological skills and wizardry by the time they enter school. They have learned how to access social knowledge and information through the electronic media. They can work with both print and electronic modes of literacy, often in forms that are hybridised in complex new ways. Clearly, educational institutions, clinging to print-based literacy practices, need to rethink the ways in which they function. The print- based industrial model of education needs to be redesigned to take account of the reality that young people are more likely to develop complex literacy reper- toires outside educational institutions. Rather than adapting the old ways, the new technologies invite, indeed demand, the conceptualisation of new ways to suit the new conditions.

8

Through the story of the rise and fall of the New Curriculum at Brown University, George Landow illuminates the challenges of educational innovation. An initiative of the 1970s, the New Curriculum represented an attempt at educational radicalism. Despite its eventual demise, Landow does not portray the New Curriculum as a failure. It brought the university to national prominence and attracted good students. In particular, Brown became open to experimentation, interdisciplinary programmes and new subjects which provided a fertile context for the hypertext-based pedagogical innovation with which Landow has been intimately associated. As studies of innovation often reveal, there was a champion of the development of hypertext systems in education, scholarship and creative arts: Andries van Dam. Financing came from creative use of grants and contracts and there were unexpected and productive uses of the technology, some not discovered till later. Ultimately, however, the hypertext experiment collapsed mainly because the administration wasn't prepared to fund it properly and the people at the helm were largely unaware of the achievements. Landow's analysis of Brown's New Curriculum in general and the hypertext initiative in particular is salutary for other educational institutions embarking on the path of innovation.

In her chapter, Jane Yellowlees Douglas presents a micro-account of teaching an online composition class in which she identifies the advantages and limitations of this new mode of learning. Douglas contextualises her analysis in the prevailing approaches to teaching and learning that were invented for another time and place and which no longer have relevance. By looking at the roots of conventional classrooms in the extremely resource-limited medieval period during which the West's great universities – Paris, Oxford and Bologna – were founded, she explores the limitations of conventional lecture and discussion courses. She argues that the much vaunted lecture method may be little more than an historically entrenched technique that reflected more the paucity of available resources during the late Middle Ages than a method based on sound principles of learning or demonstrable effectiveness. While the Internet may help us to rethink and redesign our pedagogy, this medium, if anything, is more resource intensive and demanding than the conventional classroom. The Internet is not a panacea enabling institutions to deliver instruction more cheaply and to larger numbers of students than via traditional methods.

Chris Bigum broadens the discussion from the use of new technologies in particular educational sites to the nexus between schools and the communities within which they are located. While the world beyond schooling has been characterised by profound change, supported by the deployment of computing and communication technologies (CCTs), schools have responded mainly by purchasing hardware and software to use across the curriculum. Activities in schools associated with the use of CCTs are based on the belief that the more schools spend, the better the outcomes. A similar view was once held in business and industry. However, analyses have demonstrated that there is little or no association between spending on IT and increased productivity and profitability.

Bigum suggests that schools have embraced a 'design sensibility' (Schrage 2000) based on information and its delivery – a mindset consistent with the powerful capacities of schools to *domesticate* new technologies. Rather than rethink schooling, schools have adapted the technologies to make them school-like. Bigum argues for the development of a relationship-based design sensibility for schools that shifts the focus from how to integrate IT into the curriculum towards a consideration of schools as social organisations that have relationships with local communities, government and other schools.

The last two chapters are concerned with the big picture. In his essay, Ron Burnett calls for a carefully modelled and broadly interdisciplinary approach to literacy education to provide a new foundation for learning activities within and outside institutions. He begins by arguing that recognition of the 'impossibility' of teaching should provide a basis for the development of innovative approaches to pedagogical practice. Burnett believes we are currently witnessing shifts in what we mean by learning that will have profound effects not only on global social and political structures but also upon the ways in which we see ourselves within local communities. These shifts are affecting how we create meanings, messages and information for the proliferating networks of education that now surround us. If we do not fully examine how the history of specialisation in the educational system has often prevented new pedagogical strategies from being sustained, the introduction of new technologies will not lead to innovation. When considering the implications of using technology to solve some of the dilemmas of education, Burnett argues that it simply extends the constraints of classroom experiences. Because learning now takes place in so many different ways, in so many venues, we need a more integrative and holistic approach to pedagogy.

Douglas Kellner challenges educators to rethink education – to restructure schools in response to the social and technological changes we are experiencing, but at the same time, to make sure that we cater for the needs of peoples from diverse cultures, races and backgrounds. He argues that there is much to be learned from the critical approaches to media and pedagogy articulated by theorists working in those areas. There is also much to be learned from the tradition of progressive education, first expressed by John Dewey, with its emphasis on democracy, equity and citizenship. The Deweyean notion of pragmatic experimentation – what the new technologies can and cannot do to enhance education – emerges as a particularly generative approach to inform contemporary debates. Kellner advocates a critical theory of technology in education which avoids technophilia and technophobia but uses and redesigns technologies for democracy and social reconstruction in the interests of social justice. Effective participation in the emergent forms of culture and society requires familiarity and confidence with new kinds of literacies – to access, to interpret, to criticise. Moreover, cultivating new literacies and reconstructing education for democratisation involves identifying new pedagogies and social relations.

In the concluding chapter, building on the interdisciplinary approach integral to the collection, I discuss some recent work of several important contemporary thinkers, Zygmunt Bauman (2001) and Pierre Bourdieu (1998), whose ideas have not been invoked very much in literacy and technology studies, but who have much to offer. My aim is to consider ideas that extend our understanding of the political, economic and communication contexts in which we do our work. I pose a number of questions: What are the implications of the insights of these thinkers for literacy education? What new goals might we establish for pedagogy and curriculum in times marked by significant change and uncertainty, much of which is governed by the manifold influences of ICTs? Clearly, the task for literacy education in the electronic age is enormous, but not impossible. I suggest a number of directions. In particular, Raymond Williams' (1975) explanation of effective communication as a collective ideal seems to offer something worthwhile to work towards.

The essays in this book represent a range of approaches to literacy and technology studies. There are, however, some common threads. In their move away from psychological and cognitive models to concentrate on cultural and social aspects of language use, the essays share common ground with the New Literacy Studies (Street 1995; Prinsloo and Breier 1996; Barton and Hamilton 1998; Street 2001). The contributors conceptualise silicon literacies, not as skills and competencies, but as social and cultural practices. Attention is given to people's use of language – written, oral and visual – around computer-mediated texts, and to the ways in which the meanings and the uses of these texts are culturally shaped. A number of the writers present micro-accounts of particular silicon literacy practices in specific contexts, whether in a 'community' represented by multiple participants on a website such as eBay, young people playing the computer game *Magic and Mayhem* in Australia, or university students taking part in an online writing subject in a business degree programme at a university in Florida. But they also show how the meanings of these local literacy events are linked to broader cultural institutions and practices. Several of the writers are concerned primarily with the articulation and elaboration of macro-perspectives on the implications of the use of the new media for pedagogical and curriculum practices. Collectively, the essays demonstrate that the synergy between micro- and macro-views offers us the most potent understandings of emerging silicon literacy practices and their cultural significance.

Education is at a crossroad. As literacy educators, we have within our power the opportunity to shift our own and our students' beliefs about the new technologies – about the place of the technologies in education as well as their wider cultural importance. As the contributors to this volume argue, we need to think critically about their use and to provide students with the opportunities to acquire the skills to do likewise. It is no longer tenable to dismiss ICTs simply as new tools, using them to do what earlier technologies did, only faster and more efficiently. Such a response perpetuates acceptance of a limited notion of the technologies' cultural consequences; it overlooks their material bases and the expanding global economic dependence on them. However, when the technologies are recognised as a crucial part of the cultural and communication

11

landscape – indeed, as part of a new communication order – we render a more realistic conception of the technologies' significance and of our own and our students' place in an information and knowledge-based society.

References

Barton, D. and Hamilton, M. (1998) *Local Literacies: Reading and Writing in One Community*, London: Routledge.

Bauman, Z. (2001) *The Individualized Society*, Malden, MA: Polity Press.

Bourdieu, P. (1998) *Acts of Resistance*, trans. R. Nice, Cambridge: Polity Press.

Burnett, R. (1996) 'A torn page, ghosts on the computer screen, words, images, labyrinths: exploring the frontiers of cyberspace', in G. Marcus (ed.) *Connected: Engagement with Media*, vol 3, Chicago: University of Chicago Press, pp. 67–98.

Castells, M. (1996) *The Rise of the Network Society*, Malden, MA: Blackwell.

—— (1997) *The Power of Identity*, Malden, MA: Blackwell.

—— (1998) *End of Millennium*, Malden, MA: Blackwell.

Friedman, T. (2000) *The Lexus and the Olive Tree*, New York: Anchor Books.

Gee, J. P., Hull, G. and Lankshear, C. (1996) *The New Work Order: Behind the Language of the New Capitalism*, Sydney: Allen & Unwin.

Kellner, D. M. and Durham, M. G. (2001) 'Adventures in media and cultural studies: introducing the keyworks', in M. G. Durham and D. M. Kellner (eds) *Media and Cultural Studies: Keyworks*, Oxford: Blackwell, pp. 1–29.

Lemke, J. (1997) 'Metamedia literacy: transforming meanings and media', in D. Reinking, L. Labbo, M. McKenna and R. Kieffer (eds) *Literacy for the 21st Century: Technological Transformation in a Post-Typographic World*, Mahwah, New Jersey: Lawrence Erlbaum, pp. 283–301.

Prinsloo, M. and Breier, M. (1996) (eds) *The Social Uses of Literacy: Theory and Practice in Contemporary South Africa*, Cape Town: Sached Books and Amsterdam: John Benjamins.

Schrage, M. (2000) *The Relationship Revolution*. Online. Available HTTP: *http://www.ml.com/woml/forum/relation.htm* (26 January 2000).

Snyder, I. (ed.) (1997) *Page to Screen: Taking Literacy into the Electronic Era*, Sydney and London: Allen & Unwin and Routledge [1998].

—— (1999) 'Packaging literacy, new technologies and "enhanced" learning', *Australian Journal of Education* 43 (3): 287–301.

—— (2000) 'Literacy and technology studies: past, present, future', *The Australian Educational Researcher* 27 (2): 97–119.

—— (2001a) 'A new communication order: researching literacy practices in the network society', *Language and Education: An International Journal* 15 (1): 117–31.

—— (2001b) '"Hybrid vigour": reconciling the verbal and the visual in electronic communication', in A. Loveless and V. Ellis (eds) *ICT, Pedagogy and the Curriculum*, London: RoutledgeFalmer, pp. 41–59.

Street, B. (1995) *Social Literacies: Critical Approaches to Literacy in Development, Ethnography and Education*, London: Longman.

—— (1998) 'New literacies in theory and practice: what are the implications for language in education?' *Linguistics and Education* 10 (1): 1–24.

—— (ed.) (2001) *Literacy and Development: Ethnographic Perspectives*, London: Routledge.

Williams, R. (1975) [1961] *The Long Revolution*, Westport, Connecticut: Greenwood Press.

Part I

ONLINE LITERACY AND RHETORICAL PRACTICES

1

WHAT AM I BID?

Reading, writing and ratings at eBay.com

netgrrrl ☆ (12) and chicoboy26 ★ (32)[1]

> eBay came out of nowhere and within three years created a new
> set of rules and forms of interaction by which consumers would
> buy and sell things on the World Wide Web.
>
> (Friedman 2000: 202)

Introduction

Current educational literature is awash with talk of 'new literacies', 'technoliteracies', 'multiliteracies' and the like in response to the massive incursion of new information and communication technologies into everyday routines within modern societies. Much of this talk, however, is general and impressionistic. Considerably less systematic analysis and documentation of new literacy practices engendered and mediated by the Internet has been forthcoming, let alone discussion of what social issues and responsibilities such new practices may evoke.

This chapter focuses on the emergence of a new literacy practice: the community ratings feedback system on eBay – which is a new way of reading and writing aspects of the world important to eBay users, or eBayers. It explores this ratings system from two standpoints between which there is, increasingly, considerable tension. One standpoint is that of its creators – the owners and operators of eBay.com and their communitarian 'visionary' purposes for developing it. The other standpoint is that of eBay users, and their seeming appropriation of the community ratings feedback system for less altruistic, more self-serving purposes than those of the creators. Our aim is to capture something of the dialectic between the *strategies* of producers and the *uses* of consumers (de Certeau 1984) at play in the emergence of a distinctively contemporary practice of everyday life.

We have been investigating eBay for almost two years as 'participant observers' (Spradley 1980). On the basis of our prior observations and semi-formal categorisation of issues and themes apparent in our database, we selected four participants – two male and two female – to interview. We conducted extended e-mail-based structured interviews with these participants, who live in the US and in Australia. In addition, we closely observed official eBay message boards located on the US eBay website for a period of three months. Because eBay regulations do not permit the downloading of eBay websites to computer hard-drives, we were forced to print out only the sections of discussions we felt were significant to our research question: What new literacy practices are generated in people-to-people interactive Internet spaces such as eBay? This kind of 'purposive sampling' is a methodologically acceptable compromise when researching online interactions. Our printed-out sections totalled 100 separate messages. For the purposes of this chapter, we focus on the e-mail-based interviews and discussions drawn from the 'Feedback' message board (see eBay 2001a). To protect the identity of users, we have deliberately omitted detailed information about the messages and postings in the bibliography. We analysed the e-mail-based interviews and discussion-board messages using categorical analysis and content analysis (see Knobel and Lankshear 1999).

So what *is* eBay?

eBay was among the first person-to-person auction venues to go online. It is currently the most popular and successful Internet trading community in the world (Friedman 2000; Multex.com 2001). By mid-2001, eBay had over twenty-two million registered users, averaged one million items sold each day, and listed over three million items in more than three thousand categories – and is still growing. Categories range from premium artworks, through real estate and cars, to clothing, jewellery, toys, comics and trading cards (with one person recently auctioning off his soul …). eBay describes itself as:

> the world's first, biggest and best person-to-person online trading community. It's your place to find the stuff you want, to sell the stuff you have and to make a few friends while you're at it.
>
> (eBay 2001b)

eBay (2001c) comprises sets of Internet pages that include long lists of new and used items for sale that people have posted to the website. Sellers are responsible for writing item descriptions and for generating pictures of the items that are then inserted into an eBay page template and posted on the eBay website under a self-selected category heading (and where it is automatically allocated an item number). Potential buyers – who must be registered with eBay – browse these lists or use the eBay search function to locate items of interest. They can then bid on or 'watch' these items. Watching involves clicking on the 'watch this item' hyperlink, and the item is then hotlinked to people's personal 'eBay' space (i.e., 'my eBay').

Bidding works in two ways, similarly to conventional auctions. Bidders may make the lowest viable bid possible at that particular point in time and wait to see what happens (or place a new minimum bid after being outbid by someone else). Or, they can place a 'proxy' bid – which is the maximum amount they are willing to pay, and eBay acts for them as a proxy bidder – bidding in their place until the item is 'won' or their specified maximum amount has been exceeded by another bidder. Sellers pay to list their items with eBay. The fee depends on the starting price or reserve set for an item (e.g., a $0.01–$9.99 starting price costs $0.30 to list, and a reserve price of $0.01–$24.99 costs $0.50 to list), or on the type of item being listed (real estate comes with a $50.00 listing fee; used cars cost $25.00 to list). Commission on sold items is charged at 5 per cent of the first $25.00, and an additional 2.5 per cent after that.

eBay currently operates in eleven countries and four languages. Although it is certainly advantageous to access an eBay site in your home country (language, currency, dates, time and shipping wise), it is possible to bid from anywhere in the world when payment options and shipping agreements conduce.

What's *new* about eBay

While some people might claim that eBay is just an old physical space (auctioning) in virtual get-up, we consider that it is spawning some genuinely new social practices and new literacies associated with them.

We will make our case for the newness of some of the social practices and literacies associated with them from two angles. The first simply identifies some new features of reading relevant aspects of the world occasioned by moving the familiar social practice of auctioning into an unfamiliar space, namely the virtual space of the Internet. One or two brief examples must suffice here.

eBay calls for interesting new constellations or 'batteries' of ways of reading and writing to meet people's purposes as online buyers and/or sellers. For example, the eBay facility has a mediating or brokerage role. Nobody at eBay sees or handles what is being bought and sold. And there is nobody to tell people where to go to find what they are looking for (or might want to look for if they knew it might be available). Hence, it is not simply a matter of knowing how to read or write the text of item descriptions. Participants also need to know how to navigate through or add to the website. For example, they need to know how to read and write 'taxonomically' in the sense of knowing what is likely to be in or should be in each category – of which there are hundreds. They need to be able to read between the lines in item descriptions (e.g., a Clarice Cliff style crocus jug is *not* a Clarice Cliff crocus jug). In many cases it is necessary to be able to read digitised images accurately (e.g., know that colour is often not true-to-life in digital images of objects; understand depth of field and the effects it has on objects; be wary of out-of-focus or soft-focus images or lighting effects). Knowing (how) to convert from imperial to metric measures, or even currencies, is often required for international dealings, and so on. Fakes and forgeries are much easier to disguise on eBay than in meat spaces. Collectors appear to have developed a whole new set of criteria for judging the authenticity of an item. These include evaluating the source of the product (e.g., if the sellers are the children of a famous sportsperson, then it's likely the sports memorabilia they are selling are genuine). They also include a wariness of what some call 'overdocumentation' which is the presence of too many papers 'verifying' the authenticity of an item (Sherman 2001: 63).

Moreover, physical or 'meat' space literacy practices often *mean* different things within eBay. For example, one regular eBay user we interviewed said she loves coming across item descriptions that are spelled incorrectly. To her it means she is more likely to 'win' a bargain from this person than from someone who spells correctly. Non-standard spelling indicates people less likely to be in a professional job or to own a shop and, hence, less likely to know the real value of the ceramics they are offering for sale.

The second way of considering what is new about eBay is by reference to a distinction drawn by Jeff Bezos, founder of Amazon.com, and for whom eBay provided an exemplar of the kind of thing he wanted to do. According to Robert Spector's account of Amazon.com's rise, Bezos wanted to develop an enterprise which embodied his passion for 'second phase automation' (Spector 2000: 16):

> Bezos has described second-phase automation as 'the common theme that has run through my life. The first phase of automation is where you use technology to do the same old business processes, but just faster and more efficiently'. A typical first phase of automation in the e-commerce field would be barcode scanners and point-of-sale systems. With the Internet 'you're doing the same process you've always done, but just more efficiently'. He described the second phase of automation as 'when you can fundamentally change the underlying business process and do things in a completely new way. So it's more of a revolution instead of an evolution'.

Bezos' distinction enables us to differentiate further between processes and practices that have simply become 'digitised' and those practices and processes that exist only because digital technologies do. As we can see by reference to its community feedback ratings system, eBay is a case of the latter.

In his analysis of globalisation, Thomas Friedman (2000) identifies two possible roles available for companies, governments and institutions in the 'Evernet world' of globalised networks of communication, service and power. He calls these roles 'shapers' and 'adapters'. Shapers are agents that shape up activities within a globalised world of networked coalitions and practices – 'whether that activity is making a profit, making war or making a government or corporation respect human rights' (202). Shapers design rules, create interaction frameworks and set new standards for global practices. Adapters, on the other hand, follow shapers' leads and adapt to the 'scene' being created.

Friedman (2000) regards eBay as a foremost and highly original shaper. He sees it as having been a leader in creating a whole new marketplace and insti-gating an entirely new set of interaction protocols for buyers and sellers. eBay, says

Friedman, 'came out of nowhere and within three years created a new set of rules and forms of interaction by which consumers would buy and sell things on the World Wide Web' (2000: 202). At the core of eBay's business process, 'revolution' built on 'second phase automation', is a simple rating scale and eighty-character feedback system, through which buyers can rate and respond to the effectiveness of sellers, and vice versa. This ratings system has been integral to eBay's success in its enterprise. It has simultaneously transformed relations between buyers on the Internet, and elevated to prominence, in the identity-shaping behaviour of many individuals, the practice of pursuing a positive ratings profile.

eBay's rating system has a three-point scale – positive, neutral and negative – and stands as a public judgement of the reputation, trustworthiness and relia-bility of a person. Once an auction transaction has been completed (the winning bidder has paid for the item) the buyer can leave feedback about the seller and vice versa by means of the item number. Only the buyer and seller are autho-rised to comment on a particular transaction. Feedback consists of the actual rating (positive, neutral, negative) and a written recommendation.

The eBay website reminds eBayers that '[h]onest feedback shapes the community' (eBay 2001c). The higher the positive ratings people have, the more 'trustworthy' and 'reliable' they are in eBay terms. On the other hand, accumulating four negative ratings means individuals can be excluded from the eBay community. Exclusion is not automatic, however, since it is up to users to notify eBay that someone has received four or more negative ratings. eBay users are not the only ones to take this ratings game seriously. A case could easily be made that eBay's rating system has powerfully affected Internet-based social interactions, with numerous other interactive Internet sites now using ratings systems as public reputation markers (e.g., Plastic 2001; Yahoo! Geocities 2001).

As an aside, eBay's success has spawned a diverse range of complementary products and services, many of which entail literacies of one kind or another. For example, *eBay a-go-go*™ has been purpose-designed to be an eBay wireless auction alerting service that operates via mobile phones or pagers. It alerts users when they have been outbid, and when they have won or sold an item. There are also various auction 'tracking' and 'bidding' software programs and online services (e.g., Amherst Robots 2001; BidBlaster 2001; eSnipe 2001), online mediation services for auction transactions that go wrong, escrow and e-cash services (e.g., BidPay 2001; Billpoint 2001), a range of 'how-to-bid-successfully' books (e.g., Collier and Woerner 2000; Reno, Reno and Butler 2000), and online 'beginners' introductions' to eBay (e.g., SoYouWanna 2000). Finally, for those who are truly serious about learning how to read and write the world according to eBay, there is eBay University (2001d):

> Ever wonder how to sell an item on eBay? Want to know 'buying basics'? Wish to take your eBay sales to the next level? Register to

attend eBay University in your town and you'll soon be buying or selling like a pro!

Why *ratings*?

eBay's expressed intention in devising and implementing the feedback ratings system is to build a self-monitoring ethical community of eBay users. We would argue that the feedback ratings system can be read as an embodied ideological induction into a certain 'software space'. That is, eBay is not only a shaper within the new technologies arena, but it is also an 'educator' in that it 'teaches' people how they *should* act within this new cyber space; how they should act in relation to each other. It is, therefore, a space of induction. It plays a role in shoring up new discursive norms. It socialises people about what counts as an exemplary global space, and helps generate good global citizens by encouraging the 'right' kind of cyber practices that lead to a well-organised and civil World Wide Web.

eBayers and their ratings

eBayers are very clear about the importance of their ratings. Many go to extraordinary lengths to obtain positive ratings. Some item postings contain a 'customer assurance statement' that resembles an airline 'thanks for flying with us' patter to stand in as a 'bid confidently' statement. For example,

> A Word of Thanks. ... We at Lorelei's Jewelry would like to Thank all of our Customers for their Patronage over the last 4 years. Our number 1 priority is to give you the best Customer Service in the Business. We Know that you have choices and appreciate your business. Our Goal is to provide an Exceptional Line of Jewelry at the Absolute Lowest Prices. We are here to answer any Questions that you may have in a Timely Manner Via Telephone or E-mail. All Winning Bidders are Notified Promptly and Items are Normally Shipped the Day Payment is received. We hope that you will join our long list of Satisfied Customers. ... Over 10,000 Feedbacks and Growing Daily.
>
> (Lorlei's 2000)

The reference to 10,000 feedbacks is the clincher here. It is worn like a badge of honour (although canny eBayers will note that the company does not advertise '10,000 *positive* feedbacks' and will immediately go to the company's ratings page to verify the ratings are positive as implied). We know of at least one company that e-mails successful bidders at the end of a transaction to let them know that the company has left them positive feedback. The e-mail even contains a hyperlink to automated feedback forms. Customers need only fill in the actual rating and the written feedback line.

Many individual eBayers have constructed elaborate processes that aim at ensuring as many positive feedback statements and ratings as possible:

> I have a spreadsheet that i use to keep track of my items, buying and selling and there is a space for me to check off that i have left feedback for a buyer/seller. When the buyer/seller leaves feedback for me in return, i circle the check mark, letting me know the transaction has come full circle. when i sell something, i include a thank you card with the item number listed, my ebay name and a note stating that i have left positive feedback for them and would appreciate the same in kind and i still have problems getting them to leave me feedback! So every month, i go down the spreadsheet and e-mail those who have failed to leave feedback asking them why they have not done so and if there were problems i was not aware of. this is very time consuming but it has worked on most of the delinquents. it more or less embarrasses them into leaving feedback.
>
> (eBay 2001a)

Even one instance of negative feedback is perceived as bad for business:

> [Ratings and feedback] are very important as it's the only real way of knowing how good sellers are. I have never bought off someone with a bad rating and there are quite a few of them out there ... I have had to give out a few bad ratings to people who have won auctions and have never paid me or contacted me for that matter.
>
> (*arkanoid2020* e-mail interview 12/02/2001)

> [Ratings] are extremely important. I don't want to buy from vendors with negative feedback, and I don't expect people to want to buy from me if I have any. Those comments are listed in red, and they show up like a neon sign!!
>
> (*bea1997* e-mail interview 25/09/2000)

Ratings have actually become a 'currency' for the eBay community, assuming the kind of role local community networks and character references have in physical space. One of our interviewees, *susygirl*, says:

> I really take pride in [my ratings]. And for me it is the alter ego – it is susygirl's not mine. And so I get pissed [off] if someone doesn't send me a positive feedback. But I never write and ask them to. Some sellers do that and I usually don't respond to that.
>
> (e-mail interview 1/02/2001)

Others, like *bea1997*, a long-term and very experienced eBayer, have preferred to be 'duped' by buyers than risk negative feedback. *Bea1997* explains:

> Sometimes I lose money from customers who break an item and ask for money back. I just don't want to risk having my good reputation ruined for a few lousy bucks so I just take the blame and send their money back.
>
> (e-mail interview 25/09/2000)

bea1997's experience tallies with others reported elsewhere. For example, Erick Sherman recounts:

> Both buyers and sellers get burned from time to time, but usually not badly. Shamus remembers someone who bought a $25 trading card from him on eBay then returned it, but with a corner newly bent. He said, "That's what you sent me." Shamus didn't argue because the amount was too small and negative feedback would hurt his future sales.
>
> (Sherman 2001: 63)

Others have fought vigorously with eBay to have what the eBayer regards as unjust negative feedback removed – almost impossible to achieve – and various eBayers have established entire websites devoted to explaining the events underlying any negative feedback they have received. Someone we'll call 'Pam' created a webpage showcasing the e-mail exchanges between a customer and herself to show how the negative rating given to her by the customer was unjust. Ironically, the exchange proves the opposite – further evidence of the advantage of being proficient in a range of literacies in order to participate successfully in eBay.

Ratings are considered by most eBayers to be so important that the dedicated discussion board attached to the eBay auction website for discussing ratings is a popular and much-used service (eBay 2001a). This 'board' is a web-based service that allows people to post messages (or responses to messages) about their ratings and feedback problems, warnings about 'deadbeat' sellers or buyers, complaints about 'sniping' (bidders waiting until the very last moment to place a winning bid), how to go about lodging a complaint about an unfair negative rating, and so on. Despite eBay's emphasis on community, however, the ratings and feedback system has not made for harmonious relationships.

Reciprocity is a key value enacted within eBay in relation to ratings. As *susygirl* observed, she is 'pissed [off]' if she completes a transaction and the seller doesn't leave feedback for her. Reciprocity in ratings is likewise important to *arkanoid2020*:

> I have also had the problem of people not giving me a rating after a successful transaction, which is a shame because I always make the effort.
>
> (e-mail interview 12/02/2001)

Other eBayers express their feelings about a lack of reciprocity strongly. Much of the eBay chat about ratings is taken up with who should leave feedback and a rating first, and why. For example,

> I figured out feedback right away. When I receive an item I immediately leave feedback. That's my way of keeping track of things. I then immediately e-mail the seller and thank them for good service (I've been very fortunate in this regard) and ask them to leave feedback. It seems to me that sellers will only leave feedback if requested to do so and *if* I leave positive feedback. Sellers should leave feedback when they get my prompt payment in my opinion. Why do I have to gently nudge them and leave my feedback first? They get my money first.
>
> (eBay 2001a)

In bad-case scenarios, the threat of leaving negative feedback is held over buyers or sellers. For example, when a buyer has received an item and for some reason wants to return it to the seller, but the seller does not agree to receive it back, the buyer may threaten to leave negative feedback if the seller does not comply with her wishes. eBay members refer to this as 'feedback hostage taking' – where the seller (or buyer) is held hostage to receiving feedback (e.g., 'I'll leave you feedback only when you've left me feedback'). In worst case scenarios, this is called 'feedback extortion' by eBayers – and is something taken very seriously by eBay (the company).

In a context where ratings have become important currency, but where people's 'good reputation' aspirations are often not met or realised, and where participants spend much of their time on discussion boards 'working through' issues raised by their participation in a ratings and feedback system that can be – and is – subverted by unscrupulous people, new language terms or lexical items are emerging. Many of these new terms are pejorative. Content analysis of our downloaded discussion board messages suggests that of the nine lexical items we identified confidently as being 'new', seven were unquestionably pejorative in nature. The list of disparaging terms we encountered in our message board sample included: 'feedback bombing', 'feedback padding', feedback extortion', 'retaliatory negative feedback', 'to be neutraled', to be 'NEGed', and 'deadbeat bidder or seller' (also referred to as 'deadbeats'). The ambiguous or non-inflammatory 'new' lexical items included 'snipe' and 'positive'. Sniping refers to the practice of bidding in the closing seconds of an auction, with the intention of winning the bid by only one increment (or less). For some people, sniping is an exhilarating and 'fun' dimension of participating in eBay auctions; for others, sniping is 'unjust' and 'sneaky'. The practice of giving someone a 'positive' rating is generally referred to in a short-hand way, where the adjectival use of 'positive' becomes nominalised; for example, 'I got a positive' or 'I gave a positive'. Although the terms we identified within our collected texts may not be representative of all (new) terms produced in the eBay space, they certainly signal a very visible and significant trend within the eBay community.

Not surprisingly, exchanges on the feedback discussion board get heated at times, with little evidence of the kind of tolerance expected in a community of the kind eBay aims to foster:

> and i agree if you knew the answer why bother asking? i get lots of people asking stupid ? [trans: questions] like what does it measure? when it is already posted on my auctions ... i tell them to go back and read the description. i don't find that to be rude.
>
> (eBay 2001a)

And responses from two different people:

> Not rude? must be why you have so many successful transactions ... Why not just answer the question and accept that stupid people make up a big percentage of customers?

> The guy's sarcastic, not rude. Read his very limited, posted feedback for a good laugh.
>
> (eBay 2001a)

The reference to the first person's 'successful transactions' and 'very limited, posted feedback' are snide comments on his beginner status: one positive rating. From these kinds of reactions, it is safe to assume that not only are the ratings on eBay read as integral to people's public reputation, but also as an indicator of 'wisdom' and knowledge where all things eBay are concerned.

Moreover, such exchanges are not limited to the feedback discussion board or the various eBay chat spaces. They also appear regularly within the actual feedback spaces of an eBayer's ratings page. In the following example, the 'complaint' was posted by the seller, the bidder responded, and the seller followed up. This appeared on the bidder's ratings page:

Complaint: BEWARE! BIDS AND RETRACTS! 7 TIMES! WON AUCTION – NEVER PAID! REPORTED TO EBAY!

Response: Discovered this seller was selling refurbished merchandise as new after the auct

Follow-up: BEWARE! Bids, but NEVER buys! READ ad, BID, WON, then REFUSED to PAY – JERKOFF!

Interestingly, the ratings page also shows that the seller in this particular exchange has been deregistered and can no longer use this alias on eBay (although there is nothing to prevent the seller from registering a new alias).

eBay's response to the soap opera-like dimensions of the community feedback and ratings system is to continue holding out for a self-regulating, 'trustworthy' and intelligent community:

Hello folks,

Thanks for the discussion. Let me offer you eBay's perspective on Feedback for consideration:

The real value in Feedback is in the trends that it reveals. While it is an admirable goal to work towards a perfect rating, it is IMPOSSIBLE to always please everyone all the time anywhere in life, right? An occasional isolated negative will not impact the VAST majority of users when they are deciding whether or not to bid or accept a bid. (I would say 'ANY' users, but then someone would post to prove me wrong, hehehe.)

We hope you will use the Feedback forum faithfully, despite the risk of receiving a negative that you feel you don't deserve, because in this way our whole community is served best. The purpose of Feedback is to help keep the site safe. If we use it appropriately, the good guys are always going to have FAR more positive comments than the less-scrupulous users who will quickly earn track records that show their true colours for all to see, as well.

Daphne will step down from her soapbox now. :)

Daphne

eBay Community Support

(eBay 2001a)

eBay has recently instituted a feedback service that alerts participants to items they have yet to leave feedback on. It is also possible – using a little URL tweaking, since at present it is not a formal eBay service – to access a list of feedback each user leaves others. This makes for interesting exchanges in the discussion spaces of eBay.

Complexities

The point at which we began, with the idea of eBay being a new socialising space, shaping people to become appropriate users of new cyber spaces, now appears much more complex – perhaps even contradictory.

On one hand, eBay's community feedback ratings system has been an important factor in its stunning success to date. In part, this is because it has helped establish eBay's mission and identity as a helpful broker, with its clients' best interests at heart, and as a responsible cyber force with which people, wanting to be part of the project of building a successful and responsible tradition of e-commerce, seek to be associated. Moreover, as emulators like Amazon.com have found, engaging participants in active roles as evaluators encourages further participation, 'hooking' them in by valuing their contribution. In addition, however, it appears that part of the ratings system's integral role in eBay's success has to do with the fact that it helps meet a range of personal needs, including those relating to identity and esteem. It actively recruits membership to an affinity group with which people can identify, and offers individuals and organisations a way of attaining a visible and enviable presence. *susygirl* sums up this aspect of eBay nicely:

> For me it is a kind of therapy. I like it too because i become susygirl and not some English professor. I like to hide behind my new identity.
>
> (e-mail interview 12/02/2001)

And even in meat space, when eBay crops up in a conversation between people who have met recently, we have found one of the most frequent responses to be, 'Oh great! What's your rating? Mine's *x*.' In other words, besides providing a means for mediating responsible and satisfying commercial exchange, the ratings system also offers a service to personal identity formation and to what is fast becoming a highly valued 'currency' – an exemplary personal ratings profile.

On the other hand, however, the practice of promoting written feedback and ratings has become a space in which many participants engage in activities that do not merely contradict the 'cyber civic' goal of eBay, but that actually involve a range of malicious, preying, nasty, hurtful acts toward others (some of whom doubtless contribute to their own pain by investing more than is wise in the discourse and otherwise taking their 'profiles' or 'identities' more seriously than the context merits). Some of the data we have presented smells of interpersonal power-tripping, petty acts of malice, and the desire to belittle others (which is endemic in Internet spaces).

These latter cases raise a host of issues germane to moral education and civic development, and questions concerning the extent to which the school is an appropriate place for addressing moral and civic values and practices in terms specific to the Internet. Such questions are beyond our scope here. More to the immediate point, however, is the fact that in its complexity and contradictoriness, the 'ratings game' is par for the course so far as literacy and technology practices are concerned. This point is simple and well-rehearsed, but bears reinforcing within the present context, since there are still many people who think the Internet unleashes all sorts of undesirable forces that are not equally present in the social practices of physical space.

Literacy and technology are never 'singular', never the 'same thing'. 'They' are always 'so many things' to so many different people. The same alphabetic code can be used for writing notes to children or for publishing sophisticated experimental findings in learned journals. It can be used for writing good wishes to friends and for writing extortion notes to intended victims. The same kind of ambiguity and range is open to practically any tool or body of knowledge and information we care to name. The same is true of more specific literacies, including different forms of feedback and rating genres. We need only to think of the uses to which various kinds of referees' reports can be put for the point to be perfectly clear. The particular 'silicon literacy' of producing (or withholding) ratings and feedback shares the formal character of all literacy practices (different people put them to different uses, understand them differently, etc.). It is susceptible, then, to the same 'play' of moral, civic, and emotional forces – the way that people are and how they live out their (in)securities, pleasures and pains, values and aspirations, and so on.

Reading the social practice of rating others and feeding back

Among the multiple options available for describing and understanding some of these complexities, we find Michel de Certeau's (1984) concept of consumer 'uses' particularly fruitful.

De Certeau develops a distinction between 'producers' and 'consumers', which incorporates our usual distinction between producing and consuming commodity items, but is much wider. Producers are those who have the power and a 'place' (a 'proper') from which to shape discourses and discursive forma-tion in all spheres of human life. An institution like the university can be seen as involved in production in this sense. It is a site where social actors in the form of recognised scientific experts are seen to have the right to determine, monitor and uphold what counts as 'science'. Consumers include scientists themselves who go along with scientific discourse as defined by participating in it ('playing' according to the rules). Consumers also include all who use the services of scien-tists, who study science, and who go along with a way of life shaped by prevailing definitions of the nature and role of science. In other words, de Certeau's distinction between producers and consumers works all the way down to the level at which consumers consume specific artefacts of commodified popular culture, such as television fare packaged as entertainment.

De Certeau's distinction is important because it moves us away from a narrow focus on particular acts of consuming artefacts toward a wider and deeper understanding of social *practices*. Our individual acts of making and consuming *participate* in these practices, but they do not *constitute* them. The 'operations' of producers are deeper and larger than we often think: producers actually *produce* the discourse that *constitutes* a TV programme as *entertainment* in the first place; they do not merely produce *the programme*. By the same token, the 'operations' (*practices*) of consumers are also deeper and larger than we often think.

De Certeau develops a set of concepts that provide a framework for investi-gating the nature and politics of cultural production within the practices of everyday life. These concepts include 'strategies', 'uses' and 'tactics'. De Certeau wants to challenge perceptions of consumers as being just passive effects (or 'reflexes') of the practices of producers. At the same time, he does not want to deny that power differences play out across social and cultural groupings every-where. Nonetheless, he wants to identify, understand and explain the means by which the 'weak' actively manoeuvre within the spaces constituted strategically by producers to make them 'habitable' and to meet their own purposes as best they can.

Producers can develop *strategies* to manage relations with an *exteriority* composed of targets or threats. Strategy is an 'art of the strong'. Through strategic practices, producers define spaces to be lived in by all. On the other hand, consumers (the 'weak') cannot strategise. Instead, they can manoeuvre within the constraining order of regulatory fields within which they are obliged to operate. They can do this in two main ways. One is by 'making use of' the constraining order. The other is by employing 'tactics'. We will focus here on the idea of consumers' 'use'.

De Certeau illustrates 'use' by examples like that of North African migrants being obliged to live in a low-income housing estate in France and to use the French of Paris or Roubaix (see de Certeau 1984). These people might insinuate into the system imposed on them 'the ways of "dwelling" (in a house or in a language) peculiar to [their] native Kabylia' (de Certeau 1984: 31). This process introduces a degree of plurality into the system. It also confirms that consumers are *active*. They *work* to make such spaces 'habitable'. At the same time, they remain *subordinate* to the strategies of producers.

We want to suggest that this 'dialectic' is present in every case of literacy and technology. In the present context, eBay's 'feedback and ratings' practice and the specific practices of literacy it engenders, is a case in point. Where Friedman (2000) talks of eBay as a 'shaper', we may equally speak of eBay as a 'producer'. eBay is employing strategies to define what constitutes proper practice in the field of commercial exchange in cyberspace. It has introduced the community ratings and feedback mechanism as part of its overall strategy. This is intended to serve as part of a 'constraining order' – a discursive order (currently in the process of being established) that will constrain participants to act in certain ways and not in others. It makes no difference that eBay may be seeking to do this in 'good' and 'civil' ways. There is nothing inherently 'wicked' about producers and their productions. We are talking here about contingencies of power rather than about ethics *per se*. One can choose whether or not to be a 'consumer' within this space, but if one chooses to participate in this space, then its order applies.

What we think we see in the snippets of data presented above are varying 'ways' of consumers 'making use of' the ratings game. They are 'insinuating' into the system produced for them ways of 'dwelling' with which they are familiar, adept, or which they otherwise find satisfying or reinforcing – no matter how unpleasant we may find some of these. The 'silicon literacies' of ratings and feedback can best be understood as endlessly complex and multiple. They are 'flexed' into myriad uses by consumers. They are susceptible to policing and 'moralising' on the part of producers and other consumers alike. In this respect they are exactly like the literacies of physical spaces like schools – where the 'players' involved are also inclined to invoke notions of fairness, propriety, and 'getting it right'.

In the end, eBay's community feedback and ratings system is an illuminating microcosm of literacies and social practices at large. It can be used as a reference point from which to consider the dialectics of production and consumption of official literacies of school. Some of the producers are ministers and high-ranking federal and state government educational officials who frame literacy policy. Others are those who interpret this policy, who produce guidelines for its specific implementation, who oversee curriculum and syllabus development and who police its implementation in schools. Still others are literacy researchers and theorists (the 'experts') who either collaborate with the 'major' producers, or who operate from their own comparatively powerful 'places' ('propers') to try and define what will be the constraining order of school literacies. Roles are some-times ambiguous. For example, are those who 'write' the guidelines and syllabus content to the requirements of their superior officers best seen as producers or consumers? We tend to think of them as consumers, since the power of strategy is not theirs. Teachers and learners and their caregivers are likewise consumers (along with most other 'members of the school community'). To be a producer is, ultimately, to arrogate the 'right' to shape how others will *practise* literacy and *be* literate.

It is important for those of us involved in literacy education to consider where we, personally, are positioned in all this. In the final analysis there is one crucial difference between eBayers participating as consumers in ratings and feedback literacies and learners participating in school literacies. eBayers choose to partici-pate. Learners are compelled. They are forced to operate on producer terrain. Teachers are employed to perpetuate producer terrain. The question is how we who are consumers can most effectively negotiate the cultural politics of literacy education.

The consumer 'uses' of eBayers provides a potentially illuminating perspec-tive on these things. Teacher-consumers may find it helpful to be able to recognise learner-consumer uses when they occur, and to find ways of building on them pedagogically. On the other hand, we have dealt here with only half of the picture so far as de Certeau's account of consumer practices of everyday life is concerned. The other half involves 'tactics'. It makes for a very interesting story, but one that unfortunately must wait for another day.

Note

1   netgrrrl ☆ (12) and chicoboy26 ★ (32) are users of eBay. In meat spaces they are known as Michele Knobel and Colin Lankshear.

References

Amherst Robots (2001) *Auction Data Analysis and Delivery*. Online. Available HTTP: *http://www.vrane.com/* (21 March 2001).

BidBlaster (2001) *BidBlaster*. Online. Available HTTP: *www.bidblaster.net* (11 June 2001).

BidPay (2001). *BidPay*. Online. Available HTTP: *http://www.bidpay.com* (11 June 2001).

Billpoint (2001). *Billpoint*. Online. Available HTTP: *http://www.billpoint.com* (11 June 2001).

Collier, M. and Woerner, R. (2000) *eBay for Dummies*. Second edition, New York: Hungry Minds.

de Certeau, M. (1984) *The Practice of Everyday Life*, trans. S. Rendall, Berkeley, CA: University of California Press.

eBay (2001a) *Feedback Message Board*. Online. Available HTTP: *http://forums.ebay.com/dws?14@1007150370092@.ee7b9c6* (11 June 2001).

—— (2001b) *Welcome Page*. Online. Available HTTP: *http://www.ebay.com* (27 February 2001).

—— (2001c) *eBay Feedback FAQ*. Online. Available HTTP: *http://pages.ebay.com/help/basics/f-feedback.html* (27 February 2001).

—— (2001d) *eBay Education*. Online. Available HTTP: *http://pages.ebay.com/education/index.html* (11 June 2001).

eSnipe (2001) *eSnipe*. Online. Available HTTP: *http://www.esnipe.com/* (11 June 2001).

Friedman, T. (2000) *The Lexus and the Olive Tree*, New York: Anchor Books.

Knobel, M. and Lankshear, C. (1999) *Ways of Knowing: Researching Literacy*, Newtown, NSW: Primary English Teaching Association.

Lorlei's (2000) *Customer Care Assurance*. Online. Available HTTP: *http://cgi.ebay.com/aw-cgi/eBayISAPI.dll?ViewItem&item=412824070* (11 May 2000).

Multex.com (2001) *Market Guide: Business Description. eBay Inc*. Online. Available HTTP: *http://yahoo.marketguide.com/mgi/busidesc.asp?rt=busidesc&rn=A1C7E* (27 February 2001).

Plastic (2001) *Plastic*. Online. Available HTTP: *http://www.plastic.com* (19 January 2001).

Reno, D., Reno, B. and Butler, M. (eds.) (2000) *The Unofficial Guide to eBay and Online Auctions*, New York: Hungry Minds.

Sherman, E. (2001) 'The world's largest yard sale. Online auctions: the sale of collectibles is migrating to the web', *Newsweek*, March 19: 62–64.

SoYouWanna (2000) *SoYouWanna Use eBay (And Not Get Ripped Off)?* Online. Available HTTP: *http://www.soyouwanna.com/site/syws/ebay/ebay.html* (12 March 2001).

Spector, R. (2000) *Amazon.com: Get Big Fast*, Sydney: Harper*Business*.

Spradley, J. (1980) *Participant Observation*, Fort Worth: Holt, Rhinehart & Winston.

Yahoo! Geocities (2001) 'Yahoo! GeoCities Ratings and Reviews'. Online. Available HTTP: *http://www.us.geocities.yahoo.com/* (16 June 2001).

2

WRITING THE VISUAL

The use of graphic symbols in onscreen texts

Chris Abbott

Scenario one: 1967

A studious schoolboy in the south of England, proud to be Head Librarian for his school, works long into the night on the designs for a new alternative school magazine. The magazine is to challenge the orthodoxy espoused by *The New Wordsworthian*, the official school magazine. Influenced by the burgeoning alternative press of the 1960s, the schoolboy and his friends aim to create in *Veritas*, named for the school motto *Veritas in Caritate* (Truth through Charity), a channel for protest and free speech. The young editors design the pages on paper and then trace them onto wax stencils before printing the magazine on an ancient ink duplicator, a lengthy and messy process. The first issues are taken to be approved by the Head Teacher, and much discussion follows. Eventually a compromise is reached: all that might be libellous or offensive is removed, and a rather sanitised *Veritas* – 'half-truth' perhaps would be a better title – hits the tuck-shop sales counter. Only 200 copies are sold in this grammar school which has more than 600 students. Within a few weeks, it is forgotten. Within a year, almost no copies exist.

Scenario two: 2001

In a neighbouring county, in the south of England, a young person of the same age, also of a studious nature – the label 'nerd' would suit him well – works on his website. He's had an idea of how to impress visitors to his website: to present an enhanced image of the technology supposedly underpinning the site. He works on some new pages which will show a system of interlinked computers based in a high-tech office. He collects images from around the Web to back up this explanation of the technology, and makes sure that the images create the desired impression. Within an hour or two, he has created a visual representation of his office, an inaccurate and much exaggerated picture, but one which he then publishes through his website so that anyone with Internet access can view it. His potential readership runs into millions; and his actual readership is in the thousands since he has built up a wide range of contacts who visit the site to read his journal, view his webcam, browse his gallery and talk in his chat areas.

The World Wide Web and literacy practices

The young schoolboy in 1967 was me; the student in 2001 is one of the young people whose Web activities I have written about in the past few years (Abbott 1998a, 1999a, 2000a). The principal difference between the two scenarios could easily be seen as a matter of technology. The reprographic and publishing facilities which each young person had available were very different. In 1967, access to ink duplicators was not generally possible and photocopiers were in their infancy. Literary practices such as writing for the school magazine were encouraged; alternative publications were barely tolerated and closely controlled, at least in the UK. By contrast, in 2001, young people with Web access – either at home, at school or in a public library – could publish their thoughts in words, images, moving video, animation and audio at minimal cost with no adult interference or control.

But changes in the devices of production and the social practices by which they are controlled are not my concern here: the focus for this chapter is the content and nature of the messages transmitted through those practices. In this chapter, I consider the extent to which the artefacts young authors produce are changing, and the degree to which the visual channel is becoming ever more paramount in what they create.

Previous generations have grown up in a world circumscribed by text. The publications young people read may have been illustrated, but those illustrations were, in the main, subservient to the text rather than offering enhanced or alternative readings. Signs are emerging, however, that contemporary texts are more likely to privilege the image in ways which are new, but also in ways which provoke debate. This debate has often taken place around changing conceptions of literacy, or literacies. In an influential article in the *Harvard Education Review* (New London Group 1996), a number of eminent literacy theorists argue that literacy, previously seen as a discrete concept, is actually more properly described as a set of practices, that is, as 'literacies'. The notion of literacy practices (Street 1995, 2000) is one to which I will return as it is helpful when considering the concerns of this chapter.

The New London Group (NLG) produced the article, 'A Pedagogy of Multiliteracies', at a time when the Internet was just beginning to be seen not only as a medium for locating information, but also as a medium for publication. The group was centrally concerned with the ways in which literacy practices enable young people to get involved with the processes which control their lives. Multiliteracies, the term adopted by the group to denote those practices, has been criticised by those who believe, as I do, that while literacy is changing, it is not simply fragmenting into a series of different but allied literacies. For example, Street (1999, 2000) contrasts the group's notion of multiliteracies with what he describes as multiple literacies. Street argues that a multiple-literacies approach enables these practices to be seen as socially grounded rather than as technologically determined. He portrays these literacy activities as rooted in the ideologies that underpin the societies in which their authors live, rather than being an outcome of the provision of particular hardware or software. This point is relevant for decision makers who seek to change practice merely by providing the necessary technical equipment; a literacy-practices approach would suggest that major shifts in ideological underpinnings are needed before such practices can become part of the repertoire of target groups.

By contrast, the term dynamic representational resources, used by the NLG to describe resources such as websites, is useful. Kress (1996) links the notion of representational resources with other fields of development within discourse analysis and linguistics, seeing connections with social inequities. His call for an ethnography of the representational resources used by different groups is still pertinent and has been only partly addressed.

Young website owners – developing a typology of use

Some of the young people whose online practices were studied in the early years of the Web (Abbott 1998a, 1998b, 1999a, 1999b, 2000a) grounded their literacy practices in their social lives and relationships. A typology of use I proposed then, and teased out later, attempted to characterise three main types of use prevalent in the mid- to late 1990s: the Technological Aesthete, the Community Builder and the Professional Activist (Abbott forthcoming). These types of use tended to be separate and specific in the early, innovative phase of the Web, but as it has become a more widely used medium they have merged and intermingled with each other. All three types of use, however, have contributed to the move to the visual, a powerful outcome of the development of these practices.

I have characterised Technological Aestheticism as the use of a website to create an artefact which can be admired and which will, in particular, reflect well on its author in the eyes of others. Adherents to this type of use could at first impress through their command of the programming code in which webpages are written, but with the advent of Web authoring programs, Technological Aesthetes required a new challenge, and the manipulation of graphics, audio and moving images offered exactly that. Technological Aestheticism in the mid-1990s might have consisted of merely creating and updating an extensive website; by the end of the decade, it was more likely to involve the creation of databases of audio files, graphic libraries and introductory sequences based on feature-film practices.

Animated, audio-enhanced, introductory sequences increased in popularity in the late 1990s when software tools made them possible, broadband connections became more common and the informal communities of learners within which young people operated enabled the necessary knowledge to be acquired. Typically involving a build-up of sound and movement, these sequences follow many of the conventions of feature-film trailers, themselves migrating to the Web at the time and now widely available through this medium.

Community Building as a type of website use revolves around the potential of the Web to unite people through the searching mechanisms that it makes available. Whatever the interest of a particular enthusiast, whether this be keeping Californian rat snakes or collecting vintage tractors, a Web search will almost certainly throw up further enthusiasts. Community Builders use their websites to reach out and make contact with others who have similar interests. Developing practices such as the creation of webrings – groupings of websites the owners of which have recognised their shared interests by choosing to be listed together – have supported this use of the Web. Illustrative material has become crucial to these sites; the list of old tractors which might have been on the site in 1996 is now more likely to be a series of graphics.

Professional Activists have suffered most from the ever-increasing commercialisation and globalisation of the Web. Although they can quickly publicise their cause or contact each other, they are increasingly unable to operate as they once did, now that they find themselves to be no longer in the free and unregulated environment which they took for granted in the early years.

Symbol use, special educational needs and information and communication technologies

At the same time as these developments were taking place, and attracting far less attention from the popular press or the academy, symbol users, many with special educational needs, found that the use of information and communication technologies (ICTs) could enable them to reach undreamed-of levels of communication and literacy in their everyday lives. Symbolic communication involves the use of one of the several symbol sets which are now found across the world. Perhaps the most widely used is Rebus (see Figure 2.1), a symbol set which is largely comprehensible even to people seeing the symbols for the first time. Other sets use symbols, which are less stylised and closer to small illustrations, and thus very accessible to the average user, although perhaps less so to people with particular special needs. Such people may well use one of the specific sets of symbols such as *Makaton* or *Bliss* which are designed specially for them but may be less understandable by the public at large.

Although symbols have been in use in special needs educational settings for a long time, the emphasis has usually been on the communication of basic wants and needs. More recently, the ready availability of symbols through ICTs has extended opportunities for students with special needs to develop their literacy practices, become more independent and learn more effectively (Detheridge and Detheridge 1997; Detheridge 2000). Tina Detheridge is now involved in the use

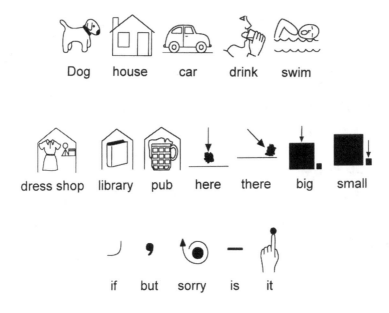

Figure 2.1   Rebus symbols (Widget Software)

of symbols to transcend textual language barriers, and the Rebus symbols are being revised so that they are international.

Symbol use varies widely and involves a broad range of consumers and practices. A recently published collection of case studies (Abbott 2000a) describes many of these. It also raises questions about the issues that arise from symbolic communication and literacy.

> Peter ... has an autistic spectrum disorder and is hyperlexic. He is a very fluent reader but although he is able to read anything, even very complex material, he has no understanding of what words mean. Staff at his school added symbols to his texts, from which he has been able to learn what the text is about and to begin to read with some understanding.
>
> (Abbott 2000a: 10)

The move to the visual discussed here has had a powerful effect for Peter: the addition of visual information to the text that he can process, but not understand, has enabled him to extract meaning in a way which was previously impossible. Staff might well have identified his needs in this respect earlier, but it is largely due to the availability of computer software with the capacity to automatically insert symbols, such as *Writing with Symbols 2000* (Detheridge 2000), that they have been able to implement this course of action.

Many people who have autistic spectrum disorders seem to have an ability to process visual information where they may be unable to gain meaning from

macaroni cheese and tuna bake

Ingredients

1 lb butter   1 1/2 oz flour   15 fl oz milk 8oz cheese 1 tin of tuna 2 teaspoons

mustard salt and pepper 2 tomatoes

Method

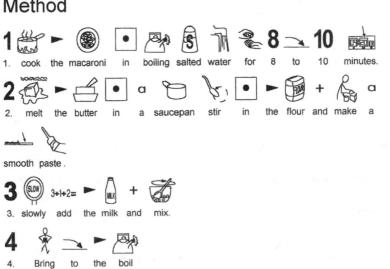

1.   cook the macaroni   in   boiling salted water   for   8   to   10   minutes.

2.   melt   the butter   in   a   saucepan   stir   in   the   flour and make   a

smooth paste .

3. slowly   add   the milk and   mix.

4.   Bring   to   the   boil

Figure 2.2   Recipe written in symbols (Widget Software)

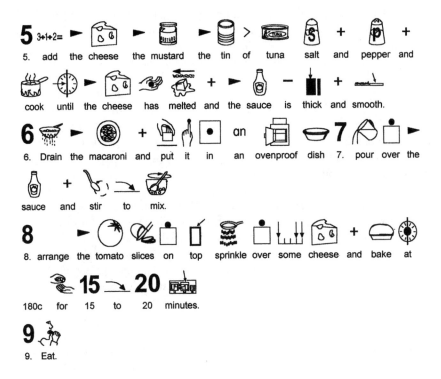

5. add the cheese the mustard the tin of tuna salt and pepper and cook until the cheese has melted and the sauce is thick and smooth.

6. Drain the macaroni and put it in an ovenproof dish 7. pour over the sauce and stir to mix.

8. arrange the tomato slices on top sprinkle over some cheese and bake at 180c for 15 to 20 minutes.

9. Eat.

Figure 2.2   continued

verbal text. This is not an uncontested proposition, however, and attitudes to autistic spectrum disorders vary as widely as do the suggested ways of assisting people who have these needs.

> A symbol is concrete, visual and permanent. The TEACCH system, developed in North Carolina, considers autism a culture and has identified that people with autism find visual, permanent communication systems much more easy to understand than aural, temporary ones.
>
> (Abbott 2000b: 44)

Further, it seems that not only those people whose needs fall within this spectrum can be helped: society's increasing ability to communicate visually offers significant improvements for many situations. Inclusion, the process by which all needs are catered for so that those with special needs do not need to be segregated and dealt with separately, can also be supported by the use of visual communication through symbols (see Figure 2.2).

The Forum @Greenwich is a community centre that runs a cafe project for people with learning difficulties. Workers at the cafe are helped with symbols on the menu board when taking orders, on notices and signs. Rebus symbols are also used in training materials covering issues such as catering hygiene and life skills.

(Abbott 2000b: 70)

Symbols can also give a voice to those who may not otherwise be heard. Making a complaint or politely declining to take part in a planned activity are not options that are available to many people with special needs; symbols can change that as demonstrated in Figure 2.3.

In Devon, the Total Communication Partnership has produced a number of leaflets to help service-users become involved in self-advocacy. The complaints form produced by the Partnership takes up two sides of an A4 page and is designed for users who can access some text. Boxes are provided for answers that mostly consist of completing sentences. Symbols appear alongside the questions to communicate alongside the written word-based text.

(Abbott 2000b: 75)

Teachers, carers, parents and symbol users have worked together to develop new practices in the use of symbolic communication and literacy. These prac-

How to complain

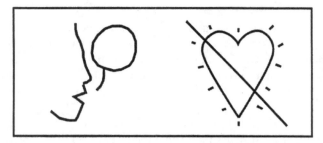

Say what you don't like

Figure 2.3 Front of a symbol booklet about complaining (Widget Software)

tices have been documented (Detheridge and Detheridge 1997; Abbott 2000a; Detheridge 2000) and user groups meet regularly to develop good practice and share expertise and innovation.

The shift to the iconic

In the ways described, whether in the form of a computer program enabling symbolic communication or via a freely available world-wide publishing medium like the Web, the use of ICTs is changing the literacy practices of people in many countries around the world. An important proviso must be added here, of course: this can happen only where access to computers and the Internet is available. It is one of the paradoxes of what is often referred to as the digital divide that many of those people who have most to gain from such technologies are often those least able to get access to them. Issues of access are not the main topic here, although they do loom large in any discussion of how these developments can be spread more widely if they are to be of benefit to different groups of people.

What, then, are the links between these two parallel developments: young people publishing visually literate websites and people with special needs communicating through symbols? An obvious connection would be the increasing number of websites using symbols either in addition to, or in replacement of, written word-based texts. This development began in schools and centres where symbol-users could be found in large numbers. Meldreth Manor School in Hertfordshire, UK, is an example of an environment in which symbol use and iconic communication predates the World Wide Web, but where the Web is now an essential part of that communicative environment. The school website (Walter 2001) gives a clear example of this in the various pathways and alternatives it provides (see Figure 2.4). Although the first screen offers textual routes for some users, others click on the symbolised link and

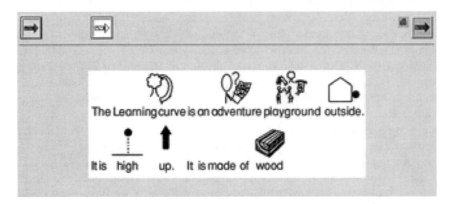

Figure 2.4   Screen from the website of a symbol-using school (*www.meldrethmanor.com* [accessed 6 June 2001])

quickly find themselves in a familiar symbol world. The school's Intranet operates extensively in this way, with the use of audio and video to support the symbolic visual information contained there.

Many schools and centres for people with special needs have begun to use symbols on their websites in this way, but strikingly, other Web-based projects, aimed at quite different target groups, have begun to privilege the visual as opposed to the word-based text as the primary navigatory and sometimes discursive environment. Majaky (the Czech word for Lighthouse) is a project set up to provide Internet access to children and young people in hospital. Although it is based in the Czech Republic, the project is now moving into an international phase, and will become even more important as it offers an interface which is meaningful to speakers of different languages.

As it happens, the interface originally chosen for the project (Sulovsky 2001) is essentially visual. The lighthouse of the title can be seen shining across the ocean, a metaphor which adds a certain mystery to an interface originally designed for a land-locked country. When new users register they choose an avatar, a visual representation of themselves, which may or may not bear any relation to their actual appearance. They then become mariners, are welcomed by the Captain (the owner of the site) and can begin to send messages and take part in discussions. Online discussions usually follow the threading metaphor originally developed on bulletin boards, and the same is true here, although with the vital difference that the discussion is portrayed symbolically. In the Message Harbour, a row of sailing ships can be seen. Each ship sails into the harbour when its owner, one of the mariners, starts a new discussion. The ship stays in the harbour if the discussion continues, but if no-one wants to continue with the topic, the ship slowly sinks. Similar visual representations are used throughout the site: the News Bay is where the latest information is available, and if you want to write some news you are taken to a room with pencils and pens on shelves and images of written materials (see Figure 2.5).

In Finland, Verkkosalkku, which means Education Portfolio, is the name chosen for the lifelong learning Web portal which is to be the entry point for Finnish citizens seeking educational provision. The portal (Verkkosalkku 2001) is likely to develop further following the initiation of the process in 2001, but an early decision was taken on the extent to which alternative access should be built in for users with special needs. It was expected that this would consist of a separate area on Verkkosalkku, but discussions between myself and other members of the project team have resulted in the decision to attempt to build a lifelong learning portal for all which uses symbols and other visual information. In this way, it is hoped that all Finnish citizens will be able to access the site. Such a plan complies with the spirit of inclusion but will also offer significant challenges in the years ahead, especially if those who are happier in a word-based text environment are to feel confident with the system.

The development of a visual interface at Verkkosalkku is not typical of government-led Web portals within education. While many other content

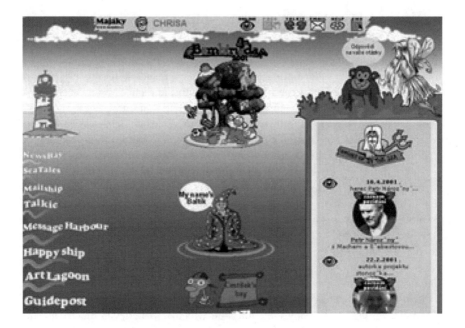

Figure 2.5 Opening screen from the Majaky website (*www.majaky.com* [accessed 6 June 2001])

providers on the Web have recognised the need to communicate in this way, others have taken refuge in a simple transposition of information from previously paper-based media to an online version. An example of this is the UK National Grid for Learning, a sober and serious place in which the irreverence, vitality and liveliness of the Web is markedly absent. The central images on the site (DfEE 2001) are of two female students, gazing delightedly at the printed material in their hands, and a map of the UK with the constituent countries, each with its own version of the Grid, marked by colour changes as the mouse passes over them.

A look at some of the rival and corporately owned sites aimed at education indicates very different approaches to the visualisation of online literacy. Some, like Schoolsnet (Schoolsnet 2001), adopt a similarly restrained approach, perhaps to avoid competing with the banner advertising who is paying for the site. Learning Alive (Research Machines plc 2001), on the other hand, uses more lively graphics, an informal font style and occasional animations. BBC Bitesize, a site intended to help students revise but which is frequently used by teachers as well (BBC 2001), takes the process a step further. The site uses animations, brightly coloured backgrounds, an irreverent style and shows a recognition that technologies like text messaging are part of the everyday life of many young people in the UK.

41

The durability of the shift to the visual

When I have spoken at conferences about the changes described here, some members of the audience assert that these changes are transitory and have no like-lihood of causing any permanent changes. However, such responses were more common in the mid-1990s than they are now, and audiences today seem more ready to recognise that real change is taking place and that they see it in their own lives. Just as in UK schools, only when a majority of teachers became owners of computers did they recognise the potential of the technology for their teaching, so it is that when people begin to communicate themselves in visual ways do they recognise that it represents something different from what has gone before.

It may still be true that the photocopier remains the most revolutionary tech-nology in the developed world. Thus it is no surprise that some of the totalitarian countries have banned access to such machines. Photocopiers were first used to copy word-based texts, and academics in Eastern Europe know what it is to not be able to share texts in this way. Until the late 1980s, texts not approved by the government had to be typed out using as many as twelve sheets of carbon paper; photocopiers could have brought down governments far more quickly.

If images have not been copied as frequently as words it is perhaps because of the thorny problem of copyright, an issue which also bedevils much Internet practice. It has become the convention in many countries that, at least for a certain period of time, the rights to reproduce an image are owned by the origi-nator and first publisher of the image. Such a policy is increasingly under attack and seems nonsensical when applied to the Web, where creative bricolage is the dominant mode and most sites are assemblages of words, images, sounds and code from elsewhere. Some have argued that these practices are culturally rooted, as do both an American writer and a Scots writer when they discern 'a Scottish ambivalence about the nature and worth of home-grown words' (Sloane and Johnstone 2000: 156). Their description of a writing tradition which involves frequent borrowings, credited or not, is a persuasive model for transposi-tion to the Web, yet I remain unconvinced that such practices are any more entrenched and ideologically rooted in Scots culture than they are in many other contexts. At times, the authors stray dangerously near to the romantic notion of the wild Scots adventurer which so often tempts those who feel a yearning for their ancestral links to the Highlands:

> [O]ne strand of the rich tapestry that comprises Scottish writing is a tradition of writers borrowing words, ideas and themes from beyond its borders.
>
> Scottish writing is rich, diverse, and has multiple preoccupations and perspectives. When this strand is transposed onto the Web, we can observe and answer more completely the question of how cultural values are embedded in any writing.
>
> (Sloane and Johnstone 2000: 157)

If the producers of the *Writing with Symbols* software had chosen to restrict the use of their Rebus symbols, the program would have been unusable except in a limited sense. Their recognition that the symbols must be freely available and freely reproducible has enabled symbol practice to grow and develop. Similarly enlightened steps need to be taken by the international bodies currently attempting to harmonise copyright law.

Publishing on the Web is not just a change in the choice of technology, but neither is it related only to the move to an environment where vast resources are available to be re-used and re-purposed by citizen publishers. More radically than this, it is an apparently open and free environment, and yet the 'messy complexity – and the oftentimes contradictory nature – of these new literacies suggests ... a more complicated postmodern vision' (Hawisher and Selfe 2000: 277). With the important proviso, in regard to inequities of access, many people around the world can now choose to publish if they wish to do so. This has not been the case in the past, although changes in reprographic technology have often been accompanied by significant social change, even if this is limited by the control of that technology exerted by elite groups (Eisenstein 1983).

It does seem less the case now than it was in the mid-1990s that the Web, in particular, is quite the openly accessible, uncontrolled and freely available site for publication that it was once portrayed to be. Understandable concerns about offensive material and a growing awareness on the part of the corporate sector that there must be a way to make money from this medium have conspired to create a climate in which some form of control, less anonymity on the part of users, and increasingly effective payment models all seem to be part of online life in the early years of the century.

The implications for schooling

It is important to recognise that much of the text-based world, especially in education, has remained largely unaffected by moves to a more visually-based set of literacy practices. It has often been pointed out that, perhaps paradoxically, much ICT practice seems to increase rather than decrease the number of printed pages in homes, schools and offices:

> [A] great deal of this technology is devoted to the storage, organisation and processing of text. On-line help systems are often heavily text dependent. Also, information technology appears to generate a huge amount of ancillary printed material.
>
> (Hannon 2000: 22)

Predicting the imminent demise of the book may be fun if you are a tabloid journalist with a deadline to meet, but no one of any credibility in the academic world is predicting such a development in the near or even medium future. That is not to say that changes are not happening, but that those changes are considerably more complex and complicated than lazy journalism might suggest.

Much writing about electronic texts has related to the ways in which the words themselves may be changing or used in different ways. An increasing number of commentators, however, are recognising the incursion of the image. Reinking (1994), in his explanation of the differences between electronic and printed texts, includes the use of images, particularly to assist in navigation. Kress goes further and writes persuasively of the changes he sees in communicative practices:

> Technology, multiculturalism, the new economies of information and services, in the context of globalisation ... are making image more significant than writing in many domains of public communication.
>
> (Kress 2000: 8)

Colour printing, too, has never been a part of serious book production in an academic sense; it is within the genre of children's books that the colour image has reached its zenith. Colour evokes powerful associations, however, and its use on the Web alongside carefully chosen images can enhance and extend the message contained in word-based texts (McConaghy and Snyder 2000). Raised as they were on full-colour illustrated narrative books, young people easily select and manipulate colour and tone in the electronic artefacts they produce.

Websites differ from books in other ways than just their greater reliance on the image as communication. In particular, they do not offer that sense of completeness and terminus that books normally indicate by their fixed limits, what Bolter has called 'the sense of closure that the codex and printing have fostered' (Bolter 1991: 87). Young people at school today do not seek that closure in the same way that previous generations might have done, since the present generation of children – the network or N-generation as they are sometimes called (Tapscott 1998) – have become used to the mores, circumlocutions and practices of the Web and other online spaces.

Children today communicate visually with ease and understanding. Papert (1996) suggests that schools have failed to change as quickly as have children and families. Endless educational conferences have begun with the now clichéd tale of the surgeon and teacher of 1900 who both travel into the future for a hundred years: the surgeon is totally at sea faced with a transformed profession but the teacher feels at home. There is a kernel of truth in the story – at least if we are concerned with what the teacher sees in the classroom – but there are considerable changes to be found if that teacher were to spend some time listening to what was going on in the school.

Schools are changing because of the use of ICTs in general as well as because of the ascendancy of the visual in electronic resources. The development in the UK of open learning centres based around the use of ICTs is part of a general shift, certainly in Europe, away from nine-to-four classrooms and towards a genuine attempt at lifelong learning at times and in places that suit the individual (Abbott 2000a). Most pilot projects in this area, in countries such as Finland and the Netherlands, tend to focus on the later years of compulsory schooling. In the UK a different approach is being attempted, although aimed at the same age group. A large government contract awarded to the BBC and Granada, a multi-national publishing group, will enable the creation of a digital curriculum in six subjects for students aged 14 to 16 years. From 2003, all six subjects are to be available, by way of digital television or the Web. At that point the questions are bound to be asked about the necessity of that age group attending a large building called a school every day at the same hours, if much of the resources they need to access are more readily available online at home or in a library or local learning centre.

How visual those subject resources will be remains to be seen, but if the publishers and broadcasters involved want their resources to be both popular and effective, they would do well to recognise that the present generation of young people expect their learning resources to be multimedia, individualised and not over-reliant on word-based text. The computer screen has been described as 'the domain of the image, of the visible as image' (Kress 2000: 9). The young person who watches digital TV, downloads Mp3 music onto a personal player, checks e-mail on a personal organiser and sends symbolised messages to the mobile phone of a friend, will not be satisfied with a 500-word revision guide for GCSE physics. And when those young people become adults, who begin sharing their views with others, how willing will they be to contribute to a future volume such as this – or will the changes affecting young people and schools now lead to trans-formations in the academy and the publishing world? I hope so.

References

Abbott, C. (1998a) 'Making connections: young people and the Internet', in J. Sefton-Green (ed.) *Digital Diversions: Youth Culture in the Age of Multimedia*, London: UCL Press, pp. 84–105.

—— (1998b) 'New writers, new audiences, new responses', in M. Monteith (ed.) *IT for Learning Enhancement*, Oxford: Intellect, pp. 96–105.

—— (1999a) 'The Internet, text production and the construction of identity: changing use by young males during the early to mid 1990s', unpublished doctoral thesis, King's College, London.

—— (1999b) 'Web publishing by young people', in J. Sefton-Green (ed.) *Young People, Creativity and the New Technologies*, London: Routledge, pp. 111–121.

—— (2000a) *ICT: Changing Education*, London: RoutledgeFalmer.

—— (ed.) (2000b) *Symbols Now*, Leamington Spa: Widgit.

—— (forthcoming) 'Some young male Website owners: the Technological Aesthete, the Community Builder and the Professional Activist', *Education, Communication and Information* 1 (2).

BBC (2001) *BBC Bitesize*. Online. Available HTTP: *www.bbc.co.uk/education/gcsebitesize* (6 June 2001).

Bolter, J. D. (1991) *Writing Space: The Computer, Hypertext and the History of Writing*, Hillsdale, New Jersey: Lawrence Erlbaum Associates.

Detheridge, T. (ed.) (2000) *Introduction to Symbols*, Leamington Spa: Widgit Software.

Detheridge, M. and Detheridge, T. (1997) *Literacy Through Symbols: Improving Access for Children and Adults*, London: David Fulton.

DfEE (2001) *National Grid for Learning* Online. Available HTTP: *www.ngfl.gov.uk/index.html* (6 June 2001).

Eisenstein, E. (1983) *The Printing Revolution in Early Modern Europe*, Cambridge: Cambridge University Press.

Hannon, P. (2000) *Reflecting on Literacy in Education*, London: RoutledgeFalmer.

Hawisher, G. E. and Selfe, C. L. (eds). (2000) *Global Literacies and the World Wide Web*, London: Routledge.

Kress, G. (1996) 'Representational resources and the production of subjectivity', in C. R. Caldas-Coulthard and M. Coulthard (eds) *Texts and Practices: Readings in Critical Discourse Analysis*, London: Routledge, pp. 15–31.

—— (2000) *Early Spelling: Between Convention and Creativity*, London: Routledge.

McConaghy, C. and Snyder, I. (2000) 'Working the Web in postcolonial Australia', in G. Hawisher and C. Selfe (eds) *Global Literacies and the World-Wide Web*, London: Routledge, pp. 74–92.

New London Group (1996) 'A pedagogy of multiliteracies: designing social futures', *Harvard Educational Review*, 66 (1): 60–92.

Papert, S. (1996) *The Connected Family: Bridging the Generation Gap*, Atlanta, Georgia: Longstreet Press.

Reinking, D. (1994) *Electronic Literacy: Perspectives in Reading Research No. 4*, National Reading Research Center, Athens, Georgia and College Park, Maryland: Universities of Georgia and Maryland.

Research Machines plc (2001) *Learning Alive*. Online. Available HTTP: *www.learningalive.co.uk/* (6 June 2001).

Schoolsnet (2001) *Schoolsnet*. Online. Available HTTP: *www.schoolsnet.com* (6 June 2001).

Sloane, S. and Johnstone, J. (2000) 'Reading sideways, backwards, and across: Scottish and American literacy practices and weaving the Web', in G. Hawisher and C. Selfe (eds), *Global Literacies and the World-Wide Web*, London: Routledge, pp. 154–185.

Street, B. (1995) *Social Literacies: Critical Approaches to Literacy in Development, Ethnography and Education*, New York: Longman.

—— (1999) 'New literacies in theory and practice: what are the implications for language in education?', *Linguistics and Education* 10 (1): 1–24.

—— (2000) 'Literacy "events" and literacy "practices": theory and practice in the "New Literacy Studies"', in M. Martin-Jones and K. Jones (eds) *Multilingual Literacies: Comparative Perspectives on Research and Practice*, Amsterdam: John Benjamins, pp. 17–29.

Sulovsky, J. (2001) *Majaky*. Online. Available HTTP: *www.majaky.com* (6 June 2001).

Tapscott, D. (1998) *Growing up Digital: The Rise of the Net Generation*, New York: McGraw-Hill.

Verkkosalkku (2001) *Verkkosalkku*. Online. Available HTTP: *www.verkkosalkku.net* (6 June 2001).

Walter, R. (2001) *Meldreth Manor School Website*. Online. Available HTTP: *www.meldrethmanor.com* (6 June 2001).

READING, WRITING AND ROLE-PLAYING COMPUTER GAMES

Catherine Beavis

Literacy, learning and computer games

Questions about the implications of the new technologies for literacy, literacy teaching and literacy practices provoke diverse and contradictory responses in the media, in policy documents, in state and national literacy assessment surveys and amongst teachers. On the one hand, the need for literacy to be reconceptualised and redefined in the face of rapid change seems overwhelming – more a matter of recognition and retrospective adjustment to reflect already established practice and ongoing change. On the other, definitions of literacy, particularly as they are enacted in curriculum and assessment policies and in schools, for the most part remain largely print-based. Fears attached to the redefinition of literacy to include visual and digital forms suggest such expansion will lead to the embrace of anything digital at the cost of critical thinking and of values associated with print literature and literacy.

The moral and cultural dimensions of these arguments have been well rehearsed in debates about the nature of the English and literacy curriculum and the role of popular culture in relation to texts regarded as mainstream. So, too, has the need for teachers to be better supported in working with the new technologies and designing and teaching a curriculum that reflects the rapidly changing nature of literacy practices associated with their use. Linked to this are repeated calls for the curriculum to find ways to strengthen the relationship between young people's in-school and out-of-school worlds. What might it mean to take seriously the proposition that artefacts of electronic popular culture such as computer games be included in the literacy curriculum?

The world of texts inhabited by young people, the literacies the texts teach and the nature of the texts, are significantly different from those with which English and literacy teaching practices and curriculum have been traditionally associated. The dimensions of difference range across the multimodal ways in which meanings are made, narratives constructed and stories told, participants' high levels of energy and commitment, and the global context in which games are played and linked to other genres. Features such as interactivity, the social nature of game playing and the centrality of the games world to youth culture and peer groups in young players' habitus, make these texts highly attractive and significant for young people. This is in marked contrast to the less immediately engaging forms of print text and literacy generally on offer in schools.

In their out-of-school lives, even in the earliest years, children's experiences and expectations of literacy are no longer necessarily paper-based. The diverse range of texts and literacies with which they become familiar prior even to entering school has implications that challenge assumptions and expectations about early literacy curriculum. Socially, culturally and in the kinds of literacies they entail, games such as *Pokemon*, *Magic Cards* and *War Hammer* present young people in the early and middle primary grades with complex, highly developed mythologies and symbol systems. Children as young as five learn to read and negotiate multilayered narratives. These narratives include large casts of players on opposing sides, each with a range of skills, attributes and weaponry brought into play in different encounters in increasingly sophisticated ways. They are often accompanied by densely written manuals, which provide detailed information about characters and scenarios. At the same time, these manuals function as catalogues for future purchases while providing essential 'background' to the games, in the manner of much children's television where advertising and narrative are also fused.

The classic instance of this phenomenon in the late 1990s amongst young children was the multiplatform game *Pokemon*. Initially a gameboy game with cards, and a spin-off of the *Magic Cards* series, it soon became popular with older children. *Pokemon* exemplifies the ways in which digital popular culture inducts young people into a multimodal literacy world. To enter the world of *Pokemon*, to become a member of the game-playing community, a complex set of operational literacies and knowledge is required. In the game, children in the role of 'trainers' are invited to collect and train as many *Pokemon* creatures as they can. To do this, players need to learn to read complex combinations of print and icons, and to find ways to insert these and themselves into the narrative and trading structure of the game. They need to recognise and make use of the skills, strengths and attributes of some 150 different creatures/characters. They need to know and utilise information about the features of each character specific to their 'element', 'type', 'techniques' and 'evolution', as well as information about who they are 'good against' and 'bad against'. In doing so, players are referred to print and visual information available across a range of platforms – cards, game-boys, television and film, and print manuals, handbooks and guides.

These literacy materials are further supplemented by saturation advertising in every corner of the children's market (clothes, toys, stationery, etc.) and perhaps most importantly, by the social context in which the game is played. Membership of the game-playing community, signalled by knowledge of specific characters and features, confers social status and marks players as initiates in a highly desirable and often multi-age world. Game playing and card trading involve skills, knowledge and capital in the form of cards, but also risk taking and social negotiation with peers and with older and younger children.

As a literacy activity, *Pokemon* exhibits many of features of literacy viewed as social practice, where ways of speaking, reading and writing are seen as always shaped by the social, cultural and political contexts in which they occur. In this view, language use carries with it or generates particular kinds of meanings and values, and is always purposeful. It constructs views of reality, and relationships between addressor and addressee, and has real-world effects in terms of relationships, perceptions and power. The ideology of the game, with its contradictory politics of cooperation and aggression, identity and commercialism, clearly constructs a set of values as the context for play, while a further set of dynamics is established between children in the trading component of the game. In both instances, these ideologies are embodied in and activated by the literacy practices through which the game is played.

The sophistication of young people's knowledge of out-of-school literacies generated by their engagement in texts such as these is increasingly being documented with respect to the early years (e.g. Downes 1999; Healey 2000; Moulton 2000). Research in this area raises questions about the implications of the mismatch between school expectations and definitions of literacy and the kinds of knowledge young children bring for their future development in literacies, both print and digital. Similarly, while the findings of literacy assessments such as the *National Australian Schools English Literacy Survey* (Australian Council for Educational Research 1997) report only on print-based forms of literacy, statistics on reading and writing, which show boys at Grades 3 and 5, for example, to be less 'literate' than girls, may not represent the full picture of literacy abilities more broadly defined. A definition of literacy that includes digital texts and competencies may well show both boys and girls to be far more competent than assessments limited to print-based reading and writing currently provide.

Linking print and digital literacies

To point to evidence of many children's and young people's knowledge of (multi)literacies (New London Group 2000) is not to argue for the displacement of print texts and literary culture in schools by computer games and digital texts of related kinds. However, it does suggest that we need an expanded set of understandings of texts and literacy, and to recognise the literacy skills many children bring with them to school and develop in their out-of-school worlds.

A number of studies have examined the degree and extent of young people's facility with computers, and their immersion in digital popular culture in their leisure time. The Australian study, *Real Time: Computers, Change and Schooling* (Meredyth *et al.* 2000) found that almost all of the 6,000-odd students surveyed were able to perform more than half of the information technology skills they specified as basic:

> the ability to use a mouse, turn on a computer, use a keyboard, shut down and turn off, exit/quit a program, save a document, print a document, start a program, open a saved document, delete files, get

data from floppy disk or CD-ROM, create a new document and move files.

(Meredyth *et al.* 2000: 27)

Two-thirds of them were able to perform them all. More than half the students had 'advanced' skills, including the ability to:

play computer games, draw using the mouse, use a computer for creative writing, letters, etc., use spreadsheets or databases, use the World Wide Web, search the Web using key words, create music or sound using a computer, send an e-mail message, copy games from a CD-ROM or the Web, create a program, use virus detection software, create a multimedia presentation and make a Web site/home page.

(Meredyth *et al.* 2000: 27)

Studies into young people's use of leisure time also suggest the importance of computer culture, as well as high levels of familiarity and expertise. Notwithstanding disparities of access and opportunity, Australian Bureau of Statistics (ABS) figures for *Children's Participation in Cultural and Leisure Activities* (ABS 2001) bear out the widespread engagement of most young people with information and communications technologies (ICTs) in their out-of-school time. In the twelve months prior to interview in April 2000, 95 per cent of Australian children aged 5–14 used a computer; 71 per cent of these at home. Sixty-nine per cent played video or computer games and 47 per cent accessed the Internet during or outside school hours. Activities included using e-mail or chat rooms (51.5 per cent), playing games (39 per cent) and browsing the Internet for pleasure (49 per cent) or for other purposes (6.3 per cent).

These figures complement research into young people's usage of electronic entertainment undertaken by the Australian Broadcasting Authority with the Office of Film and Literature Classification (OFLC), *Families and Electronic Entertainment* (Cupitt and Stockbridge 1996), the Victorian Government Parliamentary *Inquiry into The Effects of Television and Multimedia on Children and Families in Victoria.* (Family and Community Development Committee 2000) and the OFLC study, *Computer Games and Australians Today* (OFLC 1999). All four studies confirmed that ICTs are a familiar part of most young people's leisure time activities. As such, the texts of the new technologies, particularly computer games, provide the occasion both for social and enjoyable relaxation, and for the development of a range of ICT-based understandings and skills.

Designing curricula around computer games

One way to link print and digital literacies is to develop the work begun in relation to media and visual literacy to encompass digital texts as well. This would mean that in addition to developing students' capabilities in formal areas of computer literacy, such as those Meredyth *et al.* (2000) describe, schools and the English/literacy curriculum could explore opportunities for the development of textual analysis and critical perspectives on texts such as computer games with which young people are so avidly engaged. A '3D' model of literacy-technology learning (Durrant and Green 2000), whereby students engage with cultural, critical and operational dimensions simultaneously, provides a generative example of how this might be achieved.

In 1999, Deakin University colleague Noel Gough and myself and a group of teachers undertook a research study with two Victorian secondary schools to explore what incorporating computer games into the literacy curriculum might entail (Beavis 2000). Our focus was on what it might mean to extend the range of texts studied in English to incorporate games, consistent with the inclusion of 'everyday' and 'electronic' texts amongst those specified as appropriate for study in the *Curriculum and Standards Framework 2*, Victoria, Australia (Board of Studies 2000), on the nature of computer games as narratives and text, and on changing constructions of literacy as they were reflected in this instance in the planning, teaching and evaluation of the unit on computer games as texts of the new technologies. The teachers were in schools that were already actively reshaping their curriculum to take account of digital technologies. One was a private school with an established laptop programme, the other a networked state school with computer labs regularly utilised by students in most subject areas. Two of the four English teachers with whom we worked were also teaching Information Technology.

Following the initial contact, one or both of us visited each school for joint planning sessions with the teachers. Once we had described our interest in working with games as texts within the context of expanded literacy, the teachers designed a curriculum that would reflect these goals and fit in with their existing text study and curriculum. We attended and in some instances taught classes in both schools during the unit, collected student work, observed and interviewed students. At the conclusion of the unit, we returned for an extended reflection and evaluation session with the teachers, and at one school, with the students as well. We audiotaped and transcribed interviews, classes and discussions, and together with the students' written work, read them for instances of how print and electronic literacies were constructed by teachers and students, for expanded notions of reading, writing and text, and for the pedagogical and textual implications of the teachers' and students' work.

Planning at the first school centred on the theme of fantasy. The aim was to find computer games that would complement and extend students' understanding of the fantasy genre, in relation to their study of the class text, *A Wizard of Earthsea* (Le Guin 1968). We worked at junior secondary level (Year 8) with groups of games along a principle similar to wide reading. The ultimate task was to adapt the novel to a computer game. En route, students were required, amongst other things, to play a variety of games in groups, and to present a review, incorporating both print and digital literacy and verbal and visual analysis about graphic and informational technology demands. At the second school, we worked with middle-secondary students (Year 10) around *Abe's Exoddus*, (GT Interactive 1998) and asked students to undertake a variety of tasks under the rubric of 'text response'. The research provided a number of findings about computer games, pedagogy and literacy, which I discuss below.

A prior step, however, is to consider the nature of games as text, and the ways they rewrite narrative structures and the reader's role. Discussing websites as emergent cultural forms, Rivett (2000) makes the point that in any critical textual analysis, attention to the form of texts as text, as 'aesthetic and cultural form' (Rivett 2000: 36), is as much needed as a focus on the 'content' of individual texts. Such attention has long been the target of literary study in schools. Computer games, like other new media, rework older forms in a process Bolter and Grusin (2000) describe as 'remediation'. In the case of narrative role-playing games, such as those we introduced at the two schools, this reworking includes both older media, such as television or film, and elements of fantasy literature, three-dimensional graphics, and, argue Bolter and Grusin, the tradition of realistic, perspective painting (Bolter and Grusin 2000: 94). In the section that follows, I discuss two games explored in the research as objects of classroom study. In the event, as a 15+ game, *Magic and Mayhem* (Mythos Games 1998) was rejected for the fantasy unit despite its eminent suitability. *Abe's Exoddus* (GT Interactive 1998), on the other hand, went on to become the focus of classroom work with older students.

Magic and Mayhem

Magic and Mayhem (Mythos Games 1998) is a highly visual and literary game, drawing on mythic narratives and locations ranging from Classical Greece through Arthurian Albion. It exemplifies many of the qualities characteristic of role-playing games in the fantasy genre. These include an explicit set of intertextual resonances that the game relies on for much of its richness of texture, and an attention to space and surfaces and their exploration. Analysis of key features of the game give some indication of the multiple modes in which meaning is made, and what 'reading' in this context entails.

The game begins with a detailed three-dimensional animation in which players are introduced to Lucas, the character they will 'play', in his uncle's magic workshop. Here, Lucas takes a map, a magic book or 'Grimoire' and a staff before embarking on a balloon voyage accompanied by a raven (his uncle's familiar) in search of his uncle who has disappeared. The balloon crashes, and the location shifts to the first level, still in animation, where Lucas encounters and dispatches his first enemy. The animation ends, and players find themselves in the same location, now presented with a tutorial showing them how to play. This includes explicit instruction about selecting and moving characters and the creatures the players command. Players are taught how to read and use the icons such as the 'mana' surrounding the icon of Lucas' head in the bottom right-

Figure 3.1 Opening screen from the computer game, *Magic and Mayhem*

hand corner, or spell ingredients such as the fireball. Other icons include ones for creatures such as redcaps and zombies. At the same time, they are given more details about the plot structure and what players are required to do. The game goes to considerable lengths in the opening segments to locate players within the central narrative. In the first instance, players are taught how to play but, more importantly, they are also taught how to learn. In this respect, computer games resemble children's picture books in the ways 'they teach what readers [players] learn' (Meek 1988: 82).

To begin the game, the player needs both to look through the screen surface and to enter into the world of the narrative, but also to attend to that surface with its 'multiplicity of mediated objects' (Bolter and Grusin 2000: 94), in this instance the range of icons in the bottom right hand corner (see Figure 3.1).

Attention to place and surfaces, and play with literary antecedents, are hallmarks of the game from the point of entry. Information is presented in a variety of modes – verbal, visual and symbolic – indicating levels of difficulty and icons significant in the play (see Figure 3.2). Areas highlighted as active signal further information that works hypertextually – the provision of further information to the player, via the Grimoire, or instructions for proceeding with the game (see Figure 3.3). The screen is presented as a parchment page or map, with the diagonally branching path inviting entry and suggesting dimension and perspective in the classic style of landscape paintings. The Grimoire, a magic book, opens

Figure 3.2 Screen from the computer game, *Magic and Mayhem*: Enter region – Forest of Pain

Figure 3.3 Screen from the computer game, *Magic and Mayhem*: The Grimoire – Forest of Pain

with a creak of leather, and repeats the texture of the parchment page, with icons this time recalling medieval miniatures and information on the ingredients of spells, creatures and other lands. Tabs on the right indicate the kingdoms of Agea and Albion, creatures, spells and spell ingredients. The book is closed by clicking on the tab in the top left-hand corner.

As Fuller and Jenkins (1995) argue, games such as these represent a shift from narrativity to geography, with parallels concerning the navigation, mapping and colonisation of physical and cyberspace. In this game, the two are fused. Geographic regions provide the occasion for battles and conquest; they mark the means by which progress is made and also supply the mythic detail that becomes the raison d'être for the creatures encountered and spells used. Icons within the Grimoire signal the existence of these lands and beckon players forward, but the page to which they are indexed remains blank until players have achieved the level required. In this sense, the story writes itself as the game is played. Although there are markers along the way, and the narrative is prestructured and unidirectional, there is, nonetheless, a sense of openness and possibility presented to the player. 'The enemy will adapt', promises the box: 'No two campaigns will ever be the same' (Mythos Games 1998).

Abe's Exoddus

The game *Abe's Exoddus* (GT Interactive 1998) was the focus of a second set of activities with older students in a Victorian secondary school. The *Oddworld* series (Oddworld 2001), to which *Abe's Exoddus* belongs, is similarly intertextual but heavily ironic in a mock horror epic style. It's a game with a well-developed context and scenario, with characters, narrative and design elements creating a detailed comic universe. The central theme and motivating action for the game is to help the anti-hero, Abe, rescue his race, the Muddokens, from their oppressive overlords, the Glukkons. In this instance, the bones of dead Muddokens are used to make SoulStorm Brew, the 'nauseating elixir from SoulStorm Brewery'. A two-page advertisement for the game in the print magazine *Hyper* (1998) introduces potential players to the game's scenario and features, and establishes a tone of heavy irony and exaggeration. The advertisement exemplifies the intermeshing of visual and verbal elements that contribute to the game's humour and appeal as well as the multiple forms of semiosis this new literacy entails. Abe appears at the bottom left-hand corner of the page, in a bottle held by a Glukkon or a Slig, thus introducing the main characters of the game. The bottle, lifelike in its contours, lid and contents detail is itself an advertisement for SoulStorm Brewery and the game, while down the right-hand side, a string of icons provide meta-information about the classification, format, platform and copyright of the game.

The advertisement, like the game, is witty, outrageous and sophisticated, addressing a reader well versed in popular fears associated with computer games. The text is knowing and ironic, both verbally and visually. It sets out to shock and confront, but also to undercut confrontation by alerting readers to its character as parody or satire. It implies an informed and reflexive reading from players, and assumes and teaches detailed readings at literal and subtextual levels.

Like a number of other popular texts, the game sits uneasily in relation to real-world politics and texts of a more serious and threatening kind. The violence and scenario are always comic, but at the same time part of the power of the visuals comes from echoes of other associations, ranging from deep-space movie texts such as *Alien* to twentieth-century footage and film about forced labour camps. In a highly ambivalent gesture, the *Oddworld* website (Oddworld 2001) includes amongst its 'inspirational links' the Save Tibet and Amnesty sites – links which muddy the waters disturbingly in the makers' attempts to have it both ways.

Computer games, literacy and the classroom

The exploration of how notions of literacy might be expanded towards the digital and this new literacy integrated in current practice were central features of the research. The expansion of 'texts' to include computer games was readily embraced. On the other hand, both the teachers and ourselves were very conscious of the ways in which existing literacy assumptions and technologies constrained our capacity to move beyond print and verbal parameters in envisaging possibilities for student response. At the laptop school, early discussion turned on how students might use images rather than words as the basis of their analysis and response, and on the possibilities of creating a new level or new game, using specialist software in the computer-design class. The translation of the novel into a game was a 'real-world' compromise, which attempted to retain some of these features, as was the review, which in one class took the form of a visual presentation and discussion using data-projection technology.

With *Abe's Exoddus*, working with Year 10 students, the relationship was conceived differently. We deliberately took a literary approach to the non-literary game to underline the workings of the text as narrative and to highlight continuities between games and other forms – novel and film primarily – in the construction and reading/playing of the game. Students were asked to think of themselves as readers, and the game as story, in their discussion and writing about the game.

The question of how students read games, what literacy strategies and practices they bring to bear, and what strategies and practices might be generated in turn, were central issues in the research. The strategies and reading practices students drew on were particularly evident when they were faced with a new game, as they were at the school using games as wide-reading texts with analogous experiences. Contrary to popular beliefs, playing games in this situation was intensely social and interactive, with three to four students grouped around a single screen, working the controls, reading the instructions, taking notes of what appeared on screens, trying out solutions, arguing and so on. Much of this was quite traditionally print- and writing-based, with information provided on screen often itself in verbal form. However, there was not a linear reliance on print or even visual text after the initial attempts to get a feeling for the game. Rather, students seemed to leap off at some point into almost intuitive play.

Teachers in the research were more than happy with the incorporation of digital features into the literacy curriculum. The units were seen as fitting readily into existing English curriculum and priorities, providing opportunities to integrate print and electronic literacies and texts, or to study electronic texts in their own right. The units also provided opportunities to be critical and creative, and to utilise 'both' literacy forms. All four teachers were very positive about expanding definitions of text and literacy to incorporate electronic forms. The units generated enthusiasm, and provided for ongoing collaboration in a constructive atmosphere. There was a high level of interest for most students, although frustrations arose in relation to particular games. Students in the non-laptop school had less access to the technology, and hence tended to be less involved.

There were logistical difficulties in both schools, though in neither instance were these insurmountable. In the non-laptop school this required running the game through a data projector, and organising split lessons so that all students who wished to could play the game. Presenting student work through data projection at the laptop school also required the manipulation of extra technical equipment, which had to be brought in, set up and trialed. In both schools copyright issues needed to be carefully negotiated.

The study echoed concerns about issues of access and equity raised increasingly in relation to the use of ICTs in schools. Gender differences were readily, although not universally apparent. As Gilbert notes, 'Girls' lack of engagement with technology and technology subjects at school is consistent with their more general lack of engagement with computer culture, particularly electronic gaming' (Gilbert 2001: 4). It seems that computer games in particular are geared to boys. In this study, teachers commented on the higher levels of interest, involvement and collaboration from less academically strong, less attentive or less school-oriented boys. Some boys produced their 'best work' for the year. The teacher in the non-laptop school commented that students usually less involved in English work became more involved, but that conversely, some of those who usually participated more actively had less to say. The involvement of girls was much more variable. In one class at the laptop school, girls seemed equally involved and interested as the boys; in the other two, not. At the non-laptop school, with a larger population of males, some girls responded enthusiastically but others continued to make it plain that computer games were not for them.

These distinctions, between digital and print literacy, and between school and popular texts, raised difficult questions of literacy and equity, through inverting some students' orientation to class work in unexpected ways. On the one hand, some usually disengaged and disenchanted boys became deeply engrossed, and contributed their best work for the year. On the other, a number of very literate students, particularly girls, found themselves disenfranchised by this immersion into alien waters, where they had little literate or cultural purchase. One teacher at the laptop school, who had been most enthusiastic about introducing digital texts into the curriculum, nonetheless abandoned the last task, of turning the class novel into a computer game, and instead set written tasks. She commented:

> I made mine finish it off with a piece of writing, much against what I had said I was going to do, because I suddenly realised that the pendulum had swung so much that I kind of disenfranchised the same people all the time, who were usually successful, and I thought I'd better allow for people to do hand-written responses, so that would balance it all up.

In terms of literacy, for the most part, students produced thoughtful and high quality work, impressive both in its creativity and analysis and in its proficiency in both electronic and print forms. The tasks at the laptop school required students to build on digital literacy abilities (e.g., search the Internet for a review, incorporate columns and graphics into their own review) as well as utilising more traditional word-based forms. Discussion at the non-laptop school was looser, but showed a sophisticated understanding by many students of aspects of the structure and marketing of games, and of debates about media effects.

The game playing itself was the centre of a great deal of related literacy activity. Small-group work around the screens involved reading and discussion, note taking, negotiating and planning. Supplementary texts, such as game manuals, reviews from computing magazines and the backs of computer game boxes were read and discussed and used as models. Written tasks included reviews, creative and imaginative responses to the games and discussions of issues such as the significance of computer games ('for and against'), and reflections on technology and its place in the community.

Practical issues to emerge ranged from issues of suitability and censorship through to matters of logistics and copyright. As we quickly found, not all games reward close analysis in an extended way. Games closest to film and literary texts, with strong narrative structures, extensive intertextual referencing and sophisticated graphics and game play seem particularly amenable to analysis of this kind, and often fall within the fantasy genre. A related point concerned the issue of 'suitability' and age. In the classroom context, issues of censorship and age ranking are pertinent, particularly given the diversity of games assigned an M-rating, and the need to respect principles of age appropriateness in selecting texts.

Conclusions: magic and mayhem

The findings from this study supported those of other research (e.g. Lankshear *et al.* 1997; Barnett *et al.* 1999; Bruce 1999; Comber and Green 1999) on the disruption of pedagogical practices and classroom relations produced by the introduction of information and communications technologies. However, they also provide a sense of new possibilities. In both schools, the fluency of some students relative to others with computer games introduced further complex and potentially troubling disruptions in relation to what it is that students know, and what and how that is valued. Unexpected and paradoxical questions arose for teachers in both schools about how to support students already fluent with print who seemed disoriented and at a disadvantage in this context through their unfamiliarity or clumsiness with digital literacy. Issues of equity and assessment were in many ways turned on their head, as students normally disengaged in school became highly focused and involved, while more print-oriented, literary students were for the moment marginalised if they could not also operate in this visual, digital world.

As Sefton-Green observes, teachers need to recognise that their roles and authority have changed, and that 'entry into and use of literacies is a pluralistic, complex, uncontrollable part of everyday life' (Sefton-Green 2001: 174). There are many ways that schools might acknowledge the technological and textual knowledge gained by young people in their out-of-school worlds. Incorporating computer games into the literacy classroom is one approach, with powerful implications for pedagogy as much as for literacy, in terms of building links between young people's in-school and out-of-school worlds, in developing understandings about reading, reading positions, ideology and critique, and in reframing the literacy classroom in ways less excluding of many groups. Computer games in the classroom do bring 'mayhem', not least in the technological, copyright and classifications (ratings) involved. Questions of consumption, ideology and identity are foregrounded, with tricky balances to be struck between pleasure and resistance in the reading and teaching of the text as in much teaching of popular culture. Yet at the same time, there is also 'magic': in the texts themselves, in the engagement of many students more commonly bored or marginal with traditional texts and subject matter, and in the opportunities offered to both teachers and students to explore in serious, scholarly and playful ways questions of the nature of reading, and of literacy and narrative in new times, with new technologies.

References

Australian Bureau of Statistics (2001) *Children's Participation in Cultural and Leisure Activities.* Online. Available HTPP: *http://www.abs.gov.au/ausstats/abs%40.nsf/5087e58f30c6bb25 ca2568b60010b303/0b14d86e14a1215eca2569d70080031c!OpenDocument* (5 July 2001).

Australian Council for Educational Research (1997) *Mapping Literacy Achievement: Results of the 1996 National School English Literacy Survey*, Camberwell: Australian Council for Educational Research.

Barnett, J., Bill, D., Cormack, P., Hill, S., Homer, D., Nixon, H., O'Brien, J., and Thomson, P. (1999) 'Six site studies, More than just literacy? A situated research study of information technology, literacy, pedagogy and educational disadvantage, with specific reference to six South Australian public schools', in B. Comber and B. Green, *The Information Technology, Literacy and Educational Disadvantage Research and Development Project Report to DETE SA, Vol. 2*. Adelaide: University of South Australia.

Beavis, C. (2000) 'Computer games as class readers: developing literacy skills for the twenty-first century', *The English and Media Magazine*, 41: 31–35.

Board of Studies (2000) *Curriculum and Standards Framework 2*, Carlton: Board of Studies.

Bolter, D. and Grusin, R. (2000) [1999] *Remediation: Understanding New Media*, Cambridge Mass: MIT Press.

Bruce, B. (1999) 'Speaking the unspeakable about 21st century technologies', in G. Hawisher and C. Selfe (eds) *Passions, Pedagogies and 21st Century Technologies*, Urbana, IL and Logan, Utah: National Council of Teachers of English and Utah State University Press, pp. 221–228.

Comber, B. and Green, B. (1999) *The Information Technology, Literacy and Educational Disadvantage Research and Development Project Report to DETE SA, Vol. 1*, Adelaide: University of South Australia.

Cupitt, M. and Stockbridge, S. (1996) *Families and Electronic Entertainment*, Sydney: Australian Broadcasting Commission.

Downes, T (1999) 'Children's and parents' discourses about computers in the home and school', *Convergence: The Journal of Research into New Media Technologies*, 5: (4): 104–111.

Durrant, C. and Green, B. (2000) 'Literacy and the new technologies in school education: meeting the l(IT)eracy challenge?' *Australian Journal of Language and Literacy*, 23 (2): 89–108.

Family and Community Development Committee (2000) *Inquiry into The Effects of Television and Multimedia on Children and Families in Victoria*, Melbourne: Parliament of Victoria.

Fuller, M. and Jenkins, H. (1995) 'Nintendo and new world travel writing: a dialogue', in S. G. Jones (ed.) *Cybersociety: Computer-Mediated Communication and Community*, Thousand Oaks, California: Sage Publications, pp. 57–72.

Gilbert, P. (2001) 'Redefining gender issues for the twenty-first century: putting girls' education back on the agenda', *Curriculum Perspectives* 21 (1): 1–8.

GT Interactive (1998) *Abe's Exoddus*, New York: GT Interactive Software.

Healey, A. (2000) 'Children reading in a post-typographic age: two case studies', unpublished doctoral thesis, Queensland University of Technology.

Hyper (1998) Advertisement for 'Abe's Exoddus', *Hyper* 62: 14–15.

Lankshear, C., Bigum, C., Durrant, C., Green, B., Honan, E., Morgan, W., Murray, J., Snyder, I. and Wild, M. (1997). *Digital Rhetorics: Literacies and Technologies in Education – Current Practices and Future Directions*, Three volumes. Canberra, ACT: Commonwealth of Australia, Department of Education, Employment, Training and Youth Affairs.

Le Guin, U. (1968), *A Wizard of Earthsea*, Penguin: Harmondsworth.

Meek, M. (1988) 'How texts teach what readers learn', in M. Lightfoot and N. Martin (1988) *The Word for Teaching is Learning*, London: Heinemann Educational Books, pp. 82–106.

Meredyth, D., Russell, N., Blackwood, L., Thomas, J. and Wise, P. (2000) *Real Time: Computers, Change and Schooling* Australian Key Centre for Cultural and Media Policy/Department of Employment, Training and Youth Affairs. Online. Available HTTP: *http://www.detya.gov.au/schools/Publications/IT_skills/IT_Real_Time_home.htm* (25 April 2001).

Moulton. K. (2000) 'Constructing emergent literacy: negotiating literacy technologies in preschool-school transition', unpublished doctoral thesis, Deakin University.

Mythos Games (1998) *Magic and Mayhem*, London: Virgin Interactive.

New London Group (2000) [1996] 'A pedagogy of multiliteracies: designing social futures', in B. Cope and M. Kalanatzis (eds) *Multiliteracies: Literacy Learning and the Design of Social Futures*, Melbourne: Macmillan, pp. 9–42.

Oddworld (2001) *Oddworld*. Online. Available HTTP: *http://www.oddworld.com/* (18 July 2001).

Office of Film and Literature Classification (1999) *Computer Games and Australians Today*, Sydney: Office of Film and Literature Classification. Online. Available HTTP: *http://www.oflc.gov.au/PDFs/Comp_Games_Aust_Exec_Sum.pdf* (5 July 2001).

Rivett, M. (2000) 'Approaches to analysing the Web text: a consideration of the web site as an emergent cultural form', *Convergence: The Journal of Research into New Media Technologies*, 6, (3): 34–56.

Sefton-Green, J. (2001) 'The "end of school" or just "out of school"? ICT, the Home and Digital Cultures', in C. Durrant and C. Beavis (eds) *P(ICT)ures of English: Teachers, Learners and Technology*, Adelaide: Australian Association for the Teaching of English/Wakefield Press, pp. 162–174.

4

LANGUAGES.COM

The Internet and linguistic pluralism

Mark Warschauer

> It is just incredible when I hear people talking about how open the
> Web is. It is the ultimate act of intellectual colonialism. The
> product comes from America so we either must adapt to English
> or stop using it. That is the right of any business. But if you are
> talking about a technology that is supposed to open the world to
> hundreds of millions of people you are joking. This just makes the
> world into new sorts of haves and have nots.
>
> (Anatoly Voronov, Director of the Russian Internet
> service provider, Glasnet, in Crystal 1997: 108)

The spectre of an Internet-charged global English, riding roughshod over other
languages, is haunting the world. This spectre first appeared in the mid-1990s,
when more than four-fifths of the first generation of webpages were written in
English ('Cyberspeech' 1997). Today, even though more languages are represented, English remains the default tongue of international discussion online, as
well as of e-commerce ('The Default Language' 1999), and many people
continue to fear the consequences of this dominance for linguistic diversity.

An examination of language use online reveals that the issue is complex.
While the Internet has strengthened the need for an international *lingua franca* –
and that *lingua franca* is most frequently English – there are present other online
dynamics that contribute to new forms of language pluralism.

To illustrate these dynamics, I draw on research I conducted in Egypt,
Singapore and Hawai'i. My approach for analysing online language use in these
three contexts is not that of seeking 'impacts' but rather of examining dense
webs of interrelationships. Language use online forms part of a large matrix of
technological, social, political and economic contexts that shape communication
in the current era. While I reject the notion of technological *determinism*, which
suggests that a technology causes certain results, I also reject notions of technological *neutralism* which deem media as value-free vessels that can be used toward
any ends. The Internet, like other technologies, is neither good nor bad. Nor is it
neutral (Kranzberg 1985). The Internet's history and design are replete with
certain values: for example, the ASCII code, upon which computing and the
Internet were first based, privileges romanised languages such as English over

those using other alphabets or ideographs. However, these values do not determine a particular result; rather, they shape a social struggle – in this case, how individuals and communities construct and express their identities online using language.

These issues provide the focus of this chapter. I begin by exploring the changing role of language in the post-industrial era. I then discuss some examples of online language use in three diverse places: Hawai'i, Egypt and Singapore. I conclude with some thoughts about the implications of online language diversity for literacy practices in schools.

Language and identity in the era of globalisation[1]

The post-industrial era – marked by the broad social and economic changes of the late twentieth century following the development of modern computing and telecommunication systems – is characterised by a central contradiction between global networks and local identities (Barber 1995; Castells 1996, 1997). On the one hand, global flows of money, media and markets – mediated by transnational corporations and multilateral institutions – are increasingly influencing people's pocketbooks and lives, weakening or at least altering the traditional sovereignty of the nation state. Other customary sources of identity, including time-honoured gender roles, permanent careers, and even distinct racial identity, are also being challenged by the social, economic, political and demographic changes wrought by globalisation (Warschauer 2000a). On the other hand, and in response, a wide array of social movements and organisations have arisen to define and defend local identities, via religious fundamentalism, indigenous movements, men's or women's groups, and other new social movements from all sides of the political agenda (Castells 1997). As Touraine explains, 'In a post-industrial society, in which cultural services have replaced material goods at the core of production, *it is the defence of the subject, in its personality and its culture, against the logic of apparatuses and markets, that replaces the idea of class struggle*' (Touraine 1994: 168, emphasis in original).

Castells (1996: 3) explains further the central role of identity:

> In a world of global flows of wealth, power, and images, the search for identity, collective or individual, ascribed or constructed, becomes the fundamental source of social meaning. This is not a new trend, since identity, and particularly religious and ethnic identity, have been at the roots of meaning since the dawn of human society. Yet identity is becoming the main, and sometimes the only, source of meaning in a historical period characterised by widespread destructuring of organisations, delegitimation of institutions, fading away of major social movements, and ephemeral cultural expressions. People increasingly organise their meaning not around what they do but on the basis of what they are.

Within this contradictory mix of global networks and local identities, language plays a critical role. The intersection of language with international networks and globalisation is perhaps most evident. Put simply, global trade, distribution, marketing, media and communications could not take place without a *lingua franca*. These processes of globalisation over the last thirty years have propelled English from being an international language – like French, Spanish, Chinese, or Arabic – to becoming a truly global one, spoken and used more broadly than probably any other language in world history. According to Crystal (1997), 85 per cent of international organisations in the world make official use of English, at least 85 per cent of the world's film market is in English, and more than 65 per cent of scientific papers in several important academic fields are published in English. Given the vast global presence of English at the time of the birth of the Internet, as well as the leading role of US scientists and engineers developing the telecommunications industry, it is not surprising that English rapidly became the de facto *lingua franca* of online communication. Today, English is probably used on about 50 per cent of websites (see discussion in Graddol 1997) and perhaps upwards of 90 per cent of sites used for international e-commerce ('The Default Language' 1999).

But while English serves to grease the wheels of global networks, language is also critical to the defence of local identity. With other cornerstones of social authority, such as nation, family and career, battered by the processes of globalisation, language can become 'the trench of cultural resistance, the last bastion of self-control, the refuge of identifiable meaning' (Castells 1997: 52). The struggle over bilingual education in the US; the Québécois, Basque, and Albanian separatist movements in Canada, Spain and the Balkans; the battles over language and citizenship in post-Soviet countries; and language revitalisation movements in Ireland (Gaelic), New Zealand (Maori), Morocco (Tamazight) and many other countries indicate the powerful role of language-based identity in today's world.

It is not surprising that language and dialect have assumed such a critical role in identity formation. The process of becoming a member of a community has always been realised in large measure by acquiring knowledge of the functions, social distribution and interpretation of language (Ochs and Shieffelin 1984). In most of the world, the ability to speak two or more languages or dialects is a given, and language choice by minority groups becomes 'a symbol of ethnic relations as well as a means of communication' (Heller 1982: 308). In the current era, language signifies historical and social boundaries that are less arbitrary than territory and more discriminating (but less exclusive) than race or ethnicity. Language-as-identity also intersects well with the nature of subjectivity in today's world. Identity in the post-modern era has been found to be multiple, dynamic, and conflictual, based not on a permanent sense of self but rather the choices that individuals make in different circumstances over time (Henriquez *et al.* 1984; Weedon 1987; Schecter *et al.* 1996). Language, though deeply rooted in personal and social history, allows a greater flexibility than race and ethnicity, with people able to consciously or unconsciously express dual identities by the linguistic choices they make even in a single sentence, for example, through code-switching (see Blom and Gumperz 1972). Through choices of language and dialect, people constantly make and remake who they are. A Yugoslav becomes a Croatian, a Soviet becomes a Lithuanian, and an American emphasises his African-American linguistic and cultural heritage.

The rapid growth of languages other than English online is a reflection of several phenomena, including a demographic spread of the Internet from its early base in North America to much of the rest of the world. This is also a reflection of a broader media trend known as localisation. Just as CNN and MTV first globalised their distribution (in English), and then 're-localised' in a variety of languages, so are Yahoo, Google and other Internet giants relocalising their product in different language versions.

However, the growing use of languages and dialects other than standard English reflects more than just demographics or marketing. It also reflects the important role of diverse languages and dialects in assertion of meaning and identity. Even people who use English as a principal means of communication may well choose to also use other languages (or non-standard varieties of English) to express different sides of their identity. This phenomenon will be examined through three examples: in the first, English is spoken as the main language (Hawai'i); in the second, as a foreign language (Egypt); and in the third, as a second language (Singapore).

Hawai'i: the Internet and language revitalisation

An important component of the struggle for linguistic rights online is the work of many indigenous groups to make use of the Internet for language revitalisation. Members of indigenous and minority groups in North America (see, for example, Office of Technology Assessment 1995), the Pacific (see, for example, Benton 1996), and elsewhere are making use of computers and the Internet to try to preserve and revitalise endangered languages.

One outstanding example is provided by the efforts of native Hawaiians. About 20 per cent of the people in Hawai'i have some native Hawaiian ancestry, but due to a century of linguistic and cultural persecution, the Hawaiian language has nearly died out and today has only a few hundred native speakers (Wilson 1998). In the 1970s, native Hawaiian organisations began a revitalisation effort, centred in a collection of Hawaiian-immersion pre-schools and K-12 schools. However, these schools, and also the broader revitalisation effort, faced a number of obstacles. First, there were few Hawaiian language resources available to the community, and these were mostly found in one or two libraries and thus inaccessible to a people who are spread out in small communities over six different islands. Second, other than on the tiny island of Ni'ihau, with only 200 inhabitants, there is no other location with a critical mass of Hawaiians who can communicate with each other in their own language. Third, Hawaiian families sometimes lack motivation for the serious effort required to learn and use

Hawaiian, especially when most are in dire economic circumstances and require the English language to get jobs and survive. (See further discussion in Warschauer 1998a and Warschauer 1999.)

Native Hawaiian educators have made use of the Internet to try to overcome each of these difficulties. A Hawaiian-language bulletin board system, Leoki, was created to post and share resource materials in the Hawaiian language. Leoki includes a resource area for sharing of Hawaiian-language stories, articles and songs; a news site with current and back issues of a Hawaiian-language newspaper; a dictionary section with up-to-date vocabulary lists; and a newsline with announcements and information about upcoming events (Warschauer and Donaghy 1997).

Perhaps, more importantly, Leoki brings together a community of speakers, which uses the open discussion forum, chat line and Hawaiian-language e-mail system. These popular features are used by teachers and students in the immersion schools to allow for Hawaiian-language discussion and project-work by students at different schools spread out over several islands (Warschauer and Donaghy 1997).

Finally, Hawaiian language educators feel that the very existence of Leoki, which has an entirely Hawaiian interface, creates a boon for the Hawaiian language, as it demonstrates that Hawaiian is a modern language appropriate for use via information and communication technologies. Keiki Kawai'ae'a, a director of curriculum materials, explains:

> Without changing the language and having the programs in Hawaiian, they wouldn't be able to have computer education through Hawaiian, which is really a major hook for kids in our program. They get the traditional content like science and math, and now they are able to utilise this 'ono' (really delicious) media called computers! Computer education is just so exciting for our children. In order for Hawaiian to feel like a real living language, like English, it needs to be seen, heard and utilised everywhere, and that includes the use of computers.

The use of the Internet for language revitalisation in Hawai'i has not proceeded without obstacles. Neither Windows nor Macintosh provide a Hawaiian-language operating system, so the installation of Leoki is a technically complicated step that not all schools and universities have been willing to undertake. In places where Leoki is not installed, educators make use of other communication and Web-publishing programs to allow for Hawaiian-language computing (Warschauer 1999). In addition, many native Hawaiians lack computers or even phone lines in their homes, thus making it difficult to expand Hawaiian-language Internet use throughout the broader community. Few believe that the Internet can overcome all the problems that indigenous groups face in maintaining and revitalising their language, but it does provide an additional and valuable tool for this effort.

Egypt: English vs. Arabic online

In Egypt, English is the dominant language of Internet use, both on the World Wide Web and in computer-mediated communication (for example, e-mail). However, a romanised version of Egyptian colloquial Arabic has emerged as a competitor to English in informal communications, and it is predicted that standard modern Arabic will be used more frequently in the future once Arabic operating systems become more widely available.

The early and extensive advantage of English on the Internet in Egypt can be explained in a number of ways. First, many key sectors of the Egyptian economy and educational system already function in English (Schaub 2000). At universities, courses in computer science, engineering, medicine and information technology are taught largely in English. Early adopters of the Internet thus learned to use computers in English and may not even know how to type in Arabic. The Internet also arose quickly in Egypt's international business sector. These companies may have foreigners working for them or must maintain communications with foreign suppliers, distributors or clients. Much of the written communication in these companies already takes place in English. Finally, communication in Arabic on the Internet remains difficult, and a single standard of Arabic communication has not yet arisen. Many computers in Egypt even lack Arabic operating systems. For these reasons, most websites developed in Egypt are in English. An example is Egypt's well-known 'Otlob.com' website (Otlob.com 2001), for ordering food delivery from scores of restaurants in Cairo and Alexandria. Though targeted to people living and working in Egypt, Otlob.com exists only in English.

English is also the dominant language of e-mail in Egypt, at least among the young professionals who were the early users of the Internet (Warschauer *et al.* 2000). Some 80 per cent of young professionals surveyed use English exclusively in formal e-mail messages (for example, related to work purposes). However, approximately half of the professionals use a romanised version of Egyptian colloquial Arabic in their informal e-mail messages, and more than half use that same version of Egyptian colloquial Arabic in online chatting. This is especially significant in that Egyptian colloquial Arabic is seldom used outside of the Internet in written form, and almost never in a romanised written form. The strong motivation of Egyptians to communicate in their own tongue has thus given prominence to a language form that was seldom used before. This new form even includes the use of numbers to represent phonemes that are not easily rendered in the Roman alphabet. Sometimes communication takes place completely in Egyptian colloquial Arabic:

latif: enty akhbarek eih? shofty ra2eess el ouezara elgedeed
Meshtehi: allah a7la klmah sma3tah alyoom
Alawahad: tkalam ya al 7bab

[*latif:* what's new with you? did you learn about the new Prime Minister
Meshtihi: wow! that's the best thing I've heard today
Alawahad: why don't you say something you louse]

(discussion on an Egyptian online chat forum)

At other times Egyptian colloquial Arabic and English are combined in a single message:

> Hello Dalia,
>
> 7amdellah 3ala el-salama ya Gameel.we alf mabrouk 3alal el-shahada el-kebeera ...
> Keep in touch ... I really hope to see you all Sooooooooooooooon (Maybe in Ramadan).
> Kol Sana Wentom Tayyebeen.
> Waiting to hear from you ...
>
> Laila

> [Hello Dalia,
>
> Thank God for the safe return, my sweet. Congratulations for the big certificate. Keep in touch. I really hope to see you all Sooooooooooooooon (Maybe in Ramadan).
> Happy Ramadan.
> Waiting to hear from you ...
>
> Laila]

(A sample informal email message in Egypt)

When combined, terms used in Arabic are usually those that have strong cultural connotations, related to greetings, humour, religion and Egyptian customs.

In summary, the predominance of English on the Internet in Egypt is due to a variety of factors and corresponds to the broad use of English in other business and technological domains in the country. However, a diglossia exists in online communication in Egypt, with people using English in more formal e-mail communications and a combination of English and Egyptian colloquial Arabic in informal e-mail messages and online chats. As Arabic operating systems continue to improve and expand, it can be expected that more websites will be created in modern standard Arabic and people may begin to write e-mail messages in Arabic script.

Singapore: plural Englishes

An important question to be asked about the Internet and language diversity deals with variation within languages. Put simply: Will the Internet contribute to standardisation of languages or greater diversity within them?

An intuitive answer would be that the Internet will contribute to standardisation, since, by fostering international communication, it will also necessitate common standards. If people in the US, India, Nigeria, the Philippines and South Africa are all communicating with each other online using English, logic has it that they would have to conform to certain common standards to understand each other. But, as with other issues related to the Internet and language diversity, the answer is perhaps not as simple as it seems. An example of the complex interrelationship between the Internet and English-language variation is seen in Singapore.

The vast majority of Singaporeans speak a highly colloquial dialect of English known as 'Singlish', which is almost incomprehensible to English speakers outside of Singapore (Pakir 1997). Most, but not all, Singaporeans can also speak standard Singaporean English, which varies only slightly from standard forms of British or Australian English, and are thus bidialectal.

What then is the relationship between new media technologies and the competition between Singlish and standard Singaporean English? While it is too early to know, it is clear that new media technologies are creating greater incentives to advocates of both language varieties. On the one hand, educational and government leaders are aggressively pushing for an end to Singlish and for the sole use of the standard variety. They motivate their appeal on the basis of the new opportunities for international business and communication that take advantage of modern media (see, for example, Goh 1999), if Singaporeans can communicate in a form of English comprehensible to people around the world.

On the other hand, the Internet provides a very powerful means for grass-roots communication, and, as was seen with Egyptians (above), Singaporeans mostly prefer to use their own colloquial dialect as a means of expression in their informal communications such as online chatting. Singaporean chat rooms are filled with Singlish, causing great concern to Singaporean educators.

One Singaporean put to verse his strong defence of Singlish, especially in the age of information technology, in a poem written (of course) in Singlish and distributed (of course) on the Internet. The anonymous poet explains his views in the verse that follows:

Wah

I heard we all now got big debate.
They said future of proper English is at stake.
All because stupid Singlish spoil the market,

want to change now donno whether too late …
Other people hear you, say you sound silly.
So like that how to become world-class city?
Basically Singlish got good and got bad.
Aiyah! Everything in life is all like that.
Actually Singlish got one bright side.
I am talking about our national plight …
Other people all say we all got no culture.
All we got is a lot of joint business ventures.
So we got no culture to glue us together.
End up we all like a big bunch of feathers.
Wind blow a bit too strong only we fly away.
Everybody all go their own separate ways.
Now we must play Internet otherwise cannot survive.
Next time the only way to make money, or sure to die.
When other countries' influences all enter,
we sure kena affected left, right and centre.
Sekali our Singaporean identity all lost until donno go where.
Even Orang-Utan Ah Meng starts thinking like a Polar Bear.
But still must go I.T. otherwise become swa koo,
only smarter than Ah Meng of the Mandai Zoo.
Wait the whole world go I.T., we still blur as sontong,
next time we all only qualified to sell laksa in Katong.
But actually we all got one 'culture' in Singlish.
It's like rice on the table; it is our common dish.
I know this funny 'culture' is not the best around
so we must tahan a bit until a better one is found.
Not all the time can marry the best man,
so bo pian got no prawns, fish also can.
I donno whether you agree with me or not?
I just simply sharing with you my thoughts.
Singlish is just like the garden weeds.
You pull like mad still it would not quit.
Sure got some people like and some do not like.
Singlish and English, they'll still live side by side.

Although some words may be difficult to understand, the poet's overall meaning is clear. The influx of information technology is threatening to overwhelm Singapore with global culture, and Singaporeans must, more than ever, hang on to Singlish as a way of protecting their local identity, or else they will lose their identity just as would Ah Meng – the popular orang-utan in Singapore's national zoo – if she started acting as if she were a polar bear.

Global networks and local identity

Linguistic diversity is a complex social phenomenon that will not be determined by a single medium or technology. In any case, technologies more often serve to amplify trends that already exist, or create new possibilities, rather than to bring about particular results.

What trends then might the Internet be amplifying? The examples discussed in this chapter represent some of the broad social trends that characterise today's post-industrial information technology society. As Castells (1996, 1997, 1998) notes (see also Barber 1995; Friedman 1999), the central contradiction of our time is between global networks and local identities. The Internet promotes global networking through international communication in English. At the same time, though, it provides an important vehicle for grassroots one-to-one and many-to-many interaction and publishing. That interaction will frequently take place in a wide variety of languages and dialects, in correspondence with the cultural and identity needs of the diverse peoples of our planet.

The Internet is not a neutral tool, indifferent to how it is used. Its history and design have tended to privilege the wealthy (who could afford computers and telecommunications), the well-educated (who were both literate and skilled at computers), and the English speaking (since the English language functioned well in the 'ASCII' code of modern computing). However, identity is a powerful phenomenon in today's world, and communities around the globe have broken up the monopoly of standard American and British English online. The existence of native language such as Hawaiian, local languages such as Egyptian Arabic (written, if necessary, in romanised form), and non-standard varieties of English (such as Singlish) are all testimonies to the strong will of diverse peoples to communicate in their own voice and culture online.

Finally, it is important to consider the significance of this diversity for language and literacy practices in schools. In the education of culturally and linguistically diverse students, a long-time debate has taken place between advocates for the *voice of power* (by giving people access to standard English) and advocates for the *power of voices* (by valuing students' diverse languages and cultures (see Auerbach 1997). The communicative experiences reported here suggest that this is a false dichotomy. First of all, the growth of other languages on the Internet is representative of the general importance of multilingualism in today's world. The spread of English as a global language has not lessened the importance of other languages for media, marketing, and communications internal to other countries. And in a world where many well-educated people speak English, what special language advantage does a monolingual American or British person have, in competition with a bilingual German, Japanese, Chinese, or Egyptian? A linguistically diverse world requires multilingual citizens.

And, in a sense, the same dynamic applies to diverse dialects of English. As Graddol (1999) demonstrates, the majority of English speakers in the world are not native speakers, but are rather those who have used English as a foreign or native language. Just as the British lost their exclusive privilege as the owners of

71

English to the Americans and Australians, so will the broader Anglo-Saxon community lose its 'ownership' of English to Singaporeans, Nigerians, Malaysians, Filipinos, and the many other diverse speakers of global English(es). Understanding the nature and value of dialectical diversity – and even being able to communicate in a variety of dialects and genres appropriate to the circumstances – is another indication of a well-educated English speaker in the twenty-first century (Warschauer 2000b). The objective should not be to squelch languages and dialects, but to give students choices – to select the languages, dialects, genres and media most appropriate to making a particular point in a particular circumstance (New London Group 1996). That may involve informal interaction leading to a very formal finished product – or the incorporation of informal and formal genres and varieties of language in an appropriate manner in a single piece of art (see Warschauer 1999). Indeed, one of the more sophisticated examples of student media production I have seen is that of a native Hawaiian student who developed a multimedia formal Hawaiian language hypertext to provide a sociolinguistic analysis of a local English Creole (see Warschauer 1999). And one of the sadder moments I've seen in a classroom is when a student, using the Internet for the very first time, tried to write a short, informal (but medium- and genre-appropriate note) to a friend, only to be told sternly by the teacher that such types of communication were not allowed (Warschauer 1998b).

This is one further example of how literacy is much more complex than the simple ability to decipher texts. Rather, being literate has always referred to 'having mastery over the processes by means of which culturally significant information is coded' (de Castell and Luke 1986: 374). In today's world, that information is coded not only in a plurality of media, but also in a plurality of dialects and languages. A pedagogy of multiliteracies is needed to address both these forms of plurality, encouraging reading, writing and communication in diverse media, genres, dialects and languages (New London Group 1996; Cope and Kalantzis 2000).

In summary, if today's world is characterised by a contradiction between global networks and local identities, let us as teachers use the Internet to serve both. Standard English used online can help to provide students' access to the 'voice of power', whereas online communication in diverse languages and dialects can help students find and express the power of their own voices.

Notes

1   This section draws on my previous discussion of language and identity in Warschauer 2000a.

References

Auerbach, E. (1997) 'The power of voice and the voices of power', in T. Menacker (ed.) *Literacy for Change: Community-Based Approaches – Conference Proceedings* Centre for Second Language Research, University of Hawai'i, Honolulu, pp. 1–15.

Barber, B. R. (1995) *Jihad vs. McWorld*, New York: Ballantine Books.

Benton, R. (1996) 'Making the medium the message: using an electronic bulletin board system for promoting and revitalising Mäori', in M. Warschauer (ed.) *Telecollaboration in Foreign Language Learning*, Honolulu, Hawai'i: Second Language Teaching & Curriculum Centre, University of Hawai'i, pp. 187–204.

Blom, J. P. and Gumperz, J. J. (1972) 'Social meaning in linguistic structures: code-switching in Norway', in J. J. Gumperz and D. Hymes (eds) *Directions in Sociolinguistics*, New York: Holt, Rinehart & Winston, pp. 407–434.

Castells, M. (1996) *The Rise of the Network Society*, Malden, MA: Blackwell.

—— (1997) *The Power of Identity*, Malden, MA: Blackwell.

—— (1998) *End of Millennium*, Malden, MA: Blackwell.

Cope, B. and Kalantzis, M. (eds) (2000) *Multiliteracies: Literacy Learning and the Design of Social Futures*, London: Routledge.

Crystal, D. (1997) *English as a Global Language*, Cambridge: Cambridge University Press.

'Cyberspeech' (1997) *Time*, 149: 23, June 23.

De Castell, S. and Luke, A. (1986) 'Models of literacy in North-American schools: social and historical conditions and consequences', in S. de Castell, A. Luke and K. Egan (eds) *Literacy, Society, and Schooling*, New York: Cambridge University Press, pp. 87–109.

Friedman, T. (1999) *The Lexus and the Olive Tree: Understanding Globalisation*, New York: Farrar, Straus and Giroux.

Goh, C. T. (1999) 'Moulding the future of the nation', *Online Excerpts of Speech*, Singapore Ministry of Education. Available: *http://www1.moe.edu/sg/speeches/sp270899.htm* (1 October 1999).

Graddol, D. (1997) *The Future of English*, London: The British Council.

Graddol, D. (1999) 'The Decline of the Native Speaker', in D. Graddol, D. and U. H. Meinhof (eds) *English in a Changing World (AILA Review 13)*, Guildford, UK: Biddles Ltd, pp. 57–68.

Heller, M. (1982) 'Language, Ethnicity and Politics in Quebec', unpublished doctoral dissertation, University of California, Berkeley.

Henriquez, J., Hollway, W., Urwin, C., Venn, C. and Walkerdine, V. (1984) *Changing the Subject*, New York: Metheun.

Kranzberg, M. (1985) 'The information age: evolution or revolution?' in B. R. Guile (ed.) *Information Technologies and Social Transformation*, Washington, DC: National Academy of Engineering, pp. 35–54.

New London Group (1996) 'A pedagogy of multiliteracies: designing social futures', *Harvard Educational Review*, 66: 60–92.

Ochs, E. and Shieffelin, B. (1984) 'Language acquisition and socialisation: three developmental stories and their implications', In R. Shweder and R. Levine (eds) *Culture Theory: Essays on Mind, Self, and Emotion*, Cambridge: Cambridge University Press, pp. 276–320.

Office of Technology Assessment (1995) 'Telecommunications technology and Native Americans: opportunities and challenges', *Report No. OTA-ITC-621*, Washington, DC: U.S. Government Printing Office.

Otlob.com (2001) *Welcome Page*. Online. Available HHTP: *http://www.otlob.com* (29 June 2001).

Pakir, A. (1997) 'Education and invisible language planning: the case of the English language in Singapore', in J. Tan, S. Gopinathan and Wah Kam Ho (eds) *Education in Singapore*, Singapore: Prentice Hall, pp. 57–74.

Schaub, M. (2000) *World Englishes*, 19 (2): 225–238.

Schecter, S., Sharken-Taboada, D. and Bayley, R. (1996) 'Bilingual by choice: Latino parents' rationales and strategies for raising children with two languages', *Bilingual Research Journal* 20 (2): 261–281.

'The Default Language' (1999) *Economist*, p 67.

Touraine, A. (1994) *Qu'est-ce que la démocratie?*, Paris: Fayard.

Warschauer, M. (1998a) 'Online learning in sociocultural context'. *Anthropology & Education Quarterly*, 29 (1): 68–88.

—— (1998b) 'Technology and indigenous language revitalisation: analysing the experience of Hawai'i', *Canadian Modern Language Review*, 55: 140–161.

—— (1999) *Electronic Literacies: Language, Culture, and Power in Online Education*, Mahwah, NJ: Lawrence Erlbaum Associates.

—— (2000a) 'Language, identity and the Internet', in B. Kolko, L. Nakamura and G. Rodman (eds) *Race in Cyberspace*, New York: Routledge, pp. 151–170.

—— (2000b) 'The changing global economy and the future of English teaching', *TESOL Quarterly*, 34: 511–535.

Warschauer, M. and Donaghy, K. (1997) 'Leokï: a powerful voice of Hawaiian language revitalisation', *Computer Assisted Language Learning*, 10: 349–362.

Warschauer, M., Zohry, A. and Refaat, G. (2000) 'Language and literacy online: a study of Egyptian Internet users'. Paper presented at the Annual Meeting of the American Association for Applied Linguistics, 13 March, Hotel Vancouver, Vancouver, Canada.

Weedon, C. (1987) *Feminist Practice and Poststructuralist Theory*, London: Blackwell.

Wilson, W. H. (1998) 'I ka 'olelo Hawai'i ke ola, "Life is found in the Hawaiian language"', *International Journal of the Sociology of Language* 132: 123–137.

5

THE WEB AS A
RHETORICAL PLACE

Nicholas C. Burbules

I

It is a significant feature of the World Wide Web that hyperlinks operate as both semantic and navigational elements. On the one hand, links suggest meaningful associations between webpages or webpage elements, and can facilitate the tropic creation of new meaningful associations.[1] These links and associations can be read critically, suggesting ways of thinking about the relations between webpages or webpage elements that the authors may or may not have intended.

On the other hand, these hyperlinks are also navigational pathways: avenues of movement from page to page, throughout the Web. In this context many questions can be explored about how links facilitate or inhibit such movement: for example, how software filters, by blocking access to certain sites, inadvertently also block access to other sites they link to, including sites that can be reached *only* via blocked sites.[2] Issues of access, issues of implicit encouragement of movement along certain paths and discouragement of others, issues of path markers that help users know where they are in the Web space, as opposed to those that tend to let them get lost, are all crucial matters of design not only because they can frustrate or discourage users (especially novice users), but also because they determine avenues of discovery that are facilitated or closed off. A critical and reflective attitude toward such experiences can ask *how* and *why* they happened, and in this can reveal important characteristics of the Web and how it is constructed. Many have written about the experience of getting lost in the Web, but there have been few explorations of how this experience of getting lost itself constitutes a key potential learning moment.[3]

These two dimensions of hyperlinks, the semantic and the navigational, play a key role in relation to each other. In this essay I will discuss how they are inseparable, and how this inseparability in the context of the World Wide Web helps constitute the distinctive kind of *place* the Web is.

This inseparability thesis is not all that remarkable. Indeed, the very terms we use for rhetorical associations often imply movement: 'trope' comes from 'turning', 'metaphor' comes from 'carrying over' meanings from one term to another, 'metonymy' is often explained as a relation of semantic *contiguity*; we talk about 'turns of phrase' (in other words, many rhetorical terms are themselves figurative). But it is revealing to see this connection played out in the context of the World Wide Web because the Web is *contested territory*. Struggles over building or controlling 'portals' that shape avenues of access to the Web, the ways that search engines direct lines of inquiry into certain sites rather than others, and the various devices used by designers to gain 'eyeballs', that is, maximising the number of visitors who click on the site (whether they intended to come to it or not), all raise the stakes of shaping pathways of navigation for the sake of advertising revenues or for the self-fulfilling notoriety of being a definitive or 'most frequently visited' site. The effects of filters to *shut off* certain parts of the Web, just mentioned, have the opposite sort of influence. Either way, the strategies of channelling and directing navigation through the Web always have significant semantic implications because they shape and constrain the range of possible meanings users can derive from their investigations. While there seems to be a high degree of choice in how and where users move within the Web space, the pragmatics of limited time and resources, of inexperience, or of minimising inconvenience and complexity can all conspire to encourage more passive navigational strategies, and, as such, susceptibility to a higher degree of semantic manipulation. Hence it is even more important today to teach (especially novice users) a range of searching and investigative strategies, as well as a certain degree of critical distance from what they do – and do not – find as they explore the Web.

II

What are some general features of hyperlinks as they currently operate within the World Wide Web? Several characteristics are immediately apparent. First, these links are bi-directional – users can go from page A to page B and return from B to A – but this relation is not symmetrical. Users must usually perform extra work within the browser's conventions to return from B to A, and (especially having seen A already) the movement from B to A does not have the same semantic effect as the movement from A to B. For example, moving from a page about IQ and intelligence to a page about the ideas of leading figures in eugenics may make users think about the implications of 'innate' theories of intelligence for selective breeding; moving from a page about the ideas of leading figures in eugenics to a page about IQ may make users wonder how intelligent those thinkers actually were.

Second, hyperlinks are one-to-one links: from a point within one webpage to a point within another webpage (normally, to the webpage as a whole, sometimes to a particular passage or term within it) or, as in tables of contents, to later points within the same webpage. This point-to-point movement suggests a binary semantic relation, and not a multiple one; of course, there can be lists of links, and links to links, but each association is still a linked pair. This may not be regarded as a problem if we take an analytic, atomistic view of meaning; but if we view meanings as multiple, mutilayered, and semantically complex (and even internally inconsistent or conflicted), this binary form may have a limited capacity to represent such complexity.

Third, hyperlinks are, given current technologies, static: the same link will always take users to the same URL unless the author changes the underlying HTML code (of course, what is found at that URL may change, may be frequently updated, etc.). Fourth, this relates to another aspect of links – that they are author-driven. While there are emerging ways for users to modify links, annotate them or add to them, in practice most users take the links they are given for granted. Because they are static and operate almost instantaneously, they tend to be invisible as moments themselves. Even pointing out that links are not simply navigational tools but ways of conveying meaning comes as a surprise to users who regard them simply as short cuts to move around the Web (as with 'worm holes', Web users go in one place and instantly come out another).

Fifth, there are different ways in which a hyperlink, and the content of the link, can be represented. Often, for example, a link is simply described by the URL to which it will carry users; or it is described by the title of the page, or a key word, or the name of the page's author or sponsor, and so on. Sometimes the link is represented graphically, even when the content that it is linked to is not graphic at all. There are many possibilities here, but speaking broadly the designer can create certain expectations about the site linked to, by how the link is represented; this interpretative set may be ironic, critical, or humorous, but typically it is 'literal' in the sense that the representation in the link is intended to tell users more or less straightforwardly what they should expect if they go there. Still, this is not necessarily the case, and here again there are possibilities for semantic playfulness and complexity.

This brief survey of the structure of hyperlinks as they currently work in webpages suggests some of the ways in which their semantic possibilities are limited by their navigational features. The binary, static form of hyperlinks tends to encourage more associationist relations of meaning. Their forms of representation and their author-driven constraints tend to encourage more literal interpretations of what the links are connecting. Users can reinterpret these associations, can question them, can add to them their own meanings, or they can use the links in ways that go at cross-purposes to what the authors might have intended – but all of these responses require some additional effort and, usually, some consciousness of what the intended purposes of the link were, as well as a decision or choice to use it or interpret it differently. Such responses involve raising to consciousness the fact of the link as a non-neutral design decision, and as an occasion for critical analysis and reflection.

I have discussed elsewhere these second-order activities of actually questioning and critically interrogating links, and resisting the associations that they invite users to make without thinking.[4] When users do this, new possibilities emerge, not only for avoiding manipulation or being led to connections that insinuate meaningful relations without arguing for them, but also for forging more dynamic and creative understandings of the material at hand. This suggests that the function of critically hyperreading is not just negative, rejecting misleading or manipulative associations; it also creates room for new ways of interpreting the links users encounter, which is in one sense a part of forging new links of their own. But as I have stressed, these semantic possibilities relate to, and can be constrained by, navigational possibilities. Some connections are simply closed off (you can't get there from here), as when filters intervene; there are meanings to be derived from *that fact*, but users cannot work with material that is not available to work with. When links offer only the options of going forward or back along a linear sequence, they constitute a relatively more closed semantic system than when A goes to B goes to C and beyond (this might be termed a more *rhizomic* architecture). Bookmarking sites, and organising those bookmarks in a browser, is one way of clustering linked sites and creating an idiosyncratically meaningful way of relating them; but this is a limited technology and, unless users post these in a way that is accessible to others, they have no influence on how those links will be read generally.

III

When I call the Web a rhetorical *place*, I am choosing that term over rhetorical *space* for an important reason. A place is a socially or subjectively meaningful space; it shares both the navigational and the semantic elements I have been discussing. It has an objective, locational dimension: people can look for a place, find it, move within it. But it also has a semantic dimension: it means something important to a person or a group of people, and this latter dimension may or may not be communicable to others.

Calling the Web a rhetorical space captures the idea of movement within it, the possibility of discovering meaningful connections between elements found there; but it does not capture the distinctive way in which users try to make the Web familiar, to make it *their* space – to make it a *place*. Individual users do this by selecting a homepage for their browser, by bookmarking sites, by visiting the same familiar sites frequently, and by making their own webpages. Groups online do this by creating online communities, or by constituting themselves as a 'web ring' linking their pages to each other. These strategies involve carving out or creating a more familiar, accessible subset of the Web as a whole, and marking in various ways (individually or collectively) a set of meaningful relations within that zone. When users are in a place, they always know where they are, and what it means to be there.

Calling the Web a rhetorical place suggests, then, that it is where users come to find and make meanings, individually and collectively. It is not simply a huge online encyclopaedia, a font of information, or a midden. The Web can be *used* for various purposes (buying, selling, advertising), but even in engaging these more instrumental functions there is typically a result of learning something, and of learning something about the Web itself. Analogies used to describe the Web (a library, a marketplace, a classroom) often emphasise these instrumental functions – but like a library, a marketplace, or a classroom, the Web is also a place where people come to be with other people. These encounters are not always easy or pleasant, to be sure. As with other public places the Web can be a site of conflict, harassment, crime, crudity and unwanted company. To avoid such nuisances, users sometimes intentionally truncate their Web journeys; they only visit sites approved by authorities whom they trust; they limit their interactions with anyone online they do not already know. The place they have chosen or created is, they hope, a 'safe place'; but in making this choice of restricted movement they are also making a choice about restricted meanings.

It is possible to theorise more broadly about what is going on here. There are two distinctive ways in which we turn spaces into places.[5] One is by *mapping*: by developing schemata that represent the space, identify important points within it, and facilitate movement within the space. A map is never an exact replica (as the story goes, the only map that would be identical would be an exact copy of the original, which would be useless as a map) – a map always simplifies, selects and schematises the original, and it is the particular way in which this simplification, selection and schematisation occurs that makes the space a place. These are pragmatic activities; we make these, and not other, choices because they allow us to do certain things in the space that are meaningful and important to us. Certainly, there can be multiple maps, and in this sense they constitute different *places*, even when they refer to the same space.

Among these many kinds of maps, there are conceptual maps: cognitive representations that focus on key concepts and their interrelations to each other. Here what is highlighted are the meaningful connections in terms of which some ideas are explained or clarified by others; some are instances or tokens of some more general type; some share characteristics that make them seem similar to one another; and so on. These maps typically have a weblike form, and so seem to have an affinity with the links that constitute the Web. But this is only one possible way of mapping it.

There are also maps that represent patterns of use. Trails that are worn by many feet tramping through forests, or across campus greens, are maps of a sort. Again, they simplify, select and schematise a space: they identify what is important to the users, they mark out key places, they facilitate movement. They also indicate another important characteristic of maps: how they can also shape and transform the space they represent. This can be seen at work in the World Wide Web through frequency indicators: page counters, for example, as well as ratings of 'most frequently visited' sites. Such representations tend to influence patterns of future use, because they can influence how search engines pick out and identify sites, and which sites get selected for indexes. Viewed pragmatically, the representation is not discrete from the thing represented; it acts upon and is acted upon by it.

Yet another kind of map is one showing relations of relative centrality and relative periphery, from some point or points of reference. The repetitiveness of 'relative' here is not accidental: there can be no absolute centre of a space that is any more necessary than any other – in fact, it is as true to say that a centre is *defined by* the map, as to say that the map begins from a centre. And a more rhizomic map may have no single centre at all. But a map of relative centrality and periphery can still provide a way of simplifying, selecting, and schematising the pragmatic relation of what is more or less useful or relevant to a given purpose, or set of purposes. This sort of endeavour can be highly useful even if there is nothing necessary about this mapping, or even if others would map it differently – indeed, we should expect that to be true in order for such maps of relative centrality and periphery to be useful to different people (because their purposes and criteria will differ). Clearly this is true of the World Wide Web, and it partly explains why there has still been no settling on a common set of definitive or crucial websites, although there is of course a set of them that have extremely high rates of usage; even so, they might not be considered very important by their users.

These are some examples of how mapping turns spaces into places, and how these ways of thinking about mapping help us reflect on the kind of *place* the Web becomes for people. The second distinctive way in which spaces become places is through *architecture*. A space becomes a place when we build into it enduring structures. Often we live in these structures, work in them, observe or admire them. We are changed by these things we create as we change them – the relation runs both ways. Architecture here is not only the initial design or building, but the transformation of it over time; in this sense, we always help build the structures we occupy, and the structures are not fully finished until they have been used for a while (in one sense, then, they are never 'finished'). Here I do not mean architecture only in the literal sense of buildings and bridges; there are architectures also of language, of customs, of complex practices and activities (games, for example). All of these can play a role in transforming a space into a place.

Architectures transform not only a space but the patterns of activity for those who occupy them. I think that these patterns can be viewed along five polarities:

1   movement/stasis
2   interaction/isolation
3   publicity/privacy
4   visibility/hiddenness
5   enclosure/exclusion

These dynamics can be seen in the structures of the World Wide Web, and in keeping with my analyses thus far, I will highlight the navigational and the semantic impact of these polarities.

1   Structures facilitate, direct, or inhibit movement. Structures in the Web (how webpages are designed, how the multiple pages within websites are organised and interrelated, how links direct movement within and beyond a website) create the pathways through which users must travel. There are no

provisions now for reorganising these pathways short of replicating the site and rearranging it all on the user's own server – but then of course it is no longer the same site, the same space, but a new one. Doing so may serve a fruitful purpose in configuring a user's own place, but clearly it cannot be done for every site users may wish to visit. This suggests an inevitable compromise between the purposes and questions with which users approach a webpage or site, and the operations and answers it is willing to provide. It is like visiting a museum, wanting to learn about periods in art, and finding that the rooms have been organised by subject matter or styles of painting; all the information is there the visitors might want, but not in a pattern that supports the inferences they are trying to make. Which room to start with? Where to go next? The visitors' confusion and uncertainty are also a kind of paralysis, even though the design of the museum is, on its own terms, quite clear and easily navigated.

2   The design of spaces also communicates assumptions and expectations about social interaction. Architectures, by directing movement, create avenues to bring people together or barriers to keep them apart. In the context of the Web, this is manifested in the ways spaces are made into places that highlight their accessibility to numerous and diverse users, displaying for example not only a rolling indicator of how many visitors a website has received, but more substantive traces of what they found there and what they thought of it. Otherwise each new user approaches the site *as if* it had never been visited before (no matter how high the number on the counter). More actively, pages and sites can facilitate direct, synchronous forms of interaction, and clearly this has a profound impact on the impressions and meanings visitors form about the site and its content. Here, as elsewhere, this manifests a certain easing of authorial control, since these impressions and meanings will inevitably differ from each other, and from the author's original intent.

3   Publicity and privacy constitute a slightly different issue, which is the extent to which an architecture allows or inhibits the disclosure of the participants' selves, their activities, and not only their words and ideas, to others (and vice-versa). Given the opportunities for interaction just discussed, webpages or sites may allow or encourage users to reveal their identity and to encounter those of diverse others; or these features may be hidden. Of course, such 'revealed' identities can also be performances, but in many instances these performances might be no less an occasion for creative meaning-making and learning (perhaps even more so!). Architectures also influence whether such encounters, when they do happen, are simply displays, or occasions for *engaging* across such similarities and differences.

4   Visibility and hiddenness, here, refer to the transparency of architectures, to what they disclose or conceal within, and to what they disclose or conceal about themselves. Another important dimension of webpages and sites is the extent to which they make explicit to the user what decisions or choices

are built into their structures (and which could have been built differently). As discussed earlier, the avenues of navigation through a site may make such decisions and choices less apparent, even hidden – or may represent them as uncontroversial, even 'natural', which they never are.

5   Architectures also operate through enclosure and exclusion; what is counted in and what is counted out, whether this means a division of spaces, or a way of regulating who or what is allowed within. Elsewhere I have described certain websites, or clusters of sites, as 'gated communities', built to define a community made special in its own eyes by its privileged access and built to make it feel safe so that others less worthy will not interfere with it. The very attractions of such a partitioned space give rise to its limitations: the risk of complacency and numbing homogeneity. From a semantic standpoint, if we assume that certain kinds of change and development can only come from encounters with new and challenging ideas that cannot simply be assimilated, nor easily dismissed, this architecture of enclosure and exclusion starts looking less like a protective shell, and more like a self-built trap.

I have been arguing here that the rhetorical possibilities of Web spaces need to be understood in terms of the dual character of hyperlinks: as avenues of movement and as occasions for meaning-making. But these links are not all of the same type, and they do not stand alone. Links contain within them already certain kinds of navigational and semantic possibilities, and they tend to encourage some kinds of interpretation and to discourage or avoid others. Moreover, a link is also read differently when it is situated as part of a *rhetorical place*; a meaningful arrangement of Web space, a place that gives links context and shapes user expectations and tendencies toward those links.

In summary, I have explained two different ways in which spaces become places – two ways in which rhetorical spaces become rhetorical places. The first is mapping, which is in some ways a more reactive process; a process of representing a space in order to be able to move and work within it. A mapped space takes on the character of a place for those who understand and can use the map. The second way in which spaces become places is through architectures; enduring structures that reconfigure spaces. This is in some ways a more active process, in which the space is not only represented (mapped) but transformed. There are at least five ways in which this transformation affects not only the configuration of space, but the activities and the persons who operate within it. These dimensions determine the kind of place it is.

I do not mean to argue that the activities of mapping and architecture are utterly unrelated or dichotomous. Sometimes a map is prefatory to designing a structure (a blueprint is a kind of map, in fact); sometimes a large, complex architectural layout requires its own map. But the ways in which they influence navigation and meaning-making are different; and in the present discussion, they provide different contexts for thinking about how hyperlinks are interpreted and used.

IV

By way of a conclusion, I will mention three educational opportunities that seem to follow from this way of analysing the Web as a rhetorical place.

The first is that hyperlinks are not simply found. I have tended here to emphasise the ways in which existing links in webpages and websites need to be critically scrutinised and opened up to alternative interpretations. This is the process I have called *critical hyperreading*. And for most users, most of the time, this is what they will be doing: working within rhetorical spaces designed by others. Making those into more familiar and fecund rhetorical *places* will be achieved primarily by mapping activities. At the same time, nevertheless, certain kinds of learning and creativity can only be achieved when users create webpages and sites that contain their own links: links as representations of their own 'maps', and as facilitators of further new possibilities and connections (architectures). Perhaps the five dimensions of architecture described here might provide some guidelines for building more dynamic, open, and productive hyperlinked structures.

The second point is that for purposes of simplification I have tended to focus on particular features of spaces and places, as if they arose one at a time and could be analysed separately. But of course that is never the case. We are in many *places* at the same time: a room, a home, a neighbourhood – or, a language, a political group, a religion, and a friendship. Moreover, these places are not always harmonious with one another, giving rise to hybrid spaces or third spaces; positions that can yield up novel and important insights precisely because they do not fall into handy categories or distinctions. In the context of hyperlinks and the Web, this means continually resisting the binary, either/or mindset brought on by pathways that seem to take users only from point A to point B, or back again. It means trying to find within those *apparently* binary links moments of complexity and even paradox. Learning to do this means being able to adopt an orthogonal perspective on such matters, to think about what is *not* said as well as what is, and to go beyond the apparent terms of a choice to imagine it as something other than it seems to be (for example, a link between an anti-abortion page and an anti-euthanasia page).

Finally, I want to suggest, in a very open-ended way, that we conceive of learning in the context of the Web as the achievement of a certain kind of *mobility*: an ability to move within, but also across and even against the pathways that seem to determine users' options for navigation and for meaning-making.[6] We are more mobile when we have the assistance of a good map; we are even more mobile when we have the ability to forge new paths and not only follow the ones laid out for us. Mobility is a capacity to move from place to place, but also a capacity to find and create *new* places; this is what makes it a valuable model for a certain kind of learning – a kind of learning that goes beyond registering information to forming the capacities of interpreting, evaluating and adding to what is found.[7]

Notes

1   Burbules, N. C. (1997) 'Rhetorics of the Web: hyperreading and critical literacy', in I. Snyder (ed.) *Page to Screen: Taking Literacy into the Electronic Era*, Sydney and London: Allen and Unwin and Routledge [1998], pp. 102–122.

2   Burbules, N. C. and Callister, T. A. Jr. (2000) *Watch IT: The Promises and Risks of Information Technologies for Education*, Boulder, Colorado: Westview Press, Chapter Five.

3   Burbules, N. C. (2000) 'Aporias, webs, and passages: doubt as an opportunity to learn', *Curriculum Inquiry* 30 (2): 171–187.

4   Burbules, 'Rhetorics of the Web'.

5   This discussion is adapted and developed from a preliminary investigation in Burbules and Callister, *Watch IT: The Promises and Risks of Information Technologies for Education*, Chapter 8.

6   It is interesting here to note as a point of contrast the synonyms that are often given for aporia: being lost, being stuck, being paralysed, or being numb. See Burbules, 'Aporias, webs, and passages'.

7   The author wishes to thank Ilana Snyder for her excellent editorial input and for her more general support in stimulating and encouraging this project.

6

THEN AGAIN WHO ISN'T?

Post-hypertextual rhetorics[1]

Michael Joyce

I'm the wrong person to have here but then again who isn't.

With these words some time ago I began a talk to an earnest group of young web designers and cyber visionaries gathered like vultures over the cooling corpses of trendy designer pizzas around a burnished steel conference table at the Soho atelier of the neo-Bauhaus self-styled 'strategic digital communications firm with locations in New York City, San Francisco, Los Angeles, London, Stockholm, Oslo, Helsinki, and Hamburg' called *Razorfish*.

I was that week's flavour of visiting guru in a series of Friday noon 'steel table talks' meant to amuse, provoke, coddle and, one suspects, reinforce feelings of intellectual currency and even superiority among a handsome and stylish, bright and thoughtful, edgy and avant, really very winning group of multi-cultured and multi-gendered but underpaid overachievers, most of them alumni of highly selective colleges and universities and all quite conscious of being beyond the velvet rope inside the then hottest throbbing inner sanctum of silicon alley.

I'm the wrong person to have here but then again who isn't.

They paused a beat over their pizzas funghi, margarita, quatro stagione, et salmone affumatica and, thankfully, laughed.

Such a turn, as the reader knows, for I have used it likewise here, turning the remark to double duty and self-reflexivity, is what is called rhetoric.

It was the right thing to say. It did what I wanted to begin a talk about how to redeem space in cyberspace. It defused post-gen X suspicions of a balding baby-boomer professor, even one decked out in obligatory tones of Soho black Italian tweed coat, black slacks, the 'grey that is black' shirt, similar grey-black socks, soft black suede shoes, and geometric electric-yellow diamonds on the black silk field of a touchingly retro op-art designer tie.

I was talking about something I termed negative interface or interspace. I was trying to induce these young men and women to think about how they could design and ultimately sell interspace as an 'identity buffer'. Interspace, I suggested to them, buffers us from a world of choices, affirms identity and independence, and offers a progressive disclosure of zones of potential activity in lieu of pre-determined (and in the case of computer interfaces thus windowed) choices.

It might seem that I am trying to induce the reader to think about this same notion as well, although it would be quite understandable if one were suspicious of the anecdotal retelling and the faint aspect of ironic distancing which you seem to be invited to take part in. You may rightly likewise be suspicious of a sort of populist tone which turned one to you in the last sentence, and, further, which cannot but seem to diminish you however slightly even as it likewise invites you to gaze up and eastward upon the pretensions of uppercrust New York cyber-sophisticates eating brick-oven pizza in glass-walled conference rooms hidden within the upper floors of artsy cast-iron loft buildings.

Even so (or especially now) to begin by saying: 'I'm the wrong person to have here but then again who isn't', was, I think, the right thing to say to the reader as well, although one of the features of rhetoric is that speakers or writers are not supposed to claim for themselves the right to judge the success of their rhetorics but rather cede that to the audience, except in retrospect.

The question of course is how long you have to know some one, or at least how long it has to have been since you heard something, to be able to share a retrospect. It was Horace who first said that, putting it a mite more succinctly, when he wrote: 'Forsan et haec olim meminisse juvabit', which loosely translated means 'maybe some day this'll all seem a hoot to us'.

You have been promised, or at least I have agreed to offer, certain meditations which 'explore the rhetorical tradition as it is encountering computers, technology, ways of writing, ways of learning, and so forth' (as Hugh Burns phrased it to me years ago in an e-mail inviting me to speculate on such matters long before Ilana Snyder offered a like invitation for a collection devoted to similar questions). So far, however, except for mentions of web developers, silicon alley, and now e-mail – as well as a belated and apparently perfunctory mention of a writer from antiquity, always good in a talk about rhetoric – you, the reader, have little to show for it.

Although the truth is that you, the reader, are a corporate being, a representation or a virtuality if you will, whom ever you may be in that (this) sentence. The corporate (one could say composite or composed) you, of course, is filled with several feelings. Or may be.

Am I ever going to start saying something? some of you may wonder. Or rather all of you must now wonder, or at least more of you surely do wonder, now that I have planted that notion before you and watered it with the last sentence's effusion and confusion of a rhetorical turn. Maybe what he's doing is hypertext, some of you may be saying. Or rather some of you would have been saying that or something like it if you hadn't already caught on to that gambit of putting words in your mouth or ideas in your head or honey in your ears, as Horace or somebody said once of rhetoric.

You remember Horace, don't you? But wait – you might have been saying had you not etcetera etcetera etcetera – isn't putting ideas in your head and words in your mouth what rhetoric does? And doesn't that somehow really connect to 'ways of writing, ways of learning, and so forth' as Hugh Burns was said to have said in an e-mail. You remember Hugh, don't you?

I have already utilised a number of fairly idiosyncratic but nonetheless rhetorical tricks which any of you who might have read or heard me before would recognise. These include repetition of phrases, especially for self-reflexive purposes; echoes and evocations of previous situations and narratives, especially as they establish multiple perspectives for the speaker and audience; and the laying out of several registers of varying levels of discourse, from comic to metaphoric to elegiac.

Not to mention asymmetrical parallelisms at the end of tripartite formulations, which you had to read very closely to locate or have someone prompt you to recognise. Or maybe you saw right through it, and now you trust me even less. Maybe you stopped reading long ago (in which case one might wonder whether the 'you' I am writing to is you at all), maybe you are thinking of something much more pleasant, say someone's

> shoulder gleaming with ivory,
> as a cloudless moon on midnight sea sheds
> glimmering light.

You remember Horace, don't you?

That such tricks – including repetitions, echoes and evocations, and the laying out of multiple registers, not to mention asymmetrical parallelisms and parallel asymmetries including allusions to figures both historical and fanciful, and local and global (as well as nested parentheticals such as this) all on one surface – themselves form or give form to the verbal and visual pavannes and divagations (Pound 1960) which constitute electronic literacy as we know it, so far largely over the World Wide Web, should strike you. Whoever you are.

This is an essay about the rhetoric of a post-hypertextual age. As such it means to engage us in thinking how we can possibly find rhetorics fit for unforeseeable and multiple and restless audiences. How do you write for someone who is looking for an excuse to move on, a space to move in, or a moving picture? Which is to say how can we write what we seem to be the wrong persons to do so for audiences who come to us thinking they are not the persons our words are meant for, while all the while themselves beginning to think that words are a waste of time after all in a world of multimedia and that none of us have time for this, let alone for retrospect, reverie, ivory moonlight, or pizza funghi. Not to mention giving a rat's ass for rhetoric or razorfish.

Perhaps I am still talking about interspace, trying to induce you to think about how rhetoric could buffer us however briefly from a world of choices, affirm however fleetingly identity and independence, and offer us each however uncertainly time enough to think in the midst of what seems a world of pre-determined (albeit gaudily linked and trinketed) choices.

Earlier I called this a post-hypertextual rhetoric. There was a time, not long ago, when I used to be able to claim to some rhetorical effect for certain audiences that everything was hypertext, but then, with the explosion of the Web, everything *did* become hypertext and so it was no longer possible to say that to any purpose. This is one sense of post-hypertextual, a retrospect and recognition, in which post is less the actual end of something, like post mortem or post regnum, and more the virtual setting for some new something like post partum. In such a world everything is changed, pillar to post.

Yet there is another, more elegiac if not epideictic, sense of post-hypertextuality. I have written elsewhere about how the Web has discarded many of the fundamental concerns of a fifty-year history of hypertextuality characterised by attempts to find new ways to accommodate, represent, enact and commemorate multiple perspectives, tasks that rhetoric has long shared with poetics, especially narrative. However the new media of post-hypertextuality seem instead to shirk these tasks, substituting a slide show of successive perspectives for the accommodation of multiplicity, replacing memory and mortality with novelty, truncating the slow, dim process of understanding with the distribution of widely-available and swiftly minted, shiny souvenir trinkets.

The call to a post-hypertextual rhetoric is a call to find purpose in surface, to find a lasting world in our shifting sense of ordinary life. It is a call to the kind of ordinary mindfulness which has characterised rhetoric and poetics throughout the ages and which once lead an Italian fellow to see his lover's shoulder in the moonlight on the surface of a midnight sea.

It is all very well to say such things but what must we do, you wonder or will, by now either weary of the game I've been playing in such a self-reflexive summoning or made a part of it by the insistence of its purpose as it plays upon surface figures. Which is to say that one of the things we do to endow our ordinary lives with meaning is to persist in seeing them so. We watch how the light plays upon differing surfaces, whether shoulder or sea or computer screen, and we speak it.

We do speak light, you know. In a personal communication regarding an essay she published in *Art Forum*, the literary critic and feminist theorist of technology, N. Katherine Hayles (1998a), suggests that an emerging generation 'which arguably includes a majority of authors and readers presently using the Web, is marked by hybridity', by which she means that it is as much at home in visual image as in word, speaking as much in light as in sound. In her note Hayles (1998b) proposes to call the current age Gen YX which she describes as 'a generation characterised by the Y of hybridity, which modifies the X so that it no longer refers to the nondescript future Gen X'ers see for themselves but rather connotes a crossing between media'. Gen YX by no means abandons the word in Hayles' formulation; rather in her telling it is the 'verbal articulations surrounding ... images' that make images clear to us.

I would like for a while to look at two short texts which, though not terribly hybrid on first glance (or at first hearing), nonetheless cast their light upon surfaces and persistences which may perhaps help make our own images clear to us. To do so I revisit two favourite authors, Czeslaw Milosz and Hélène Cixous, both of whom I have often written about, one who offers the literal pretext for the present essay, the other of whom I have written about so frequently and in such several settings (fictional, lyrical, theoretical, hypertextual, rhetorical) that someone who has followed my work might throw up her hands and say, no not her again.

A reader may wonder why I have told you any of this. It may seem to you a needless divagation or hesitation, mere rhetorical posturing. You might, in fact, look on this moment as similar to the moment of hesitation, divagation and verbal-visual posturing (and positioning) when a webpage first loads in and, depending on the speed of your connection, you either see in outline the features and content of the page as you wait for graphics and text to load in, or, on a swifter connection, you take in the first view of the layout of the page before you, looking to understand it by its arrangement (and most likely already sizing up the array of links which point the way out). The truth is that, as this essay unfolds itself, you most likely would not know any of the personal history which surrounds these two texts of Milosz and Cixous and so I have to summon it. Then again some of you could know all the history and so my summoning would seem excessive or, worse, be something you take for granted, skip over, link away from, and thus deny the possibility of any new unfolding, thereby of course making it paradoxically even more important for me to summon you so in some way to keep you.

All this makes you an audience for which you may be the wrong persons but, now knowing as much, or at least by my making that claim, you thus become paradoxically (and actually, that is, by this act) not so wrong. My own history and the need to have you confirm it for me makes you necessary to me. The wrong audience, and then again which isn't, thus becomes exactly the right audience. Or, to put it differently, a post-hypertextual rhetoric requires us to arrange ways to call upon those who do not want to hear us, making them feel certain it is they whom we most need to hear us.

Aristotle called this *dispositio*, or arrangement, in the Rhetoric, and it is some-thing like *dispositio* which Czeslaw Milosz (1988: 437) points us toward when he speaks of myness in the first of the texts I want to consider here.

> 'My parents, my husband, my brother, my sister.'
> I am listening in a cafeteria at breakfast.
> The women's voices rustle, fulfil themselves
> In a ritual no doubt necessary.
> I glance sidelong at their moving lips
> And I delight in being here on earth
> For one more moment, with them, here on earth
> To celebrate our tiny, tiny my-ness.

Though this is a lovely poem, one which in the right mood moves me to tears – an instance by the way of an appeal to the sympathetic fallacy as well as a truth – let us first talk a bit about commas and the space they leave us and leave us in.

There are two instances of commas which immediately strike me: the one that sets off the critical phrase 'with them' in the line, 'For one more moment, with them, here on earth'; and the one which stops us in the doubled particularity of myness in the line that follows, 'To celebrate our tiny, tiny my-ness'.

The interesting thing about talking aloud about commas, as opposed to writing about them as I do here, is that you never see them and must depend upon someone else to mouth them. They are instances of exactly what Kate Hayles means by 'verbal articulations surrounding … images' that make images clear to us, although most of us are no longer used to seeing the humble comma, bent in half like a dying ant on a doorsill, as an instance of an image. Commas we believe are transparent, and if we see them at all it is as God's own flyspots, remnants of rules which buzz over language and settle upon its sweetness. In fact, however, commas are guppy mouths gulping tiny breaths midstream.

The commas in this short poem of Milosz's of course, have nothing to do with such humble beasts as ants or houseflies or guppies. Even so they do have their own humility, situating us by means of breath, within a world of parents, husband, brother, sister, a world which we might once have called the family of man, but which is here discovered in more humble words in the women's voices at a breakfast cafeteria. For one moment, comma, with them, comma, here on earth makes a simple phrase a space of wonder and in the process casts light upon our surface awarenesses and our persistences. An ambiguity grows, like zucchini or an orchid, in the space delineated by the commas. The one moment in the cafeteria is our one moment here on earth. All eternity, and all mortality, is contained in the ordinary.

And the ordinary is tiny, comma, tiny, a my-ness which heard wrongly can sound like the opposite of a plus and so requires that a speaker give it an orthography and a hyphen which the page easily endows to the eye: My-ness. M-Y-hyphen- N-E-S-S. Comma, tiny my-ness.

But the comma here does another thing besides amplifying the tiny tinyness of our my-ness. It also slows us down long enough to hear what we've gone past, or perhaps to let the sound of it catch up to us: our tiny, tiny my-ness. The word 'our' makes this my-ness a state we share and our tinyness something larger and, if not more heroic, at least not quite so much a M-I-N-U-S minus.

The first line of the poem, put in quotes, is itself a hypertext, more text than text as Ted Nelson, who coined the word, first had it. No one ever said, 'My parents, my husband, my brother, my sister.' On the other hand each of us has spoken precisely this sentence in more or less the same words. Yet someone did say these words in this poem, and perhaps even in the cafeteria where Milosz sat over tea and cinnamon toast or coffee and eggs over light and, half dreaming, listened in.

(Perhaps you don't like to think of him drinking tea or coffee or eating eggs. You'd rather think of him as 'the poet', someone above it all, full of high sentiment rather than cinnamon toast. Maybe you wish he were Horace – you do remember Horace? – looking out to sea.)

The sentence also encapsulates the voices of the assembled women whose ritual the solitary poet – his cyclops egg-over-easy staring up at him – shares in only sidelong, although erotically enough in their lips, whose moving moves him to delight at his moving unmovingness, which is to say presence, and brackets him, however briefly, in the embrace of the commas which become them, with them, here on earth.

If you have followed my reading the commas have moved in and out of the world, and indeed the actual text, of the poem, becoming ant, guppy, and the unfolding arms of women muttering rituals, who necessarily enfold us. This moving in and out of world and text is what electronic textuality, and paradoxically this poem, summon us to.

Could you get there by yourself? Would you? Who can know? It depends upon how you are disposed. Which is the meaning of disposition, our disposition is our mood, what we tend to do or think in common parlance, but it is also a gift, a giving over of control which dis-poses us, a giving ourselves over to others which takes us out of posing and into action. Another meaning of disposition is an arrangement, an array. This potential for action is laid out before us like a gift, like breakfast, coffee tea cinnamon toast and eggs-over-easy, a kind of communion. A surface sense, a rustle says the poem, which a curious phrase reins in briefly as 'no doubt necessary'. When we look at things like this in slo-mo such curiosities take on doublenesses, and their soundtracks seem echoes. 'No doubt necessary' is a man's offhand dismissal of women's chatter, but in this chattering light (we do speak light, you know), the ritual offers a saving grace and no doubt is necessary. Disposition also has a meaning of necessity, a final settlement. The poet too fulfils himself. It is a delight to be here on earth, comma, with them, comma, here on earth.

Electronic literacy is a locale for disposition in all these senses, *of* all our senses, our possibilities laid out before us like bathers on a beach. Each one who sits squinting on the beach tries to bring a story into focus, each dozing creature dreams another. They bracket us like commas and we move among them as we head to the surf.

The second text is a paragraph from an essay of Cixous' (1998) which I have taken entirely out of context in the sense that I have written about it here quite before I have read the full essay in which it appears, and without quite knowing yet just what the selection means, either to me or in the fuller context of the essay, and yet secure in a sense that I know how to know what it means, even if I do not linger long enough to do so, even if I move on without any secure understanding.

I do this partly to be a wise guy, to point out that this is how we most often read anything and especially the Web. In *Imagologies*, their printed hypertext regarding 'media philosophy', Mark Taylor and Esa Saarinen (1993) argue likewise:

> You might say that skipping through a book is as important an aspect of 'creative reading' as the cumbersome, clumsy process of actually going

through a sentence. You might say that part of professionalism is one's ability to sense intuitively those parts of the textmass that are not really worth reading, together with an ability to concentrate on the so-called essential. All this is true but does not conceal the scandal of reading: the fact is that the culture of books, printing and reading remain over-whelmingly defined by the micropowers of non-reading. For no one reads that much.

('Superficiality': 7)

Taylor and Saarinen recommend instead a kind of 'hypertextual reading … jump[ing] around at will in a given textmass' ('Superficiality': 8). In a surprising and moving meditation which contrasts the importance of watching over and smelling the fragrance of your sleeping baby with the self-important dignity, fixity, and relative unimportance of reading books, they locate the question of reading in terms of one's disposition toward life and love. 'Love is commitment, and commitment is your urge', they write, 'Who cares if you don't read all the books, most of the books, none of the books completely: the praxis of reading is but one means among others; this is an age that calls for instrumentalities to step down from their commanding status to mere means' ('Superficiality': 11).

It is in this spirit of commitment to the scent of sleeping things that I retrieve this segment from the middle of an essay I have not yet fully read. For this is how I have always come to know Cixous, in murmurs and whispers, in segments and surfaces, or, as she says here, in the isolation of a nutshell.

A suave concavity spreads out, the world is entirely hollow, we are equally hollow. One recognises the scene by its disposition, wherever it takes place, in Egypt, in Verona, in Paris, in Manhattan, in a palace room, hotel room, in the open air under the moon, on a Pantheon square, in the middle of a crowd, or in the isolation of a nutshell, an intimacy rises up and takes the two characters in its arms.

(Cixous 1998: 78)

The essay has an appropriately sleepy title for our considerations, 'What Is it O'Clock?' You will already have noticed that the paragraph I've quoted speaks explicitly of disposition in terms of exactly these dislocations and movements which we have been considering. You will also notice that in the last sentence I left off the strategy of attributing certain phrases to you directly and instead, for the second time in this essay of mine, assumed the easy mantle of a future tense shifting into a shared first person plural. You and me, and we.

As if you will recognise this space. As if we have been through something.

This, too, is a hallmark of the new rhetorics of post-hypertextuality. One often speaks of hypertext in terms of association and yet there is rather a quality of accumulation, in the way that someone moving through a field of wildflowers is stained with pollen, tagged with burrs, hooked by nettle, silked by milkweed.

You will already have noticed another second appearance here, in the arrival of yet another character on this unfolding scene of ours: a new someone named one, taking his or her place among the you and I and we which have characterised this discourse so far, becoming a family member of sorts, my parents, my husband, my brother, my sister, Horace, Cixous or Milosz, you, me, we, and one.

There have been only two further instances of the impersonal construction, 'One does suchandsuch' before the occurrence of that construction in the quoted paragraph of Cixous', where indeed you might not have recognised it. There have been twenty-seven occurrences of the word, one, since the beginning of this essay up to the beginning of this sentence and only four of them have featured this impersonal character called one. One of the missing ones occurred in the very beginning of this essay where in describing my role as a visiting guru at the steel table I slipped away from my own voice to attribute something of a criticism to the impersonal one. I was 'meant to amuse, provoke, coddle and, one suspects, reinforce feelings of intellectual currency and even superiority' I said. The second one was more self-conscious and signalled the issue, if not this discussion, of relationship between you and one. 'It would', it (or I) said, 'be quite understandable if one were suspicious of the anecdotal retelling and the faint aspect of ironic distancing which you seem to be invited to take part in'. Finally the most recent one was also a side-stepping or off-setting, a dis-positioning, of the same sort as these others: 'One often speaks of hypertext in terms of association', I wrote neatly slipping out of that garb, 'and yet there is rather a quality of accumulation'.

It has always been possible to attend to and keep track of how one is addressed by others, but the computer makes it easier to do so. We are drawn to surfaces, of language as well as image, on account of such ease. This is what the great rhetorician of both traditional and electronic literacy, Richard Lanham (1993), means by the distinction he makes between looking at and looking through. The side-stepping as I move from what I am saying to what one hears as another is almost transparent, and thus we look through it. The catalogues of ones and their uses is nubby and opaque, thus we look at it. As we look upon writing (which of course often includes visual images, both static and moving) on a computer screen, Lanham argues, our eyes oscillate between looking at and through. Yet the truth is we don't really notice the shifts, not on the page or in the ear, not on the screen or in our lives, until they are accounted to us, recounted, counted.

This kind of counting by ones is not arithmetic but rhetoric. The shifting of perspectives from you to I to one to we is characteristic of electronic literacy and post-hypertextual rhetoric. One wishes you to be many and for us to share my sense of shifting selves.

Which brings us back to Cixous and her one here who 'recognises the scene by its disposition'. This 'one' has only a moment earlier been a 'we' in the sentence: 'A suave concavity spreads out, the world is entirely hollow, we are equally hollow'. It is a lonely sentence, despite the soothing sound of the word suave. We do not like to be hollow (literature students and an older generation of readers recognise the haunting of the word from a memory of T.S. Eliot).

Thank god the hollowness is overturned, filled really, or to use the language of Milosz's poem (and why not, we are talking of hypertextuality) necessarily fulfilled by the rustle of a catalogue of places which in Cixous' prose are not unlike the names of relatives in Milosz's poem. Egypt, Verona, Paris, Manhattan, palace room, hotel room, open air under the moon, Pantheon square, middle of a crowd, isolation of a nutshell: the names shoot by us like someone's vacation snapshots or a set of linked webpages. Accumulating, they take on the quality of association, both inside and outside their own hollow sphere. The open air under the moon seems to recall our Italian friend Horace. Perhaps you think of Milosz at breakfast when you hear the mention of the hotel room; meanwhile Manhattan may make me recall the *Razorfish* steel table.

Like the Milosz text this one ends in an intimacy, and yet it is an intimacy almost robbed of its force by the curiously distancing phrase, 'the two characters', whose taking up we may celebrate but nonetheless takes us beyond the realm of rhetoric and into private language. Unlike the solitary poet with whom we 'celebrate our tiny, tiny my-ness', here 'an intimacy rises up and takes the two characters in its arms' leaving one – to put it in a nutshell – in a suave concavity.

Of course it isn't fair, one might say, to read like this, isolating a paragraph from an essay, even an essay about various isolations, and read it, as we say, 'out of context'. Indeed certain critics of technology (perhaps you know a teacher or a writer who argues this; perhaps you are one) argue that electronic literacy (from telephone to radio to television to the web) results in a lack of attention span, a loss of caring reading. I have argued elsewhere 'in response to others who claim that the so-called MTV generation has no attention span' that

> in an age like ours which privileges polyvocality, multiplicity, and constellated knowledge a sustained attention span may be less useful than successive attendings. Increasingly it is not the substance of what we say but its expression and construction which communicates.
>
> (Joyce 2000: 74)

In fact the whole of this essay means to argue in its own expression and construction as much as in what it says in its substance that electronic literacy does likewise. Much the same kind of oscillation that Richard Lanham poses in terms of looking at and looking through has characterised the discourse of rhetoricians throughout the ages regarding form and content. The glory of rhetoric through the ages is that it has shown this form and content distinction to be a sham; yet to its shame rhetoric through the ages has often been summoned to support artificial distinctions for what is essentially an organic and dynamic relationship. Indeed surface reading – the process of browsing – discloses this dynamic.

Putting aside the dirty truth (or another 'scandal of reading' to use Taylor and Saarinen's phrase) that we have always read so – flipping and browsing and constructing meaning amidst fanning pages much like someone manages to see an animation in a cartoon flipbook – the truth is that even when we read straight through like good little intellectual soldiers, page by page line by line in dress-right-dress column left-right order in full possession of our full attention span, our minds drift, swirl, veer, connect, unlink, wander, and settle like doves in flight.

In fact one could argue that reading from the surface like this is a way of valuing something even more than reading at depth. We circle the thing and let it remain, or become, itself, let it disclose itself to us successively and rhythmically. Circling this essay of Cixous' I am saving it for myself the way someone sets aside a savoury bit for the last part of a meal or a midnight snack or, in another time, for marriage. I know I will like it. In fact I come to know that exactly by these acts of setting aside and successive attending which have the function of pre-disposing me, *dispositio* again, to do so.

There is a joy to moving over surfaces. For instance with this Cixous piece, I can read first-lines backwards up the page, paragraph by paragraph, as if a monkey up a ladder, the ladder being a favourite image of Cixous (1993), reading successively preceding partial lines thusly:

> One step – love takes a step – and they are both, and at a single bound, inside the room-inside-the-room.

> Here the continent is going to open up, it is the unique continent, and it is interior.

> Continents no longer separate our two observers.
>
> (Cixous 1998: 78)

I said earlier that the call to a post-hypertextual rhetoric is a call to find purpose in surface, to find a lasting world in our shifting sense of ordinary life. That it is a call to the kind of ordinary mindfulness. Surface attentions grace human life and grant us peculiar joys in realms as diverse as music, painting, poetry or other forms of lovemaking.

Does that last phrase surprise you? One hopes so, it was meant to. To think of the arts, and especially those which use language and image to shape our concerns to each other, as a form of lovemaking, is both a rhetorical turn and a summoning. Our friend Horace – you do remember him, don't you? – is quite often accounted to have appropriated the traditional concerns of rhetoric for poetry. Poetry teaches, delights and moves us Horace (1998) tells us in his *Ars Poetica*, although Plutarch (1971) says in the *Moralia* that Simonides said this first, making our boy, like most poets, an early hypertextualist. That a poem means to convince us of something, say that the moon dapples the sea as a caress does one's shoulder, seems a natural enough connection, a link one might say. Perhaps Horace is the wrong person to attribute this link to, but then again who isn't. The list of poets who have followed him in making this distinction, from Sir Phillip Sidney to Marianne Moore to Czeslaw Milosz suggests that anything important moves through us and we author it by turns and upon successive surfaces.

In the first flush of hypertextual thinking, many of us sought to identify the process of finding purpose in surface as a kind of new authorship, one which the reader shared, or more radically shaped for herself, as she pieced or traversed successive surfaces of contiguous and contingent texts. It was a concept, or rather an array of interlinked and harmonic relationships, a network, which we wove variously, borrowing from poststructuralist, postmodernist, feminist, futurist, imagist, and postcolonial philosophers, rhetoricians, poets, critics, other artists and theorists and, most of all, each other, whatever we were, cybertheorists, hypertextualists, computer compositionists. It is a claim I am unwilling to give up on, a claim indeed I am making for you here as well. At the crossroads of the link we leave all talk of one or other behind and we look briefly at each other, you and I seen there, where the light plays upon differing surfaces.

This essay means to summon one, or you, or us to certain meditations which 'explore the rhetorical tradition as it is encountering computers, technology, ways of writing, ways of learning, and so forth'. Perhaps in such an enterprise one expects words like gif and jpeg, java and flash, chat and MOO, applet and Perl script. Perhaps you hoped for layers, frames, and the slow disclosures of server side includes or the pillowy and compliant surfaces of antialiased rollovers. Instead we have poetry and self-reflexive knots of silvery threads blurring like airplane contrails before the chill persistence of unseen winds in high cerulean skies. What you will make of it you will indeed quite literally *make*, fashioning it of and for yourself, making meaning of light and of memory despite your realisation that its ground and its duration are no more secure than the high, cold air and the strong, dark winds within the outer orbits of electrons. You are the author of what you read or hear; it is a process for which you may think yourself unsuited but then again who isn't.

Note

1   This essay was first offered as a talk as part of the Distinguished Rhetoricians Seminar at Texas Women's University, a series conceived and inaugurated by Win Horner, and coordinated by Sue Webb and Hugh Burns, to whom I am grateful for the opportunity and continuing inspiration.

References

Cixous, H. (1993) *Three Steps on the Ladder of Writing*, New York: Columbia University Press.
——— (1998) 'What Is it O'clock?' in *Stigmata: Escaping Texts*, New York: Routledge.
Hayles, N. Katherine (1998a) 'Byte Lit', *Art Forum* 37, 2: 2–3.

—— (1998b) 'Personal communication'. Online. E-mail: *m.joyce@vassar.edu* (18 August 1998)

Horace (1998) 'She doesn't yet have strength to endure a yoke', trans. S. Willett, *Selections from Horace's Odes*, Diotima web. Online. Available HTTP: *http://www.uky.edu/Arts Sciences/Classics/horawill.html* (21 June 2001).

Joyce, M. (2000) 'The lingering errantness of place, or library as library', in M. Joyce, *Othermindedness: The Emergence of Network Culture*, Ann Arbor: University of Michigan Press.

Lanham, R. (1993) *The Electronic Word: Democracy, Technology and the Arts*, Chicago: University of Chicago Press.

Milosz, C. (1988) *The Collected Poems*, New York: The Ecco Press.

Pound, E. (1960) *Pavannes and Divagations: Prose and Poems*, London: Owen.

Plutarch (1971) *Moral Essays*, trans. R. Warner, Harmondsworth: Penguin.

Taylor, M. C. and Saarinen, E. (1993) *Imagologies: Media Philosophy*, New York: Routledge.

Part II

TEACHING, LEARNING, TECHNOLOGY AND INNOVATION

7

EDUCATIONAL INNOVATION AND HYPERTEXT

One university's successes and failures in supporting new technology

George P. Landow

Why did it take so long? ... Well, the first reason is the classical inertia problem. New ideas take forever to be popularised. The second reason is, of course, that there are technology problems. It takes a long time to develop something as cheap and as user-friendly as the Macintosh, for example. ... Now the technology is definitely here, and there is certainly no excuse for waiting any longer.

(Andries van Dam, Keynote Address, *Hypertext '87*: 889)[1]

Brown University, or, successes and failures in innovation

Brown University has been a byword for innovation, particularly in the American popular media, since before I arrived there in 1971. Having spent three decades at Brown, I propose to examine a number of educational projects and draw some general conclusions about initiating and supporting innovation. The history of Brown University's New Curriculum in many ways embodies the strengths and weaknesses of an educational institution insofar as it is open to various kinds of innovation. Therefore, before discussing hypertext and other innovative uses of computing at Brown, I begin by examining the university's broad attempts at educational innovation, particularly its so-called New Curriculum of the early seventies, which was initiated as an attempt to teach students to live and learn according to the fundamental assumptions of a naively optimistic educational radicalism.

Ever since the French Revolution, political thought in the West has relied upon a division between two fundamental assumptions about human nature and the systems of power that it demands. Those on the right, to use the terms passed down to us by the French Revolution, take as an axiom that human beings have such pervasive, fundamental flaws that a principal purpose of government is to protect people from themselves – and one principal means to

101

achieve that end involves conserving whatever forces of order a society has created, however irrational their source, however inefficient and unjust their operation. These sons and daughters of Plato, who himself lived in a period of political chaos and learned to fear disorder above almost all else, believe that order is hard to come by, easily lost, and terribly difficult to re-establish.

Radicals, in contrast, believe that human beings are either fundamentally good or at least fundamentally malleable. Since they believe in the fundamental goodness of human nature, they blame the presence of sin and suffering, poverty and evil, on the System – that is, whatever form of society and government exists at the moment. It follows that changing the system will make people happy and good. Whether a Maoist or a Marxist–Leninist believing in the party's right and obligation to exercise total power for the eventual good of all, or an Anarchist believing that all political structures are evil, the Radical is convinced that change is for the better. The tens of millions of people who have died during the last century testify to the immense attraction of these beliefs – and their terrible cost.

Most political beliefs, of course, fall into the difficult-to-defend but easier-to-live-by camp of Liberalism, which variously blends change and preservation, liberation and restraint. The strictest Conservatives are so terrified of throwing out the baby with the bath water that they are not willing to throw out anything, sometimes at the expense of the baby. Radicals believe the baby is clearly suffering so much in the bath water now – and is in such immediate danger – that little is to be risked by acting hastily. Liberals know the water has to be separated from the baby, but they have just seen the Radicals drop a baby on its head and they want to proceed more cautiously. Sometimes they dither a bit about when to empty the bath water, about who has the right to decide how it should be emptied, and about how quickly the task should be done. Of course, the Conservatives grumble about taking such great risks while the Radicals, who take their greatest pleasure in being out of power and seeing the failures of Liberals, look on smugly, jab each other in the ribs, and say, 'Will you look at those idiots!'

Brown's venture into a comfy radicalism took the form of the New Curriculum, which assumed that imposed structure, and imposed rules are always bad and that students, even beginning students, know what's good for them. If students chose their courses without constraint, the reasoning went, they would work harder, be more creative, take greater risks, and sample new, 'strange' areas that might otherwise have been too threatening. Requiring students to take a Core Curriculum, like that at Columbia or Chicago, or even a mandated sampling of courses in different disciplines, was in some fundamental way educationally unsound. Brown therefore would do away with all such freshman and sophomore requirements, and, furthermore, since being graded formed another constraint, students would have the option of taking all courses ungraded.

The New Curriculum went even further, permitting students to choose not just pass/fail options but Satisfactory/No Credit (SAT/NC), meaning that failures not only received no credit but did not appear on the students' public transcripts. In fact, you did not want to tell students they had failed – that would be too judgmental – they just did not get credit. After all, students should not be blamed for failing a course – perhaps they were too busy with creative activities to come to class, the class didn't suit their needs, or maybe it was just too hard – and students shouldn't be expected to be drudges. (This was a time, remember, when at least some people exalted play over work. In the early 1970s, when I chaired the committee that supposedly supervised university admissions, representatives from student government argued in a white paper that we should avoid admitting students who worked too hard, because such 'Puritanism' with its 'work ethic' – their words – was obviously bad for the university.)

Furthermore, those choosing to take grades as an option in an individual course no longer risked receiving a grade as low as D, since the New Curriculum considered such a low grade unwise. Then, since the grade of D, which had formerly counted toward fulfilling graduation requirements, no longer existed and some students had needed Ds in the past to graduate, the graduation requirement was lowered from thirty-two courses to twenty-eight. As an additional way of lessening supposedly harmful pressures on students, they were allowed to drop a course without penalty at any time up to the final examination.

To the cynic or the Conservative, this was a slacker's paradise; to the Radical educational idealist, this was a learning paradise. Both, as it turns out, were right, and what happened next shows some of the interesting and unexpected complications of educational and other forms of innovation. The most obvious effect was that Brown University, which had always been a small regional school drawing the majority of its undergraduates from Rhode Island, Massachusetts, and Connecticut, rose to international prominence, and whereas historically it had always been at the bottom of the Ivy League pecking order, it now rose to fourth place in the rankings, just behind Princeton, Harvard, and Yale.[2] The quality of the student body certainly rose, as did campus morale and student satisfaction. Not surprisingly, an educational programme largely formulated by undergraduates proved to be extremely attractive to people of about the same age. There were other darker, never publicly acknowledged, 'benefits': since students no longer had to learn a foreign language, the language departments could be cut, and when the seventies recession brought hard times, the administration, strapped for cash (at an institution with a then-notoriously poor investment policy), quietly axed lots of instructors.

Of course, the New Curriculum was never as free as its advocates or its detractors claimed, and almost immediately upon its introduction, it began a retreat from its original form until Brown's undergraduate education came to resemble the programmes at other liberal arts colleges. First, there was one requirement: as at other schools, students had to demonstrate a minimal writing ability. More important – and as some entering students were surprised to discover – students still had to choose a major, and some departments used the introduction of the New Curriculum as a means of making their majors more stringent. In addition, although the programme was based on the assumption that students knew how and what to choose immediately upon their arrival at Brown, they were in fact never left to their own devices. Everyone immediately realised that the system could only work if students were supported in their decision-making by an elaborate system of faculty, student, and residence-hall advising. In fact, as soon became clear from directions given to incoming students and their advisers, the role of the advising system was to convince – read, 'browbeat' – students into taking precisely the kind and range of courses that other institutions required their undergraduates to take.

One reason for the increasingly rapid falling away from its original stated ideal involves a sharp divergence between the goals of the faculty and students who proposed the New Curriculum and the administration which supervised its implementation, the generally idealistic faculty who tried to put it into practice, and the widely varying conduct of the students who experienced the new system – for system it was, and where there's a system, some people quickly learn to manipulate it to their own advantage. First, the actions of the administration, or University Hall (or simply UH), as it is known at Brown: one of the crucial components of the original New Curriculum was a cadre of special interdisciplinary courses under the rubric, Modes of Thought. Their presence in the programme had made many sceptical faculty members willing to abandon distribution requirements because they were convinced that these new courses, among which students could choose freely, would more than accomplish the goals of liberal education. As it turned out, these courses, which had mandatorily low enrolments (no more than twenty-five) and were to be taught by tenured faculty, if possible, proved very expensive. In fact, they proved immediately too costly for an institution much poorer than its league rivals, and one that was also in the midst of establishing a medical school, one of the most costly educational endeavours in existence.

From the vantage of hindsight, the outcome was obvious: at the same time Brown was benefiting from publicity about its pioneering new courses, the university, which was then very inexperienced at fundraising, decided it had to cut its losses. According to an assistant professor of modern languages, who had been put in charge of the Modes of Thought programme, the then-president of the university had told him, 'Your job is to oversee the death of the Modes of Thought courses', and the administration hastened the demise of the programme by making clear to departments that wished to teach them that they would do so at their own expense: Modes of Thought courses would *not* count toward the departmental budget. Departments got the message pretty quickly, the programme died quietly, and my young informant soon left the teaching profession.

Meanwhile, the popular press continued to trumpet Brown's innovations, teaching many at the university that smoke and mirrors produced illusions as good as the real thing. To be fair, maybe in a sense they were: despite its quick demise, the Modes of Thought programme led teachers to rethink their approach to education, and it thereby produced some wonderful courses, one or two of which lasted for decades. One lesson, then, about educational or any other innovation: anything that prompts people to think about the way they do things in a new way, even if it does not succeed or last very long, can lead to beneficial change. The short-lived Modes of Thought courses at Brown provided a valuable paradigm for rethinking teaching and learning.

The most serious failure of this major attempt at fundamental educational innovation appears in its effect on students whose goals, it quickly emerged, differed greatly from those of the reformers. The Brown reformers had created a programme for the ideal student; unfortunately, real students enrolled in the university. The purpose of doing away with distribution requirements, including knowledge of math, science and foreign languages, like the adoption of no-fault grading, was to encourage students to explore, to take chances, to learn for the pleasure of learning. There is no doubt that in the first years of its adoption, many students *did* take courses SAT/NC, as the Brown jargon has it, and some of the finest students I have ever taught, a few of whom have become leading scholars at major universities, chose this route.

A grading system is, however, still a system, and students soon became adept at manipulating it to do what they, not the educational reformers, thought was to their advantage. Realising that one needed four fewer courses than previously to graduate, some students took no courses in their last term, or simply didn't bother to complete ones in which they had enrolled. Others became extremely skilful at managing their grade-point average, dropping courses when it appeared they'd likely receive only a B when they thought they needed an A for, say, law school. The ease with which a clever student can work the system at Brown has made meaningless many of the highest honours, such as election to Phi Beta Kappa. An example – a particularly egregious one: in the spring of 1974 a very bright young undergraduate talked his way into my doctoral seminar, seemed to be doing satisfactorily, and then a month or so into the course (just when scheduled to give a substantial in-class presentation), he came to the seminar and politely told me he was dropping the course. When I mentioned his name to another member of my department, I learned that he had dropped out of his postgraduate course, too. After I attended the Phi Beta Kappa induction ceremony and saw the student there, I suddenly understood: he had enrolled, as it later turned out, in *three* graduate seminars, gained election to Phi Beta Kappa, and his goal having been achieved, dropped all three without penalty! From the student's point of view, the system had not let him down.

Granted this student and those like him represent extreme cases, but faculty and administration eventually realised how common were students who cynically played the system. Largely under the leadership of Sheila Blumstein, then-Dean of the College and Professor of Cognitive Science, a series of steps were taken to prevent such abuses: students eventually had to pass a minimum of three courses each term to stay out of academic difficulty, and gradually the graduation requirements were raised too. As we have seen, the great majority of the transcripts of Brown graduates look very much like those of students at other liberal arts institutions. There is no evidence that Brown students are any more venture-some, as far as taking courses in new areas goes, than are students at comparable colleges and universities. As this innovative set of educational experiments (one really can't term it a curriculum) grows older, it has less and less of its original feeling. Students take fewer and fewer courses SAT/NC (graduate schools and employers do not look on them with favour), and many of those who do so use them to avoid a grade of C rather than to experiment with new subjects.[3]

When looking back at almost three decades of the New Curriculum, some of its apparent failures are not surprising since from the very beginning its imple-mentation revealed a lack of institutional confidence, an unwillingness to take risks, even a kind of bad faith. In a supposedly egalitarian spirit Brown aban-doned Cum Laude degrees (honours) and Summa Cum Laude (highest honours) and yet in a particularly bizarre move, kept Magna Cum Laude (high honours); and retained Brown's membership in Phi Beta Kappa, the third oldest chapter in America. Yes, students were offered the option of SAT/NC, but faculty members could give excellent students a SAT+ to differentiate them from 'ordi-nary' satisfactory grades. Similarly, Brown University abandoned pluses and minuses, but kept grades. Doing away with the D caused instant grade inflation: a C quickly became not a satisfactory grade but one that was just above failing.

Why the New Curriculum was a successful innovation

The previous narrative might lead readers to assume that I believe Brown's New Curriculum was an unmitigated disaster, nothing but sixties educational radi-calism having a comical encounter with reality. Such is not the case. The reason it is not tells us some important things about successful innovation. What did it accomplish? First, it brought a small, regional college to national attention, and in so doing, made Brown a byword for innovation – some thought it crazy or foolish innovation, but innovation nonetheless. Second, Brown with the aid of the popular media convinced large groups of potential applicants that it was at the cutting edge of precisely the kind of educational change that matched the tone of the early seventies. In the guise of radical educational reform, Brown offered undergraduate consumerism. The mix worked, and Brown began to attract a new blend of national and international students. Since recruiting top students is one of the essential components of a university, the favourable atten-tion the university received did in fact improve Brown, its reputation, and especially the quality of its incoming classes.

Yes, the New Curriculum was not really much of a curriculum after all, but it changed what had been a conservative university into one unusually open to experimentation, interdisciplinary programmes, and new courses and majors. The very climate produced by seriously debating the old curriculum and becoming willing to consider major changes produced deeper, more pervasive changes than simply abandoning the distribution requirement ever did. In partic-ular it created an atmosphere of experimentation and an exhilarating feeling that one might be at the cutting edge. Brown fairly quickly became a place of burgeoning programmes, centres, interdepartmental programmes, and majors, often with those in charge – both those in the senior administration and those in individual departments – failing to take into account the various costs eventually involved.[4] Nonetheless, virtually all those associated with Brown during the past few decades agree that the university has improved a great deal during that time.

Hypertext at Brown University – three waves of innovation

One of the areas in which Brown gained in reputation during the period following the introduction of the New Curriculum involves humanities computing, in particular the development and application of hypertext systems in education, scholarship, and the creative arts. I would like to be able to state without reservation that the atmosphere generated by the New Curriculum was directly responsible for this innovation, but although I suspect this is in part the case, it would be hard to prove. What is certain, however, is that all three waves of innovation in hypertext, humanities computing, and cyber-arts derive directly from the work of a single person – Andries van Dam, the first chair of Computer Science and an internationally known pioneer in both computer graphics and hypertext systems. Professor van Dam (or 'Andy', as he is generally known to all his friends and students) brought Ted Nelson, a fellow graduate of Swarthmore, to Brown in late 1967 or 1968, and drawing on that extended visit and the work of Douglas Englebart, the man who, among other things, invented the computer mouse, he and a team at Brown produced the Hypertext Editing System. Let's let Andy tell this part of the story in his own words from his keynote address at *Hypertext '87* (van Dam 1988: 889):

> Ted started coming to Providence, using, as he is proud to say in *Computer Lib*, his own money. We started working on the Hypertext Editing System, which was essentially dual-purpose. One purpose was to produce printed documents nicely and efficiently ... But the main purpose was to explore this hypertext concept.
>
> I want to mention a couple of numbers, just so that you can size the system. We ran our 2250 graphics display application in a 128K-partition memory, our mainframe at that time. An IBM/360 Model 50 is slower than a vanilla Mac [in 1987!] and has less memory. Yet in that one partition we ran the Hypertext Editing System, and there was a complete timesharing system in another partition. There was no virtual memory; everything was done with software paging.
>
> The undergraduates programming the Hypertext Editing System as a bootleg graphics project were paid by my IBM graphics contract. When our project monitor, Sam Matsa, saw it, he liked it, so we came out of the closet and started showing it around at a variety of sites

where IBM had large customers. It was also ported to a number of university sites. Even after the project was frozen and we went on to the next-generation system, it was sold by IBM (unbeknownst to me and Ted and others who had worked on it) to the Apollo mission team at the Houston Manned Spacecraft Center and was used to produce documentation that went up with Apollo, I'm proud to say.

(van Dam 1988: 889)

Professor van Dam's reminiscences prompt several observations, the first of which is that hypertext at Brown preceded the New Curriculum, but not by much. Second, from the very beginning, undergraduates, not postdocs or doctoral candidates, were involved in pioneering work. Third, financing for true innovation sometimes came, as it often does, from somewhat creative use of other grants and contracts; innovation sometimes happens in the gaps and shadows. Fourth, as the final sentences in the quoted passage make clear, the innovators do not always know to what uses their innovations may be put until much later.

The first of the three waves of hypertext developments at Brown that affected a large number of undergraduate and postgraduate students was not HES but the system that grew out of it – FRESS (File Retrieval and Editing SyStem). FRESS, which eventually became a kind of underground movement among a select few humanities faculty and students, turns out to have been astonishingly advanced, particularly when one considers that it had features that HTML and the WWW still do not have three decades later! It had bi-directional links with explainers, for example, worked on a wide range of devices, and was the first system to have an Undo function! Keywords were possible on every element, both for online and offline trails. Links could be 'typed' with these key words.

Nonetheless, as van Dam points out, 'Nobody said, "Hey, it's great you're building tools for humanists, that's wonderful, when can we have it?" In fact, quite the reverse' (van Dam 1988: 891). It was the senior administration at Brown that most opposed this major innovation, prefiguring a general problem that the university has faced off and on for many years. As van Dam told the story of such resistance in his *Hypertext '87* keynote address, he had 'serious warfare' with a senior administrator 'about whether the software should even be allowed on the system, because if it were on the system, then people would use it. And that would subvert the true purpose of computers, which was to produce numbers for engineers and scientists. He said, "If you want to screw around with text, use a typewriter"' (van Dam 1988: 891); van Dam tells a similar story in other public lectures: he had introduced Roderick Chisolm, one of the most famous philosophers ever associated with the university, to his innovation, and Chisolm began to use it in his work when the Provost called van Dam on the carpet for wasting the university's resources. Probably the worst, by which I mean, most depressing, of what van Dam calls 'barefoot-in-the-snow stories' (van Dam 1988: 891) of pioneer experiences is one I heard from various humanists who used FRESS and mourned its eventual passing: the university eventually refused to support FRESS on the campus mainframe, because it would cost a certain sum of money – and chose an off-the-shelf product with vastly fewer features and little user-friendliness that eventually cost twenty times as much to maintain. True? I don't have any paper documentation, but my informants were closely associated with or employed by Computing and Information Services, so one assumes they knew about the reasons FRESS was excised from the Brown budget at last.

As we shall see from the university's treatment of succeeding innovations, this anecdote reveals Brown's fundamental lack of support for the kind of innovation about which it supposedly cared so much. None of the people who failed to support FRESS and later innovations in humanities computing were bad or unintelligent or particularly mean-spirited. The problem is more institutional than personal: throughout thirty years of often brilliant innovation, the university has never managed to develop structures or processes that integrate such beneficial changes into its sense of mission. Since such innovation always comes as an institutional afterthought, no one has the responsibility of tracking and evaluating it. One important if obvious conclusion: institutional factors and conditions that stimulate innovation are not the same as those that nurture it, build upon it, or preserve it. Another: as difficult as stimulating valuable innovation might be, it is equally difficult to know what to do with it when it happens.

Long after its disappearance from the Brown mainframe, FRESS continued to function as an indirect agent for innovation by fostering a small cadre of people dedicated to humanities computing. After the software no longer could be used, the paradigm remained, influencing their lives and careers and many of the students and faculty with whom they came in contact. One of the most important indirect effects of FRESS, for example, was CHUG (Computing Humanities Users Group) a half dozen or so people, originally almost all undergraduates and postgraduate students, who created an informal organisation that without funding or official encouragement managed quickly to achieve an international reputation among researchers working in humanities computing and hypertext applications, many of whom came to Providence to deliver papers and receive the famously stringent critiques that followed. CHUG's main interests were hypertext systems and text encoding, including SGML and later the Text Encoding Initiative. Most of the founders and early members of CHUG, including Allen Renear, Elli Mylonas, Steven J. DeRose, David Durand and James H. Coombs, have established major reputations for their achievements in computing.

The second wave of hypertext and humanities computing centres on the Institute for Research in Information and Scholarship (IRIS), which existed from 1983 to 1992. The chief accomplishment of IRIS was its development of Intermedia, a proof-of-concept hypertext environment that in most ways remains the finest hypertext system with which I have worked and taught. Since, unlike FRESS, Intermedia has been described in many places (see note 5), I'll just mention a few of its key features plus parts of the story relevant to the theme of this chapter, innovation. First, in keeping with the vision of the hypertext pioneers, Vannevar Bush, Englebart, Nelson and van Dam, the system permitted readers to have a new relation to existing text, for although they could not change something written by someone else, they could create their own documents and link to it. Second, it was a system that turned the common lost-in-hyperspace dilemma, so common on the WWW, into a non-problem. Third, because it was a networked system, editing changes and new materials became immediately accessible to all users. It was successfully used for five rich years to teach courses in creative writing, biology, and English (the departmental survey course, postcolonial literature, and Victorian undergraduate and graduate seminars), even though most faculty members in the department of English were conspicuously not interested in learning about it, much less in using it.[5]

Now to the matter of external funding, university support, or the lack of it: IRIS and Intermedia were funded by substantial grants and contracts from IBM, Apple Computers, the Annenberg/CPB Project, and various hardware and software companies. Brown received a good deal of favourable publicity about Intermedia and its educational uses, all of which seemed to confirm the university's reputation as a so-called Star Wars university on the cutting edge of innovation. For those who don't understand the reference, let me explain that in the 1980s one of the national magazines proclaimed Brown, MIT, and Carnegie-Mellon 'Star Wars universities' (referring to the George Lucas film and not to the later Strategic Defence Initiative). Whereas the other two institutions have devoted considerable funding to innovations in digital culture, most famously the MIT Media Lab, and continue to support such innovation, Brown has not. My motivation for writing this chapter involves discussing some reasons this might have been the case.

Brown staked its initial claim as a supposed standard for innovation in educational and scholarly computing with two simple, interrelated, extremely bold decisions: it installed a broadband network throughout much of the campus and it gave everyone on campus – students, faculty, and staff – a computer account. As it turned out, these decisions, when combined with the presence on campus of innovators like van Dam, the computational linguist Henry Kucera, an idealistic (and often heroic) staff at the Computer Center, and a tiny number of students and faculty acquainted with mainframe computing, produced a pool of humanists amazingly sophisticated in their use of computing for scholarship and teaching. At one point in the late 1970s or early 1980s, the Computer Center decided to analyse its users and discovered to everyone's surprise that the English department had 140 active accounts, more than any other department!

Like the New Curriculum, access to campus computing facilities produced an innovative community, some of whose members carried the word outside Brown. The university administration, when it was aware of it, was delighted by the publicity, and it willingly used presentations of Intermedia and other Brown accomplishments, chiefly those by van Dam, for fundraising with alumni and major donors. Brown's presidents, provosts, and almost all other senior administrators who have run Brown for the past three decades never considered this kind of innovation central to Brown's mission – Don Wolfe, who recently resigned as Vice President for Computing, being an honourable exception – and consequently they were never willing to support this kind of work. When some funding opportunities for IRIS failed to materialise, senior administrators showed themselves willing to shut it down at a few hours' notice – this is not an exaggeration.[6]

'They give you money to build three-quarters of a bridge'

FRESS, IRIS, Intermedia, and similar innovations have a lot in common with the crucial Modes of Thought courses in the New Curriculum: although the official, statutory leaders of the university enjoyed Brown's reputation as an unusually innovative institution, they were unwilling to fund crucial elements that would have kept particular innovative projects going and probably would have produced new external funding as well. Brown has long practised a kind of creative chaos – 'creative' because during three decades university and departmental administrators have permitted many kinds of experiment; 'chaos' because the institution has no means of distinguishing between success and failure, true innovation and a dreadful mistake. Because its senior managers remained unaware of the existence of successful innovation, they could neither reward nor nurture it.

At the same time, the senior leadership and much of the university had become very complacent, apparently remaining unaware of how much simple good fortune it has enjoyed. Even when it was savouring its reputation as a Star Wars university, Brown did not seem to recognise that it had already fallen behind, not just the other innovative universities in that group, but behind many other institutions as well. In the late 1980s, for example, Princeton and other major universities already had networked residence halls that Brown was just considering as a possibility. How could an institution so capable of nurturing innovation continually fail to nurture it? One might argue – indeed, some have – that some of the innovations were simply not worth preserving or nurturing, or one might resort to the claim that it didn't have the money. Brown, it is true, has a comparatively small endowment, but clearly a university that has an annual budget around $145 million has money to spend *somewhere*. After wondering for the umpteenth time how a university known for innovation could so frequently fail to capitalise on it or support it, I heard the problem perfectly described by someone (not van Dam, let me hasten to say) who had raised millions of dollars for scholarly, educational, and creative computer projects. 'Brown', he explained, 'is a place where they give you money to build three-quarters of a bridge.' When something good happened, no one is paying attention because without an institutional mechanism to evaluate innovations, the university has no means of dealing with them.

Another factor (though one less important, I believe, than institutional organi-sation and ethos) is that Brown has had several presidents who were not familiar with the new computer technologies. At a time when digital information tech-nology threatens (or promises) to change some of our fundamental ideas about education, the creative arts, how we work, the reliability of images, intellectual property, legal jurisdiction, and so on, it is a terrible misfortune to have had people at the helm who do not understand what is going on in these key areas of change.

These various factors explain why attempts during the past decade to take advantage of Brown's reputation as a leader in humanities computing, cyber-arts, and digital culture have generally met with failure. In particular, repeated attempts over the last decade to create either a programme or a major in digital culture has met resistance and incomprehension – despite the fact that dozens of Brown undergraduates independently or covertly major in such subjects each year. Brown's own novelist-in-residence Robert Coover has long been one of the pioneering popularisers of hyperfiction and related applications of multimedia to the arts. From his and related classes have come some of the world's pre-eminent writers of such fiction. When I was teaching my hypertext and literary theory course at Brown some years back, one of my older students, Mark Amerika from the MFA programme, approached me to apologise for missing classes the following week because a festival in Berlin was flying him there to speak on avante garde writing. Another MFA graduate, Shelley Jackson, is inter-nationally known for her brilliant hyperfiction, *Patchwork Girl*. Despite such success, there has rarely been any support at the top for this part of the Creative Writing programme. After years of thwarted attempts, it has not been possible to secure full faculty appointments for instructors in the programme, which keeps hiring other faculty in more traditional forms. Every time Coover goes on leave, hyperfiction threatens to disappear at Brown.

Another instance of such general institutional problems appears in the central administration's lack of awareness about major websites, such as Massimo Riva's NEH-supported *Decameron Web*, based at brown.edu. My various websites, which receive as many as 8 million hits/month, have been endorsed by the ministries of education (or the equivalent) in France, Sweden, Scotland, England and the United States. These large websites add something to Brown's reputation. Certainly, whenever I am invited to deliver lectures about them and their rela-tion to scholarship and education, members of the audience make clear that they assume I receive support for materials development from Brown (which I do not) and that they are a result of some major university initiative (which they are not).[7] The university leadership simply is not interested in them – or aware of them. When some years ago, knowing the attention my sites were receiving, I suggested that the university take advantage of that fact and list them some-where in the Brown website, I was told that that would not be Brown policy. Most recently, I suggested to one senior administrator that we could publicise either a proposed department of digital culture or the entire university by putting a statement of Brown sponsorship in each document. I even offered to hand over management of the sites to a committee, a group of editors, whatever. This proposal was not deemed worthy of a response. Again, I do not think this lack of institutional awareness derives primarily from any particularly egregious qualities of individual administrators, or any particular ignorance. Rather, we once again encounter a lack of institutional commitment to the kind of innovations this particular institution is best at creating.

After the demise of IRIS in 1992, Allen Renear founded the Scholarly Technology Group (STG), ostensibly as part of User Services at Brown, and his vision, hard work, and skill at putting together a fine team and fundraising has produced yet another wave of innovation at the university (the third in the heading of this section). The STG website (www.stg.brown.edu) contains a great deal of valuable information about this group's projects and accomplishments. I'll just point out that after STG established itself as an internationally recognised centre of expertise on electronic text and text encoding under the leadership of Renear and Elli Mylonas, it provided a home for many cutting-edge projects, including the Women Writers Project, one of the rare projects in humanities or any other computing to be self-supporting. It has also become the new home for CHUG. But even here Brown finds itself at a crossroads, and who knows what will happen next?

The university's director of instructional computing left several years ago for an institution that promised more support for educational computing; the vice president for computing who quietly, sometimes covertly, protected so many innovative projects has chosen early retirement; some key people at the STG have accepted academic jobs elsewhere; and Renear has left Brown for the University of Illinois at Urbana. Some of the other faculty leaders in humanities computing have told me they have applied for jobs at other universities. Like so many other American institutions, Brown still does not have any way of counting hypertext and most computing work in the humanities toward tenure or promotion. Although many other leading research universities, such as Georgia Tech, Duke, and the University of Virginia, have positions, chairs, programmes, or departments in digital culture, proposals to have such at Brown, where so much of this work originated, remain unaccepted. Nonetheless, there are at least some signs of hope, and we'll have to see wait and see what will happen next.[8]

Conclusions

As I write this conclusion, Brown University, which has been without a president for a year, the last one having lasted only two, has to wait about six more months before its new president, Ruth J. Simmons, assumes office. Some claim that Brown is at risk of losing its status as a research university and returning to its earlier existence as a fine liberal arts college for wealthier members of American (and now international) society. This institution, like so many others today, finds itself at a crossroads, and the next decisions by faculty and administration will do much to determine the stature, national importance, and influence of this educational institution.

As important as such questions might be to anyone associated with Brown University, most of my readers, I assume, care more about what its history over three decades has to tell them about the possibilities for successful educational innovations, particularly those based upon networked digital information technologies. Several things are clear. First, although institutions can plan for innovation, or try to stimulate it, first-level successes – actual innovations – often come as a surprise and often involve the law of unintended circumstances. As the history of both the New Curriculum and FRESS reveal, when any innovation changes the way people think about key matters, such as teaching and learning, or organisational management, these changed attitudes, some of which are unexpected, are frequently more important and longer lasting than the original innovation. As the Brown example shows, knowing what to do next is an extraordinarily complex matter. Organisations that wish to promote innovation must have an effective means of keeping track of various innovations – they must have someone who pays attention to what is going on – and they must have someone who can evaluate any innovation in terms of institutional needs and goals. Institutions obviously cannot simply spend money or human resources on projects and then forget about them. Equally important, in an age of fast-paced expensive technological innovations, someone in a position of major authority must understand both the nature of the technology and at least some of its potential effects upon the institution. In an age of digital information technologies, those who make key decisions about goals and resources must grasp, for example, the way digital technology affects long-held conceptions of teaching, learning, scholarship, intellectual property, publication, institutional structures, and the like. In particular, those who hope to lead must realise that applying inappropriate paradigms drawn from the world of the book, however comforting, has a very high cost.

Notes

1   Van Dam, A. (1988) Keynote Address: *Hypertext '87*, Communications of the ACM, July 1988, 31 (7): 887–895.
2   The rankings to which university administrators and admissions officers refer came not from popular periodicals but from the academic pecking order based on so-called reporting percentages. If, say, 95 per cent of students admitted to Harvard and Brown choose Harvard, then Brown's reporting percentage is 5 per cent and Harvard's 95 per cent. If 51 per cent of the students admitted to both Brown and, say, Columbia, choose Brown, then it has moved above Columbia. Historically Brown ranked last among Ivy League schools. After the introduction of the New Curriculum, it moved to fourth place, where it has remained.
3   In my experience as a teacher at Brown for close to three decades, at least two-thirds of students of the comparatively few electing to take courses SAT/NC do work equivalent to a low C, often at the very edge of failure; most of the remaining third are idealistic students who would have earned As or A-s. Admittedly this is a small sample and of no statistical value.

4   President Howard Swearer, who had done his graduate work at Princeton University, liked to compare Brown with that institution, even though Princeton had far greater financial resources than Brown. Brown with half the faculty for the same size student body eventually had twice as many majors. Furthermore, the desire to allow faculty members to experiment with new kinds of courses and programmes often left basic departmental responsibilities uncovered.

5   When the department held one of its then-regular faculty seminars, only two people, one of them my former graduate student, came besides myself and the convenor of the session. When a few years later Philip Stiles, Dean of the Graduate School, invited me to give another talk, despite my warning few would come, three or four people came, none, I recall, from the humanities. When I tried to interest the Center for the Advancement of Teaching and Learning in projects for which Brown had received a small, if important, international reputation, I was assured, 'Brown faculty are not ready for this'.

6   This lack of understanding and support proved particularly sad because the remaining members of IRIS, myself included, had plans for developing what the full Intermedia group had called 'The Continents of Knowledge' with a consortium of two dozen colleges and universities. This project involved developing the content for a major interlinked, multidisciplinary educational hypertext – the prototype for the content (not software) on the WWW.

Incidentally, immediately upon the first appearance of the WWW, IRIS-in-the-basement created Brown's first humanities materials on the web, Professor Gerald Guralnik, a theoretical physicist, showed me Mosiac, offering room on his server for any documents we wished to create, whereupon David Stevenson, an undergraduate research associate, translated his *Freud Web* and *Context32*'s 'Religion in England' section from Intermedia to HTML.

7   In fact, my 'Brown' websites – the *Victorian, Postcolonial,* and *Cyberspace Webs* – were first hosted by Gerald Guralnik, Professor of Physics, on his research machines, and when the Scholarly Technology Group began, I moved the sites to their server. Since late 1999 the 'Brown' sites have actually been supported by the University Scholars Programme at the National University of Singapore, and many of their major projects, including *the Victorian Web Books*, a 2,500 document online museum of S.E. Asian art, and a similar gallery of Indian architecture, have all been funded by NUS.

8   I think one of the most hopeful signs is the recent statement (in February 2001) by the Provost that the university library system, not the computer center, will be the place for assistance in developing websites for individual courses. The library, it was announced, will assist instructors in obtaining materials in copyright and otherwise act as an information resource. As far as I know, the Humanities Computing Center, which Jerome J. McGann helped found at the University of Virginia, was the first such institute to be housed in a library and come under the aegis of a library. Virginia is also one of the first institutions to accept electronic dissertations. When Barry J. Fishman did an honours thesis on Intermedia at Brown in the late 1980s, we had to print parts of it to put in the university archives.

8

HERE EVEN WHEN
YOU'RE NOT

Teaching in an Internet degree programme

J. Yellowlees Douglas

At this very time, in such a class, all the scholars of the Empire are studying a certain page in Vergil!
(Remark attributed to Minister of Education under the Second Empire, quoted in Rudy 1984: 102)

A university is a mechanism for the inheritance of the Western style of civilisation. It preserves, transmits, and enriches learning, and it undergoes evolution as animals and plants do.
(Eric Ashby, quoted in Rudy 1984: 11)

Online distance learning is our latest great polariser: higher education's saviour or its anti-Christ, depending on your particular point of view. For administrators, online distance learning represents the means for tiny American colleges that currently register as mere blips on the higher education grid to contend for students alongside heavyweights like Stanford or Harvard. For educators, online distance learning signifies either the next step for learning after Gutenberg or classes packed with escalating numbers of students and courses over which they lack ownership of their materials. For techno-enthusiasts, digital technology automatically redistributes authority and power, making classrooms inherently student-centred. For sceptical faculty, online distance learning threatens to enshrine all the worst aspects of the university-as-corporation. And even some of the most intelligent commentators on the online distance education fracas insist that the model of 'new' pedagogy ostensibly represented by online distance education has, in fact, been operating in writing classrooms since the days of Dewey, a reflection of progressive views of education, not the radical rear-ranging of hierarchies of knowledge and authority many associate with the influence of the World Wide Web (Markel 1999).

All these views assume that the technology, its infrastructure, administration, economic and cultural values have all reached closure, the point where a tech-nology reaches the end of its cycle of innovation and revision in response to socio-technical values and pressures (Bijker 1995). The refrigerator, fax machine and bicycle have all reached closure. The World Wide Web, the prime vehicle for delivering online distance education, however, has not: witness the recent scrum of filings, judgments and appeals involving intellectual property rights, electronic copyrights, and Napster, all of which attest to the still-evolving nature of digital *again.* technologies. Moreover, few online distance education programmes adhere to anything like a singular model for delivery or even a single philosophy informing programme content, technology and curricula. The classroom lecture may have reached closure some time back in the days when Oxford University was a mere stripling and only a few universities dotted medieval Europe's intellectual land-scape. And while we may be as sure about what a classroom lecture entails in terms of pedagogy and delivery as was a certain Minister of Education about the Second Empire's scholars lingering over a single page in Vergil, even the term 'distance education' is relatively meaningless as descriptors go. In the US, distance education used to mean videotaped lectures sent in the mail, television courses and CD-ROMs that arrived via FedEx. And even the more specific descriptor suggested by Burbules and Callister (2000: 272) – 'online distance learning' – can mean, as with the Duke University Internet Master of Business Administration (MBA) programme, fifteen-week on-campus residencies for courses. When we talk about online distance education, we're not talking about a technology nearing closure. We are, instead, looking at a platform for learning, a technology in its infancy, taking its first, toddling steps, a stage historian Elizabeth Eisenstein refers to as 'incunabular' (1983: 9).

If we can't pronounce judgement on online distance education as a mono-lithic entity, we can still assess the efficacy of certain programmes, particular approaches. Reports from the front will, after all, always have some immediate value. My case study attempts to serve up, as Stake (1985: 280) puts it, enough of the 'elaborate information on which readers decide the extent to which the researcher's case is similar to (and thus likely to be instructive about) theirs'. While discussions with colleagues teaching in the same programme and follow-up interviews with class members have revealed that my students' experiences were not typical of online distance education, we can, nevertheless, understand the potential for online distance education by scrutinising the course, its content, and students' performances. In any case, as Stake suggests, a long-term study – in this example, twenty-four months of follow-up interviews and surveys – may provide us with insights we could not otherwise glean from a single semester's scrutiny.

This chapter explores the first semester of an Internet degree programme at the University of Florida by focusing on pedagogical approaches to teaching a writing-intensive course, and by providing explanations for student perfor-mance outcomes and perceptions of the course. Modelling my approach on case studies, I conclude that the change of modes from conventional to virtual classrooms can provide valuable impetus for faculty members to try new methods of teaching. Breaking away from traditional lectures, moreover, may be a smart call, particularly when relying on lectures means hours of video-taping and developmental work, burning multiple CD-ROMs for a single course, and high-cost development involving multiple support staff to produce pint-sized talking heads in seemingly endless video clips that bore to distraction students accustomed to thinking of the computer as a dynamic medium. Indeed, online environments may actually be the *best* means for teaching writing and may also provide valuable opportunities for faculty to model strategies and practices. Finally, teaching in this new environment provides us with a perspective on the resource and instructional limitations of what many see as the core of higher education itself: the classroom lecture. A backward glance reveals that the classroom lecture is merely a 'lighterweight' version of the core element in Western higher education as it first appeared approximately eight hundred years ago – classroom practices informed not by any understanding of human cognition or pedagogical methods but by a scarcity of the resources we now enjoy in abundance.

The apparatus: delivering the goods

In typical American fashion, about 20 per cent of the universities in the country probably claim to have launched the first-ever Internet degree programme. In the face of so much territory-staking, the University of Florida opted for a more modest first-ever claim: the first Internet-only Master of Business Administration (MBA) programme. The Internet-only programme – originally dubbed the Flexible MBA, abbreviated by all to 'Flex' – began in April 1999 and offered students a complete online MBA degree programme with only two days' residency for each term during which students completed exams and were introduced to the next term's faculty. While the programme used a Lotus Notes platform, the client was simply either a Netscape Navigator or Internet Explorer browser: students used the same programme for accessing course websites and resources as they did for surfing the Internet. The programme, designed to unfold over nearly three years, offered only two courses per term, with faculty in both courses free to identify the means and methods by which they delivered courses already required of students in Florida's other MBA programmes. Florida's Warrington College of Business also provided faculty with development money and a support staff dedicated solely to the Internet courses.

In Professional Writing (GEB 5213) students completed three genre assignments, spaced evenly over the sixteen-week term, and were graded on six of ten memos submitted to Economics of Business Decisions (ECP 5705), selected randomly throughout the term, to ensure students applied their newly mastered skills on all writing assignments for both courses.[1] The course also required students to assess and comment on their peers' work in detailed critiques and evaluations that were posted on course discussion databases. Peer grades were averaged with the instructor's grade, with each student receiving the average of all four grades. Students were provided with extra credit – or docked for credit – equalling one-third of a grade for each set of critiques and evaluations, added to or subtracted from their final grades, a substantial incentive to take evaluation rather seriously.

The goods – mostly

Strikingly, for a start-up programme, the Flex students proved to be a cohesive group of high-performing, hardworking students, easily the best group I have taught in my seventeen-year career in higher education. Clearly, Florida had recruited carefully for this first-ever programme with an eye toward expanding into online distance education. But the students may also have self-selected accurately for the programme, understanding that a first-time programme might turn them into the equivalents of crash-test dummies, recognising, also, that, with the flexibility and autonomy that were the hallmarks of the programme, came a greater need for responsibility and commitment to their studies and an ability to juggle graduate school and full-time jobs in professional or managerial positions. Further, the group's cohesiveness may even have stemmed from their positions as the first class of students admitted to a fledgling programme using an untried platform – the Internet – to deliver their entire graduate degree. There's nothing quite so binding as the recognition that you're all guinea pigs together in one grand experiment. If the group, however, owed its togetherness entirely to the experimental conditions the programme operated under, they exhibited virtually none of the restive, sceptical identity of subjects chafing against the administrators pulling the strings. In fact, even when one instructor later remained incommunicado for all but the last week of one term, the students simply acknowledged that the entire programme was a learning experience and pressed on.

In a series of questionnaires completed three terms into the Flex programme, students acknowledged the role played by faculty in fostering the group's identity and cohesiveness. Since Flex students see each other only six days per year, we might expect class members to have only foggy recollections of one another's names or identities, yet many in the group have forged lasting friendships, and the entire class socialises together as a group during their two evenings on campus each term. Many of the tight-knit relationships grow from the high percentage of team assignments required for most of their MBA courses, requiring students to meet frequently through SameTime Conference, an application for synchronous chat and application-sharing. Flex students also exchanged e-mails, used firetalk – using the Internet to carry their voices – or even made phone calls to complete team work. One student cheerfully acknowledged that he spends far more time talking to team members and classmates than he does to his wife. As teams rotate every term, the small size of the Flex class ensures that every member of the programme has worked together often with every other member.

Equally important, however, is the role of synchronous communication in online distance learning courses, even for students who cannot attend them due to business commitments, travel, or insuperable differences between time zones. I designed Professional Writing in Business around weekly synchronous class meetings using SameTime Conference, scheduled on Saturday mornings, to ensure class members had opportunities to query me about their unit materials for the week and to apply that week's stylistic concepts to a shared whiteboard document. Discussions, significantly, also provided the course with a distinctive tone, similar to the way an instructor's humour or wry sensibility conveyed during lectures can provide a course with a particular identity. By contrast, in conventional classrooms, the instructor nearly always establishes the course's 'tone'. As Paulo Freire would have it: the instructor speaks, the students listen (Freire 1970). In the SameTime discussions, however, the instructor merely moderates discussion, much as one would in a class workshop: directing the flow of conversation, calling attention to particularly apt questions or to the way one student has addressed a question posed minutes before by another. As students 'speak' via the scrolling chat window, the moderator must work to mould discussion by typing rapidly while reading the still-incoming responses. Classroom discussions enabled the Flex students to establish clear-cut identities that stretched beyond their jobs and prior degree histories: the thoughtful commentators, the sharp-eyed critics, and, of course, the inevitable class wise-ass.

Perhaps, most strikingly, Flex students displayed marked improvement in their writing over my other business graduate students. Students who floundered when revising a brief internal policy memo to ensure greater compliance with its edicts were, by the end of the term, writing eloquently on their corporation's operational effectiveness and turning out admirably detailed feasibility analyses. Aside from their self-selection for a rigorous and largely autonomous degree programme – and whatever benefits that might have conferred on class members' performance – why did these students perform so well?

There are four reasons why this writing course benefited from an online environment.

In the virtual classroom, as one student put it, there's no place to hide

In conventional classrooms, most discussion is carried by a handful of students, and, even when participation is considered in weighting students' final grades, every classroom has its unresponsive students. In an online distance learning environment, every word in both synchronous and asynchronous threaded discussions is recorded – and immediately made public. For a course where fostering consciousness about writing is the goal, the setting is ideal. Students can't simply be loquacious in discussion; they must use writing to convey every word, every nuance, of their critiques and comments during class discussions. And, as many instructors in subsequent terms of the Flex programme required participation in discussions, students needed to pay attention to what other students were saying and to add their own input to the ongoing discussion. Since a proportion of the grade for certain terms two and three Flex courses in Finance and Management were linked directly to the number of posts students made to asynchronous discussions, lurking or not attending to the ongoing discussion was invariably hazardous to students' pending grades.

Online writing courses are inherently recursive, since every critique, every point must be written

I probably seemed perverse to my colleagues when I waxed grateful for the ten-to-fifteen second lags that accompanied streamed video conferencing and the glitchy nature of audio online. But video would have removed the very recursiveness from the course that ultimately proved so beneficial to members of the class: every transaction in the course was written. And, as our early assignments and discussions involved the equivalent of the carpet bombing of some poorly written corporate memos, some of which circulated quarterly among major US corporations, most students had learned to take care in composing everything from their asynchronous discussion posts to their input during SameTime Conferences.

More important, however, was one of the major components of the course: a series of lengthy evaluations of each other's writing assignments. To ensure that students both wrote for a *bona fide* audience and relied on as diagnostic tools the stylistic principles we covered in the course, I assigned each student three peer critiques and evaluations for each assignment. Assignments were posted to a database that identified the author/poster only to me, and students downloaded the papers, evaluated them, providing a lengthy rationale for the grade they assigned, and posted the evaluation and grade to the database, again, virtually anonymous – identified only to me. My evaluations were, conversely, tagged with my name, so students could weigh my own remarks against the ones they had made for the same papers, and also scrutinise my comments alongside those of their peers. All four grades – three peer and instructor – were weighted equally, with assignments receiving the average of the four grades, although students had the right of appeal if, for example, I wrote a laudatory critique and awarded the paper an 'A', while their peers awarded 'C' grades or below.

Peer evaluation accomplishes three important goals. First, it ensures students grapple with the vagaries of writing for a genuine audience – and often juggle two or three mutually exclusive sets of advice on revision. Second, students in classrooms using peer critique and evaluation write under a strictly symmetrical arrangement.[2] In conventional classrooms, students write papers for their instructors' eyes; instructors write comments back, suggesting revisions but continually stressing awareness of audience. Students, not entirely unreasonably, revise the assignment exactly as the instructor has advised – not thinking one whit about what a general audience would make of their writing. Third, students have to use the very principles they've just put into action in their writing as diagnostic tools to recognise, explain, and evaluate what's going on in their peers' work. The process of critique and evaluation requires them to turn a visceral sense that something's not quite up to snuff in a report into a detailed analysis of the individual elements that, together, make for some rough, confusing, or simply inefficient and unconvincing reading. As many members of class noted during follow-up probes after the course had finished, the peer critiques of rough drafts and peer evaluations of final drafts proved the most valuable component of the course. By the completion of the course, Flex students were better able to recognise and point out to others the errors they were making in their own work. And, after the dust had settled on the evaluations, they were also more likely to subsequently recognise the same patterns of error in their own work-in-progress. As one student noted after the course had concluded:

> I definitely believe that doing the peer critiques helped me in critiquing my own writing, improving my own skills. The exercises really teach you to think analytically of your writing's purpose, structure, organisation, clarity. ... Since taking your course I have received several compliments and open praise for my writing.

Two elements ensure students take peer critique and evaluation seriously. Their judgements affect their classmates' grades as dramatically as do the instructor's, and their final grades reflect, in part, their performance on the task of evaluating. Anonymity of both author and evaluator alike further ensures that students' responses are not hampered by their relationship to the author or by the prospect of working with future team-mates still smarting from their criticism or the lousy grade they were awarded on an assignment in Professional Writing.

In courses that use asynchronous discussions, class discussions in real time, or published peer evaluations, students assist others in negotiating zones of proximal development

As Lev Vygotsky (1978) noted, when students approach a point where they are ready to traverse the boundary between one developmental stage and another in, say, acquiring a skill, an instructor can't assist them in traversing the boundary – only a more advanced peer can. Peers are, understandably, better able to point out negotiation strategies and assist students in moving from one skill level to the next than are instructors, who may have learned the same skills so long ago that they no longer recall the minutiae involved in knowing, for example, exactly how to put a positive spin on some dismaying figures in a business plan's annual profit and loss statement. Peers, having struggled between the same Scylla and Charybdis recently, know exactly what's involved. In peer critiques and evaluations, students provided scaffolding for their peers, assisting them when they hovered near a zone of proximal development, pointing out strategies they'd evolved for dealing with passive construction or for assessing the feasibility of a start-up company seeking infusions of capital. One student was particularly adroit during discussions at formulating telegraphic sentences and descriptions that aptly conveyed steps students needed to follow in their writing. For example, during a discussion of negative internal policy memos, he dubbed the memo structure a 'thin sandwich' of elements required for a well-constructed negative policy memo: a neutral opening paragraph, followed by a rationale, with the negative policy directive embedded in a dependent clause, followed by a feel-good closing paragraph. As an instructor, I was thinking about the psychological qualities of the individual elements and of clinical studies involving reader reactions to the elements in negative memos. My students, however, were thinking of building an information structure and wanted to envision what, exactly, went where. For several students, the 'thin sandwich' description one student used in his critique and during class discussion was a more comprehensible model of the negative internal policy memo's structure than my more theoretical description.

The online environment makes simple the apparatus for collaborating in teaching and curriculum design

To ensure that students applied their fledgling stylistic skills in other courses and to safeguard against regression of these skills, Professional Writing was paired with another course in the Flex MBA curriculum. Students simply submitted all writing for both courses, fully aware that the writerly equivalent of Big Brother was eyeballing their every submission, requiring students to ensure they wrote well at all times for both courses. The mechanism for handling the submissions was similarly uncomplicated: students submitted their assignments online to the Economics course, where both faculty members downloaded the initial submission, then uploaded their comment files and registered grades online. The last faculty member to complete an evaluation submitted the file as 'Graded', one of the four options for handling submissions, which kicked the file into the 'Graded' database, where its student author retrieved it. Because collaborations like this one are logistically easy to handle, faculty – especially faculty handling a writing course – can more easily work together, creating, as with the Flex Term 1 programme, syllabi that were articulated and carefully calibrated. When the work load in Economics became particularly intense, my colleague and I ensured that the work load for Professional Writing eased up somewhat and vice versa. Students, moreover, found the joint submissions ideal: they used extra opportunities to practise and maintain their stylistic skills without having to generate more verbiage for the writing course. By doubling up assignments, students enjoyed optimal exposure to course materials and methods for both courses and were, significantly, able to focus more intensively on the requirements for both courses in a single assignment than they would have been had the workload been doubled with one assignment for each course.

The conferences that never were – how minutiae count in virtual classrooms

What can we learn from the Flex programme and its students who, when last queried,[3] felt they were more in touch with faculty and getting more out of their education than they had from their conventional undergraduate degree programmes? For starters, collaborating with other faculty and linking together assignments in writing courses with core courses in the MBA curriculum worked well – a feature of the programme students commented on frequently both during and after the first term. More significantly, students were struck by how much presence faculty and other students could have in an online environment.

Of the twenty-five students surveyed in the Flex programme, twenty-three felt they knew their fellow students well and twelve felt that they knew their fellow students much better than they had known their classmates in conventional classrooms. Many of the students commented on the synchronous SameTime Conferences as a vital part of getting to know one another, remarking that they were pleased that both Professional Writing and Economics of Business Decisions had made use of synchronous meetings. There was only one problem with this enthusiastic reaction: my colleague had never held a SameTime Conference, nor had he ever held office hours using SameTime Conference. As we pored over the evaluations and puzzled over the fictitious conferences, we realised that students were reacting merely to my colleague's virtual omnipresence online. All Flex students and faculty had SameTime Connect added to the start-up files on their laptop PCs, which, whenever any member of faculty or student involved in the Flex programme logged onto the Internet, added them to a list which also indicated whether they were online. Since SameTime Connect functions much like the AOL Instant Messenger, students and faculty could chat, hold impromptu meetings, or simply take comfort in knowing that someone else in the Flex programme was online. Seemingly, no matter how late or how early you logged on, my colleague's name invariably greeted you in the SameTime Connect window, dotted with green to indicate he was active and available. Occasionally, he would join the Professional Writing SameTime Conferences to observe students' interactions and look over material for the writing course. His high visibility online, complemented by an abundance of posts and e-mails, clearly made students feel as if they were often involved in a class in real time – even when they weren't.

Similarly, in evaluations for other Flex courses and in debriefings each term, students remarked on what would usually represent minute aspects of their instructors' behaviour. The length of time between e-mail queries and replies, and the swiftness with which instructors responded to asynchronous discussion postings loomed large in evaluations of faculty performance. Lacking face-to-face cues about their instructor's attitudes toward the class or teaching generally, usually gleaned from small details like tone of voice, eye contact, and facial expressions, students merely went in search of some criteria that would stand in for the usual face-to-face cues – in this instance, speedy replies and overt attention to postings. Obviously, both elements are desirable in an instructor, for students awaiting replies and doubly for students leading dual lives as working professionals with a high regard for and need of efficiency. But the emphasis and signifying power Flex students gave these relatively small portions of their instructors' performances were strikingly different from the emphasis they receive in conventional classrooms. Far more than in conventional classrooms, every gesture, every nuance, every word looms large in online environments because students are attempting to generate from a comparatively small amount of data an overall picture of the course that fits with their experiences of earlier, conventional classrooms rife with data: vocal and facial expressions, body language, palpable enthusiasm, irritation and ennui, all of which can be detected in peers and faculty alike. With only the speed between query and reply, strictly informational postings, and terse, matter-of-fact answers to questions, students probably generate a reading of the course from minute details that would scarcely merit a minute's discussion between classmates in a traditional classroom.

Which brings us to an often overlooked point about online environments raised in the passionate refrain sounded throughout *The Cluetrain Manifesto*: what matters most is the sound of a human voice – although humour, in the manifesto, ranks one tick up the food chain from the human voice itself (Locke and Weinberger 2000). Ironically, the very paucity of inputs from other modes makes establishing a presence in an online course easier than it is in a conventional classroom. And humour, enthusiasm, or a distinctive sensibility play a particularly striking role. In any event, in an online classroom, more is decidedly more: the more posts you make to the course materials – for example, posting exemplary versions of an assignment chosen from submissions in class, posting a list of best submissions or best evaluations or strikingly good critiques – or the more you add to asynchronous discussions, or the more you involve yourself with real-time discussions, the more opportunities you have to confer a distinctive tone on the course and the greater your chances that students will judge you on something other than the mere speed of your replies to posts.

The traditional classroom as QWERTY keyboard

[A]pportion [your] time wisely, listen to all [you] are told, make copious notes, memorise the essential facts, discuss [your] problems with fellow students, and, finally ... pray for success.
(Robert de Sorbon, founder of the College of the Sorbonne at Paris, just after founding the college in 1257, quoted in Cobban 1975: 167)

At the University of Florida, the Warrington College of Business Administration had steadily been forging ahead on online distance learning before taking the leap into full-fledged online distance education. Not so the College of Liberal Arts and Sciences, the college in which I have tenure, where barometers indicating the climate in which online distance learning was viewed could be measured by my then-dean's smirk whenever he mentioned the subject. Online distance education, most of the deans and faculty held, was little more than a licence to print money – or, rather, money and degrees. Our college followed in the hallowed tradition of liberal arts education, handed down from the classical age through the founding of the great medieval universities to our classrooms.

The real problem here is more than the usual killer-technology scenario, which has technophiles and Luddites alike bellowing about the Internet replacing libraries, or hypertext fiction supplanting *To the Lighthouse* or *Middlemarch*. For starters, the list of actual killer technologies is surprisingly slender, once you start enumerating them: the light bulb, the automobile, the refrigerator, the washing machine and drier – with nary a technology of representation among them. On the other hand, the technologies that have generated noise and fanfare since their inception – daguerreotypes that were rumoured to destroy painting, cinema that was destined to squash theatre, television expected to steamroll cinema – have migrated to niches, from which they occasionally emerge to tweak the boundaries of their patches but which have never threatened to extinguish the technologies of representation that preceded them. Second, the territory we're guarding when we refer to the *liberal arts curriculum* or *traditional classrooms* may well be about as hallowed as the QWERTY keyboard. During the early days after typewriters were first invented, operators who achieved a modest keystroke rate noticed keys clumping together. The QWERTY keyboard resolved this particular sticky dilemma by separating the keys typists were most likely to use frequently, thus slowing down the keystroke rate. Within a few years, designers had entirely eliminated the sticking problem, and the new Dvorak keyboard debuted which grouped all the most commonly used keys in the typist's home row. Unfortunately for both the inventors of the Dvorak keyboard and hordes of typists thereafter, as well as all of us who use keyboards, the installed base for the QWERTY keyboard was large enough to deter manufacturers from adopting the new standard. We're stuck with an awkward arrangement of keys solely due to resource limitations skulking around during the typewriter's infancy. So, too, arguably, is the state of our classrooms burdened with a legacy that has nothing to do with ideal configurations of resources or research on optimal learning conditions and everything to do with the interaction between secularised clergy, resource scarcity and the rise of the first great Western universities – and a precedent that, like the QWERTY keyboard, enshrined a briefly useful method of instruction as a central *modus operandi* in education, based on little or no evidence of its efficacy.

Today's classroom lectures exist largely because they rapidly became a cornerstone of medieval higher education in days when manuscripts were both expensive and time-consuming to produce. Although some scholars argue that medieval *scriptoria* enabled students to rent substantial quantities of non-illuminated manuscripts cheaply (Rudy 1984), others point out that, during the early years after the founding of the universities, texts were scarce and time-consuming to produce (Schwinges 1992). During the early years, students attended dictation sessions which remedied their lack of hand-written texts (Pedersen 1997). But by the time student demand gave rise to the sweat-shop *scriptoria* that churned out manuscripts for rent, lectures had evolved into two varieties: *lectio* or lessons that involved *interpretes* or interpreters, who interpreted the text passage by passage, pointing out its origins and clearing up its obscurities, and *recitatores*, who confined their lessons to slavish progress through the text via mere paraphrase (Pedersen 1997). Significantly, the very word *lecture* has its origins in the Latin *lectio*, which actually means *reading*. In any case, lectures were enshrined as a cornerstone in higher education because the textual reading and explication closely conformed to the methods of Christian hermeneutics, where scholars produced commentaries on the origins, interpretation, and significance of religious texts (Cobban 1975). Even the way daily work is organised at modern universities is founded on the medieval university's origins in the Church. Early timetables cohered with canonical hours: *lauds, prime, tierce, sext, nones, vespers,* and *completorium*, all of which situated the seven daily prayers of the Church (Pedersen 1997). While contemporary classrooms may no longer be guided by the timing of lauds and vespers, they still unfold in blocks of time better suited to reading Scripture or taking dictation than to learning via discussion and team or lab work.

Ironically, one of the elements critical to medieval higher learning, the *disputatio* or disputation, a vestige of classical education, mostly withered into extinction. Drawing off the Socratic method, disputations involved instructors formulating *quaestiones, respondens* tackling answers, and *opponens* refuting these answers. Significantly, St. Thomas Aquinas viewed disputations as central to higher education, as they alone could be used to remove doubts regarding the accuracy of facts and could even be used as a research method to create new understandings (Pedersen 1997). Lectures, even St Hugo acknowledged in his pedagogic guide of the twelfth century, would only prove fruitful if they led to students reflecting independently on their lessons after hours and those reflections also led to deeper thoughts and insights. Since this process, however, could only be achieved via students thinking the night away, scribbling down their thoughts, or arguing with fellow students, the students' personal ethics were ultimately the deciding factor in their education – not their teachers' pedagogic methods or lectures (Pedersen 1997).

All of which brings us back to the inestimable Robert de Sorbon, chaplain to Louis IX and founder of the Sorbonne, who, nearly 750 years ago, advised his students to

> listen to all [you] are told, make copious notes, memorise the essential facts, discuss [your] problems with fellow students, and, finally ... pray for success.
>
> (Cobban 1975: 167)

Ditch the 'pray for success' part of the recipe, and you have a pretty accurate snapshot of higher education, circa 1257–2001. Although the explication of philosophical or religious texts is hardly the mission of your average course in, say, organisational behaviour or forensic anthropology, the delivery method is all but indistinguishable. Lectures have survived largely because they are cheap to produce, provide an easy means of controlling students, supply fodder for tests which can also be cheaply and quickly graded, and, perhaps, most important, can accommodate scores of students to only a single faculty member. Moreover, expectations about what constitutes 'good' teaching – including the colloquia required of many an entry-level job candidate as well as peer evaluations made during classroom visits – are heavily influenced by the lecture mode:

> A biology instructor was experimenting with collaborative methods of instruction in his beginning biology classes. One day his dean came for a site visit, slipping into the back of the room. The room was a hubbub of activity. Students were discussing material enthusiastically in small groups spread out across the room; the instructor would observe each group for a few minutes, sometimes making a comment, some-times nodding approval. After fifteen minutes or so the dean approached the instructor and said, 'I'll come back another time when you're teaching'.
>
> (Barr and Tagg, quoted in Markel 1999: 212)

Disputations, like discussions, on the other hand, spell smaller classrooms, potential control issues, and an investment in what students are saying, not to mention a rather messily subjective and possibly time-consuming evaluation process. Traditional, face-to-face classroom instruction could be something worth preserving, if most of our colleagues organised instruction around peda-gogical methods and goals – including small-group work that enables students to negotiate zones of proximal development, peer-to-peer feedback, even the active debates once enshrined in disputations.

If the Flex students' continual rounds of team work, peer critiques and eval-uations, and friendships gave them the equivalent of the network[4] many students wish they'd forged during their on-campus undergraduate and grad-uate careers, what have they lost by receiving their education entirely through online distance learning? From all appearances, surprisingly or sadly – depending on your point of view – absolutely nothing. The very costs in money and time involved in capturing lectures to video, ensures, happily, that, at least, the usual lecture mode won't be nearly as omnipresent online as in its on-campus incarnation. Certainly, like Archimedes' fulcrum and level place to stand, virtual classrooms and online learning provide a platform for us to assess and potentially nudge our traditional pedagogical practices and curricula, now ossified by millennia of habit and convention. With luck, our colleagues may discover that discussion, attention, and feedback are far less costly and time-consuming than producing marathon video lectures, capturing miniature heads on pint-sized screens which offer, anyway, opportunities for students to zap through lectures, a feature countless students have probably longed for during lectures in the flesh.

Notes

1 Stylistic skills followed the principles established by Joseph Williams (1990), principles based on studies in cognitive psychology and psycho- and sociolinguistics.
2 For a more detailed discussion of symmetry and asymmetry in writing classrooms, see Douglas (1994).
3 Students answered detailed questionnaires in September 1999 and April–May 2000.
4 Approximately 30 per cent of the Flex students, however, remarked that they wish they could spend more face time with their colleagues, with one student advocating the students pay out of pocket for an extra day or two on campus to socialise with their Flex peers.

References

Bijker, W. E. (1995) *Of Bicycles, Bakelites, and Bulbs: Toward a Theory of Sociotechnical Change*, Cambridge, Mass: MIT Press.

Burbules, N. and Callister, T. (2000) 'Universities in transition: the promise and the challenge of new technologies', *Teachers College Record* 102 (2): 271–93.

Cobban. A. B. (1975) *The Medieval Universities: Their Development and Organisation*, London: Methuen.

Douglas, J. Y. (1994) 'Technology, pedagogy, or context? A tale of two classrooms', *Computers & Composition: An International Journal for Teachers of Writing* 11 (3): 275–82.

Eisenstein, E. (1983) *The Printing Revolution in Early Modern Europe*, Cambridge: Cambridge University Press.

Freire, P. (1970) *Pedagogy of the Oppressed*, trans. M. Bergman Ramos, New York: Continuum.

Locke, C and Weinberger, D. (2000) 'E Z answers', *The Cluetrain Manifesto*, Cambridge: Perseus Books.

Markel, M. (1999) 'Distance education and the myth of the new pedagogy', *Journal of Business and Technical Communication* 13, (2): 208–18.

Pedersen, Olaf. (1997) *The First Universities: Studium Generale and the Origins of University Education in Europe*, trans. Richard North, Cambridge: Cambridge University Press.

Rudy, W. (1984) *The Universities of Europe, 1100–1914: A History*, Rutherford, NJ: Farleigh-Dickinson University Press.

Schwinges, R. C. (1992) 'Student education, student life', in H. de Ridder-Symoens (ed.) *A History of the University in Europe*, vol. 1, Cambridge: Cambridge University Press.

Stake, R. E. (1985) 'Case study', in J. Nisbet (ed.) *World Yearbook of Education 1985*: *Research, Policy and Practice*, New York: Kogan, Page, pp. 277–85.

Vygotsky, L. S (1978) *Mind in Society: The Development of Higher Psychological Processes*, trans. and ed. M. Cole, Cambridge: Harvard University Press.

Williams, J. M. (1990) *Style: Toward Clarity and Grace*, Chicago: University of Chicago Press.

9

DESIGN SENSIBILITIES, SCHOOLS AND THE NEW COMPUTING AND COMMUNICATION TECHNOLOGIES

Chris Bigum

Last year I attended a meeting of my local school's information technology committee and one of the items for discussion was the establishment of the school's webpage. Talk centred on promoting the school and having a 'presence' on the World Wide Web. When I asked about other possible uses there was a suggestion that teachers might put homework assignments online so parents could check what their children were required to do. As the conversation continued it became apparent that apart from having some promotional material about the school available for parents (Do parents go online to look up potential schools for their children?) and news about the school (Do parents go online to read school newsletters?) there appeared to be little else that the committee could identify as worth publishing on the Web.

I recount this event because it is illustrative of a long-standing pattern of schools' engagement with the new computing and communication technologies (CCTs), that is, trying to find educationally useful things to do with them. From the early 1980s to the present, schools have worked hard to engineer the use of a range of computing and related technologies into classrooms. But this is no simple task. Further, the patterns of CCT use in schools in comparison to other, more traditional practices, have proved difficult to sustain. Such a history does not auger well for schools' engagement with any new communication order. This chapter elaborates the problems with the current approaches to using CCTs in classrooms and describes research work beyond the impasse of previous practice. A key part of this strategy is to rethink the roles that schools can play in the new communication order.

Responding to orders and ordering

The word 'order' is a much worked noun among the overdeveloped countries of the world. It is often found in combination with the adjective 'new', for example,

'New World Order', 'New Work Order', and in this collection, 'New Communication Order'. 'Order' has both the sense of regimentation or making orderly, or of giving a command or instruction. It is useful in the context of this chapter to think about the word in both ways, that is, in terms of the ordering that occurs in schools *vis-à-vis* the new computing and communication technologies as well as in terms of the orders or imperatives to which schools have responded.

Since the first appearance of commercially available microcomputers in the late 1970s, schools have been responding to orders or directives both implied and explicit from the vendors of CCT products. The promotion of CCTs for education by vendors promised improvements in student learning as well as enhanced employment opportunities. In recent years, with the development of the World Wide Web, a third claim has been added – the claim that CCTs improve student access to information. The merits of these technologically deterministic claims may be dubious but their efficacy in providing the basic elements of a rationale for using CCTs in schools cannot be disputed. They are taken for granted in the conversations of teachers, principals, parents and policy makers concerned with the implementation and use of CCTs. Despite their wide acceptance among users and promoters of CCTs in education, it is important to consider the origins of the logic associated with claims of improvement because it helps to locate the more overt directives concerning CCTs imposed on schools.

When a new technology, particularly a communication technology, is developed its take-up is not automatic. How it is taken up is also a matter of conjecture (Bigum 2000). But whatever the mechanism, the user has to be convinced there is some advantage in using the new technology. Typically, persuasion is based upon improving an existing practice by making it more effective or efficient. In some businesses, it is necessary to identify the savings that will accrue from the implementation of a new technology. Paul Strassman reports that comptrollers often require 30 to 50 per cent returns on the investment before agreeing to computerising an operation (Strassmann 1997: 309). Lee Sproull and Sarah Kiesler (1991: 4) make a similar point labelling the claims about improvements, 'first level effects', which they describe as 'the planned efficiency gains or productivity gains that justify an investment in new technology'. When the new technology is put in place, things happen that bear little relationship to what was imagined. Sproull and Kiesler call these 'second level effects': 'people pay attention to different things, have contact with different people, and depend on one another differently' (Sproull and Kiesler 1991: 4). Or, as Strassman (1997: 309) observes:

> In all my years as CIO and consultant I have never come across a valid and totally independent post-implementation audit. Conditions always change, and therefore the original plan does not correspond to what is finally delivered. The observable results evade comparison with the approved proposal.

The difficulty of conducting comparative studies has not deterred many researchers from measuring improvements and differences in learning between the use of CCTs and the use of other technologies. The popularity of such studies reflects the large number of researchers who have been trained to study educational phenomena using methods drawn from agricultural botany. Seymour Papert has parodied the application of the scientific model to the evaluation of computer-based learning. He suggests that the failure to find significant differences in favour of computer-based approaches is like the failure of a nineteenth-century engineer who failed to show that engines were better than horses.

> This he did by hitching a 1/8 HP motor in parallel with his four strong stallions. After a year of statistical research he announced a significant difference. However it was thought that there was a Hawthorne effect on the horses ... the purring of the motor made them pull harder.
>
> (Papert 1972: 2)

It is clear that using CCTs in education or in any other field of human endeavour changes things. However, if proponents of CCTs were to use this fact as a rationale for acquiring computers, their success in securing funds for such bids would be unlikely. So, rather than necessarily improving an existing set of circumstances, say for example, the teaching of geography, we might expect the teaching of geography to be changed when CCTs were deployed and changed in unpredictable ways. The question of whether things have improved becomes a more difficult issue and perhaps one that is less important than understanding how things have changed and what the implications are for teachers and learners. The paradox is that to obtain the CCTs in the first place, claims about CCTs improving the teaching of geography are essential.

By contrast to these implicit directives, there are orders which are less subtle. These are the requirements of schools and users to comply to a never-ending upgrade path as newer versions of hardware and software come onto the market. These developments tend to be driven by advances in hardware such as faster CPUs, more efficient mass storage and new means of capturing digital images. While it is possible to resist upgrades for a time, in the end it becomes difficult not to comply. Compatibility with the hardware and software of other users, expressed as an ability to exchange files, typically drives such decisions.

Given the capacity of CCTs to change things in the settings into which they are introduced, there is another notion of ordering that occurs in schools when these technologies are introduced into classrooms. There have been a number of studies that have investigated the patterns of use, outcomes or effects of employing CCTs in classrooms (e.g., Becker 1994; Lankshear, et al. 1997; Coley et al. 1999). What is apparent in these and earlier studies (e.g., Bigum et al. 1987) is that most often CCTs have been made to conform to the requirements of the curriculum and the classroom. In a sense they have been domesticated, or, as Tyack and Cuban (1995: 126) put it, 'computers meet classrooms, classrooms win'. This outcome is consistent with what happened with other, earlier technologies deployed in classrooms. They also were accompanied by similar promises of improved learning but succumbed to the long-standing practices of the classroom (Cuban 1986).

It is worth considering further some of the features of ordering that are associated with taking CCTs into classrooms to get a better sense of the ways schools are able to respond to the changed circumstances in the world outside, and in particular to a new communication order.

The domestication of CCTs can be seen in terms of bringing together a resilient and long-standing paper and pencil curriculum designed and developed to serve the needs of an industrial era, with a view of CCTs as educational or learning technologies. What results is a focus on 'the how' of using CCTs in classrooms with little attention paid to 'the what' and 'the why' (Bigum and Green 1993). Seeing CCTs as significant only in terms of how to teach and learn is related to a persistent 'horseless carriage' perspective[1] on CCTs. This view regards the new, even though the new is in many respects now twenty years old, as not much different from the familiar, and continues to see it in those terms. Thus teaching, learning, curriculum and assessment are supported, aided or managed with the help of CCTs. There is little consideration of the possibility that existing teaching, learning, curriculum or assessment practices may not be appropriate for a world outside schools, increasingly shaped by the use of CCTs. Domestication produces a kind of reassurance that schools are doing something about CCTs. Such reassurances are implicit in the practices which are given labels like 'information literacy' or 'computer literacy'. They are consistent with an assumption that the new, digital world is really not that different from the world for which schools had become so rehearsed in preparing the young (Lankshear and Knobel 2000; Lankshear et al. 2000).

The ordering of CCTs in schools evidences a way of thinking about CCTs which is unlikely to respond to a new communication order in any way that is different from previous patterns of response to developments in CCTs. How CCTs are understood and imagined to be of value in schools is therefore an important element in the consideration of schools and a new communication order and warrants further examination.

Design sensibilities

Michael Schrage (1998) suggests that the positions assumed in regard to the use of CCTs in schools can be conceived as *design sensibilities* – as skews or biases in the way these technologies are understood. For instance, the assumption that IT is an educational good is a skew, a bias which informs how the technology is understood and used in schools. That these technologies can be seen in terms of earlier technologies – for instance, the word processor as a kind of typewriter or the spreadsheet as a sort of calculator – is another design sensibility that shapes practices in classrooms. According to Schrage, it is important to recognise the design sensibilities that inform particular patterns of use. He makes a case for his own position – that IT use in education still needs to be seen as a somewhat poorly understood new medium, requiring careful and critical experimentation.

I now examine a particular design sensibility to illustrate an important blind spot common in schools: one which until recently they have shared with business. Rather than being seen as poorly understood and warranting the kind of cautious exploration urged by Schrage, CCTs are subject to a simpler framing in many classrooms, one in which computer use is seen as a good and the more of this good that can be obtained the better. The ever-present concern to acquire more computers for classroom use is an indication of this bias. It can be seen as an educational application of the 'pig principle', that more is better. This principle characterised the thinking about CCTs in a broad range of human activity during the 1980s and early 1990s. In business, it was generally held that because CCTs were a 'business good' that more of them would guarantee greater efficiencies and higher profits. This logic dominated the early take up of CCTs in business and, as in education, little attention was paid to testing the veracity of the relationship between expenditure on CCTs and profits. Recent work by Paul Strassman (1997) highlights the difficulty of examining this relationship but in the end clearly demonstrates that there is no simple association. As he puts it,

> Despite much talk about the cyber economy, information age, or knowledge-based enterprise, as yet there are no generally accepted economic or financial principles to guide executives in spending money on computers. Decision makers find it difficult to reconcile the claims of computer advocates with their staff's ability to prove IT investments are profitable.
>
> (Strassmann 1997: xv)

This is not an anti-computer argument. On the contrary, Strassman is passionate in his belief in the significance of these technologies for the improvement of human existence. Unlike many of the proponents of these technologies, he carefully documents the complexity in business of obtaining improvements by using CCTs. Drawing on his analysis, he offers advice for business which works around the design sensibilities that have driven investment in CCTs in business. For example,

> View with skepticism all survey data about IT spending gathered by means of mail-in questionnaires or telephone surveys.
>
> (Strassmann 1997: 107)

134

Diminish the emphasis on technological decisions and shift attention to the costs of employee training, the effects of organizational disruption, and the causes of workplace resistance.

(Strassmann 1997: 239)

Avoid quoting isolated anecdotal cases to substantiate economic gains.

(Strassmann 1997: 40)

Similarly informed advice for schools is notable by its absence. While there is a persistent bias that CCTs are an educational good, the kinds of hard-nosed Strassman-like assessments simply don't exist. Although the business-education comparison can be taken too far, it is important to underline the continuing and broadly held belief in schools which equates investment in CCTs with improved educational outcomes.

I now return to the story with which I began, that of the school pondering what to do with its webpages. The design sensibility, the bias, perhaps, was one based on information and its delivery. It is a sensibility or mindset that is commonplace in schools and among Web users generally. A large industry has grown up around the design and development of webpages as sites for information delivery and retrieval. For schools, however, a design sensibility based upon information delivery is limited from the outset. What information can a school produce, recycle or repackage that will attract the attention and patronage of the local community and beyond? Schools are limited because traditionally they are, in the jargon of the so-called information age, information consumers, that is, they purchase resources judged to contain information appropriate to their needs. The little information that schools do produce is reflected in the limited set of suggestions made at the meeting described at the beginning of this chapter. It would be possible at this point to make a case for schools reappraising their role and considering what information they might produce, for what purposes and for what audiences. But to locate this kind of enquiry in an *information* sensibility would keep schools locked into their current patterns of consumption of both hardware and information. We need to shift the design sensibility from information. As Schrage (2000) puts it:

To say that the Internet is about 'information' is a bit like saying that 'cooking' is about oven temperatures; it's technically accurate but fundamentally untrue.

The biggest impact that digital technologies are having and will continue to have, argues Schrage, is on the *relationships* between people and between people and organisations. These altered relationships derive from the new modalities of communication, or as argued in this book, from a new communication order. This is not a new idea that CCTs or indeed any technology can be seen in terms of the relationships they affect or mediate, the new relationships they support and the relationships they terminate. What is important here is the emphasis or design sensibility that is placed on relationships rather than on information.

From CCTs to relationships

Thinking about the new information and communication technologies in schools in terms of relationships shifts the focus from the technology *per se* and problems of how best to integrate CCTs into the curriculum towards schools as social organisations, their internal relationships and those with the local community, government and other schools. In effect, the focus shifts from the question, 'What on earth do we do with this new technology?' to 'What kinds of relationships do we want to have with the world beyond our boundaries?' In other words, the key questions to be considered are to do with new articulations beyond school, that is, 'What role should a school have in a new communication order?'

This question is not intended to suggest that the existing relationships many schools have with their local communities and beyond are not significant nor that they need to be reappraised. Rather, it is both possible and valuable to think about additional relationships for schools which means in effect examining the possibility of some new purposes or roles for schools. To do that a further point about information and in particular its so-called abundance needs to be made.

In an era in which information or content is made increasingly available via an expanding number of delivery mechanisms, the scarce resource will be an ability to make sense of the plethora of material to hand. In other words, what will matter is expertise, point of view, a place to stand from which to make sense of information. As Paul Saffo (1994: 75) argues:

> 'Point of view' is that quintessentially human solution to information overload, an intuitive process of reducing things to an essential relevant and manageable minimum. Point of view is what successful media have trafficked in for centuries. Books are merely the congealed point of view of their authors, and we buy newspapers for the editorial point of view that shapes their content. We watch particular TV anchors for their point of view, and we take or ignore movie advice from our friends based on their point of view.

In a more formal way, educational institutions like schools offer experiences designed to teach students particular points of view. We call them subjects. But what is of interest in this chapter is the expertise or point of view that might be developed beyond the traditional practices of the school curriculum. The reasons for pursuing this line of argument will become apparent when I describe some of the early forays in this direction by schools.

From the point of view of a community, what might this mean? For instance, in what might a community have expertise? A way to think about this question is to consider the kinds of knowledges and information communities have. There is a focus on the individual knowledge and expertise resident in a particular community that is a kind of aggregate of the individual skills and knowledge of community members. There are other knowledges that are more collective in nature, specifically, knowledge about the community as a whole. In many communities there are examples of these knowledges. They range from the stories about community that informally circulate to more formal collections like local histories and neighbourhood surveys.

The one thing that a community can and will need to have more expertise in is knowledge about itself. In a world which appears destined to be increasingly shaped by financial and information forces which operate globally, having a rich source of knowledge about itself will provide a local community with a strong basis from which to read and act on the global influences that it encounters. In other words, the production, accumulation and dissemination of local knowledge will become more valuable to communities. At present, any formal production of such knowledge is often dependent on funding from government. When it occurs it tends to be part of a larger, often national interest, which may not coincide with local interests. Schools have a unique opportunity to play an important and possibly central role in this respect.

What follows is a preliminary account of the early exploration of some of these ideas by schools. The focus of the work is exploring new kinds of relationships beyond the school. To achieve this, schools have to move from the relatively safe, 'pretend' space of conventional curriculum to doing work that is judged by external groups as useful and valuable.

New relationships with community: schools as knowledge providers

It is important to underline that this avenue of development is exploratory. It is informed, however, by a design sensibility that does not accept CCTs simply as an educational good. It reads the external world as much changed because of the deployment of CCTs. It sees these changes in terms of changed relationships which flow from additional modes of communication. It acknowledges that schools need to examine new kinds of relationships with the world outside.

There are a small number of schools, primary and secondary, with which I am working and which have various levels of interest in this agenda. I give an account here of some of the explorations of one of these schools.

This primary school invested in CCTs to support the recording of digital visual images, both still and video. It has a modest amount of CCTs by school standards, two to three per class, with a small central facility that allows easy editing of video and still images. What is interesting is the routine way in which all students at the school currently employ digital and video cameras to do their work. For story telling occasions, students regularly opt to make a claymation movie.[2] The move to use CCTs to support writing with cameras is recent for the school. In less than a year, a broad base of expertise has developed among the staff and students that allows preparation of audiovisual presentations typically stored on CD-ROM.

The school has begun to examine the implications of having students produce knowledge products that are directed at audiences beyond the school. When the Principal was invited to talk about developments at the school to a state conference of primary school principals, she commissioned a group of Year Seven students to document the use of CCTs in the school on video and to produce a CD. The students completed the project and presented it to an audience of over 200 principals at the conference.

In another instance, in response to a class incident, a group of Year Six students designed and produced a PowerPoint-based CD to offer advice to students about bullying. They scripted and filmed six scenarios each with three alternative outcomes to illustrate the consequences of what they labelled 'weak', 'aggressive' and 'cool' responses to a bully. They launched the interactive CD at a public meeting at the school and intend marketing it to other schools.

These represent the first small steps of the school towards a fuller engagement with local community needs and interests. They should not be read as examples of the community-based research envisaged as an end point of this agenda. What matters, however, is that the school is moving in this direction, informed by a design sensibility, different from that typically found in many schools. It has adopted an approach which considers any request from outside the school in terms of the possibility of students preparing the response. On one occasion a group of local principals visited the school to inspect the approach it was employing in the use of CCTs. While teachers structured the day and spoke on some occasions to the group, there were three workshops for principals which were presented by students. One of these, how to make claymation movies, was taught by a group of Year Four students. The students were exemplary teachers. They offered encouragement, advice and gave instructions without taking over or doing it for the principals. The men and women sat on the floor in their suits and negotiated a plot with pieces of coloured plasticine and recorded over fifty images using a digital camera. The students then taught them how to convert the stills into movie format. Although this event may not be hugely significant, it illustrates the commitment by the school to examine every opportunity of having its students work on tasks that matter to those beyond the school.

Knowledge production in schools is not something new. What is different in this case is that the tasks derive from local needs or interests and are tested by an external audience. From this basis, the school is beginning to examine other forms of knowledge production that will further develop it as a site where knowledge is produced and disseminated.

Thinking about schools and the students in them as producers of knowledge, particularly knowledge that is valuable to the local community, is not a new idea. A number of agencies have from time to time made use of the labour of school students to support national and international research projects of one kind or another. Other agencies have made use of the labour of school children to do such things as counting vehicles on nearby roads, conducting surveys of community attitudes on environmental issues, monitoring local environmental indicators and contributing to national mappings of local famous identities.

The possibility is to move from a discontinuous involvement in research activities to one in which schools see research as one of the things they are good at and through which they can contribute to their local community. Coupled with this changed view, schools could see themselves as a logical location for the production, accumulation and dissemination of information about the local community. It would mean moving some student work from the 'fridge door' mindset, to one in which their work is valued by and is valuable to the local community. Many teachers already do all kinds of interesting and potentially useful data collection with their students but in a fridge door context the data are rarely kept, the analyses are not shared beyond the classroom (except on a family's fridge door) and it is unusual for the data to be stored and added to over time. With not much more effort and judicious use of computer support, this could be changed. But importantly, simply doing research, collecting data and doing analyses will matter little if the local community does not value the work. And this is the hard part. Schools would have to be at least partially remade in the minds of the local community. It would not require a wholesale change, but project by project it would be possible to build up a repertoire of research skills and products in consultation with local needs and interests.

The other elements of the research agenda would be directed at finding out the kinds of research that can be sustained by different age cohorts, the professional support necessary for teachers to work in this way and strategies to support and encourage these new kinds of school–community partnerships. Having students participate in such work would be much more than simply employing them as inexpensive labour. The rigorous and systematic study of the local community is a worthwhile educational activity. Such work *can* be done, and, what's more, done well. If taken seriously, it can provide the basis of new kinds of relationships with the local community.

In this context, CCTs have a role in supporting and sustaining new relationships. The collection, analysis and dissemination of information is work that computers can support well. In this way, schools don't 'do' computers for computers' sake. Schools can respond to a new communication order by reconsidering the role they play in the community and it is this role – that of knowledge production – that can be usefully supported by the judicious use of CCTs.

Notes

1 Horseless carriage was the term first used to describe early motor vehicles which, to the horse-using population of the time, were similar to carriages but did not require horses for movement.
2 Through the process of 'claymation' or clay animation, animated film can be produced by taking a sequence of digital still pictures of clay figures which are slightly

altered from frame to frame to give the appearance of animation when assembled into a movie. See for example, *http://library.thinkquest.org/22316/home.html?tqskip=1*

References

Becker, H. J. (1994) *Analysis and Trends of School Use of New Information Technologies*. Online. Available HTTP: *http://www.gse.uci.edu/doehome/EdResource/Publications/EdTechUse/CTBLCNT.HTM* (12 January 2001).

Bigum, C. (2000) 'Actor-network theory and online university teaching: translation versus diffusion', in B.A. Knight and L. Rowan (eds) *Researching Futures Oriented Pedagogies*, Flaxton, Qld: PostPressed, pp. 7–22.

Bigum, C., Bonser, S., Evans, P., Groundwater-Smith, S., Grundy, S., Kemmis, S., McKenzie, D., McKinnon, D., O'Connor, M., Straton, R. and Willis, S. (1987) *Coming to Terms with Computers in Schools*. Report to the Commonwealth Schools Commission, Geelong: Deakin Institute for Studies in Education, Deakin University.

Bigum, C. and Green, B. (1993) 'Curriculum and technology: Australian perspectives and debates', in D.L. Smith (ed.) *Australian Curriculum Reform: Action and Reaction*, Belconnen, ACT: Australian Curriculum Studies Association in association with Social Science Press, pp. 105–122.

Coley, R. J., Cradler, J. and Engel, P. K. (1999) *Computers and Classrooms: The Status of Technology in U.S. Schools*. Online. Available HTTP: *http://www.ets.org/research/pic/compclass.html* (12 November 2000).

Cuban, L. (1986) *Teachers and Machines: The Classroom Use of Technology Since 1920*, New York: Teachers College Press.

Lankshear, C., Bigum, C., Durrant, C., Green, B., Morgan, W., Murray, J., Snyder, I. and Wild, M. (1997) *Digital Rhetorics: Literacies and Technologies in Education – Current Practices and Future Directions*, three vols. Project Report: Children's Literacy National Projects, Brisbane: Queensland University of Technology/ Department of Education, Employment, Training and Youth Affairs.

Lankshear, C. and Knobel, M. (2000) *Why digital epistemologies?* Online. Available HTTP: *http://www.edca.cqu.edu.au/lit/re-open* (17 Jan 2000).

Lankshear, C., Peters, M. and Knobel, M. (2000) 'Information, knowledge and learning: some issues facing epistemology and education in a digital age', *Journal of Philosophy of Education*, 34: 17–40.

Papert, S. (1972) 'Teaching children thinking', *Mathematics Teaching*, Spring 58: 2–17.

Saffo, P. (1994) 'It's the context, stupid', *Wired*, 2: 74–75.

Schrage, M. (1998) *Technology, Silver Bullets and Big Lies: Musings on the Information Age with author Michael Schrage*. Online. Available HTTP: *http://www.educause.edu/pub/er/review/reviewArticles/33132.html* (26 January 2000).

—— (2000) *The Relationship Revolution*. Online. Available HTTP: *http://www.ml.com/woml/forum/relation.htm* (26 January 2000).

Sproull, L. and Kiesler, S. (1991) *Connections: New Ways of Working in the Networked Organisation*, Cambridge, MA: MIT Press.

Strassmann, P. A. (1997) *The Squandered Computer: Evaluating the Business Alignment of Information Technologies*, New Canaan, Connecticut: Information Economics Press.

Tyack, D. and Cuban, L. (1995) *Tinkering Toward Utopia. A Century of Public School Reform*, Cambridge, MA: Harvard University Press.

10

TECHNOLOGY, LEARNING AND
VISUAL CULTURE

Ron Burnett

I have been an educator and administrator for over thirty years. The disciplines I have taught range from English literature, film, cultural studies and linguistics through to new media, communications, photography, video and media studies. My research includes anthropology, video and television, science and computer science, as well as popular culture and computer-mediated communications and the role of technology in teaching and learning. I mention this interdisciplinary background because one of the purposes of this chapter is to open an interdisciplinary debate on the role of literacy, not only at a pedagogical level, but also as a broad-based cultural activity. Further goals are to explore the increasing pedagogical importance of media and visual literacy programmes, as well as the historical *lineage* of some of the major concepts that drive research on literacy and subsequent applications in the classroom.

Literacy research and the practice of teaching literacy have been framed by the desire to develop the skills that learners need to both understand and decode the world around them. Often, literacy is used as a generic term to exemplify work with texts both from a learning and a teaching perspective. This is perhaps why literacy studies has spread across a variety of areas from media right through to computers and visual culture. Of further and crucial importance is the use of technology to the field of literacy studies and to learning in general. These range from using computer-assisted learning programs in a language lab to the more complex deployment of digital technologies to facilitate interaction among students and teachers. I cannot approach these issues, however, without first reflecting on the contexts of classroom teaching and learning. In other words, I need to situate my comments on literacy, technology and learning within the experiences that I have had as a teacher and scholar.

Classroom paradoxes

In an essay written in 1982, Shoshana Felman described some paradoxical statements made by Socrates and Freud on education and learning. In the context of a discussion on pedagogy, Socrates and Freud talked at different times about the 'radical impossibility of teaching' (Felman 1982: 21). I would like to argue, in some agreement with Felman's analysis, that recognition of the 'impossibility' of teaching enables and encourages the development of new and innovative approaches to pedagogy and learning. At the root of the claim about the impossibility of teaching is my feeling that learning never progresses along a 'simple one-way road from ignorance to knowledge' (Felman 1982: 27).

The balance between where students have come from and where they are headed is rarely linear and is often not clear. There is a legitimate desire on the part of teachers to structure ideas and values, as well as knowledge and content, for the purposes of presentation and discussion. However, what must be recognised is the role of 'desire' in communication and teaching, as well as the gap between what teachers know and how well they have come to grips with what they do *not* know. This crucial gap affects a teacher's capacity to create a site of learning for students. How can a teacher address a group of students whose central obsession might be the *Backstreet Boys* from a position of shared knowledge and understanding (Luke 2000)? Why do students have to learn from people who may have very little respect for the cultural context in which students live? The same question could be asked of learners in relation to teachers. This issue of intergenerational communications and sensitivity is often forgotten as teachers and students struggle with the everyday problems that they face in schools and in their classrooms. Popular culture provides a central if not crucial foundation for the lives of students. Often, in not recognising the centrality of popular culture, teachers may be missing some of the most important elements in students' understanding of their own lives. Yet, it seems clear that an improvement in the level and breadth of communications cannot be achieved if there is not some mutual giving in all quarters. I am talking here about more than just a shared discourse. We need a shared understanding and that will require a profound shift in the ways in which culture is both seen and understood within learning environments.

The history of education is full of experiments and noble efforts at change. My intuition has always been that learning comes about when we understand what motivates or attracts us to a particular set of ideas or practices. The difficulty for the teacher is that the classroom is not necessarily the best place to discover those motivations. The classroom as an environment often does not easily facilitate the type of personal interaction that permits students and teachers to recognise the elliptical nature of the communication processes in which they are engaging. This would apply to environments in which technology is embedded as well as to classrooms in which technology is not the essential characteristic. However, when technology is invoked, it is usually to make the claim that many of these problems will be solved. 'In 1913, Thomas Edison predicted that books would "soon be obsolete in the schools" because of motion pictures. Similar predictions of epochal change in education accompanied the diffusion of radio in the 1920s and '30s and television in the 1950s' (Starr 1996). Today, the ubiquity of computers is as important as the overwhelming presence of other technologies of communications. This means that educators are caught up in the reality of technology use whether or not they understand the implications. In addition, there is so much experimentation going on to examine the potential, both negative and positive, of technology's role in education, that a mass of assumptions about this issue has become embedded in the social and cultural fabric of society and has become a basis for discussion of classroom issues.

Does technology provide some answers?

What are the implications of trying to use technology to solve some of these problems? I am fascinated with and have been involved in the development of online learning, as well as other techniques of distance education (in addition to making broad use of technology in the classroom). But much of what passes as educational on the World Wide Web, for instance, simply extends the constraints of the classroom experience. This is partially because the complexity of understanding visual cultures (Bolter and Grusin 1999) and the inter-relationships between information, awareness and knowledge cannot accommodate the grand expectations of a medium such as the Web. I say this with all due respect to the Web and to the Internet, which continue to be of great importance to me. Visual cultures, of which the Web is both a part and a foundation, are very complex. We need only imagine a visit to a mall. If we were to zoom in on each storefront, on the signage, the displays, the sounds and organisation of space, as well as the architectural design of the mall, we would have only a small fragment of the phantasmagoria that is one of the foundations for modern-day shopping. A phenomenological analysis will not provide much insight into the often times chaotic and sometimes ordered relationships that buyers/viewers have with malls. We need to probe more deeply.

The same problems arise in analysing films and television. I have regularly startled my students as well as audiences I have addressed, when I have said that a TV show like *Beverly Hills 90210* should have been required viewing for all parents and teachers. After all, if we are to find some common ground for communication and analysis with students, what better way than to watch a show which is a shaper and critic of youth culture? The same can be said for music videos or shows like *Survivor*. Visual cultures are about different orders of knowledge and knowing. Visual cultures depict, criticise and sustain the contradictions in which they are immersed. If classrooms are to be places of exchange, then students and teachers need to feel comfortable about their relationship to popular culture. This also means rethinking how the Web operates, because it is fundamentally a window into the concerns and narratives of popular culture. If we factor in the role that computer and online games have in defining a cultural orientation, then the urgency of developing creative tools to critique visual cultures is all the more central to the task of teaching and learning. Somewhere between the classroom, the home and the street, we will find that learning has moved far beyond the conventional competencies that teachers look for in their students. Driven by a combination of new and old technologies as well as social and economic change, learning now takes place in so many different ways and venues, that we need a far more integrative and holistic approach to pedagogy.

There are some fundamental guidelines that provide a foundation for an integrative approach: these guidelines may both form and inform the development of pedagogical strategies in literacy education:

1   Popular and visual cultures are immersed in technology. Learners are both the progenitors and creators of technological innovation.
2   Resistance and acquiescence drive learning. Cultural phenomena are part of a complex system through which a variety of central narratives are constructed. These narratives are the content of the media and if we are to connect learning to context, we need to know and understand these stories.
3   Classrooms are public arenas of exchange. Networked learning does not eliminate the contradictions, potential and pitfalls of the classroom experience. Technology is never a substitute for interpersonal exchange and I say this even as Internet technologies are redefining what we mean by public discourse and public spaces as well as interactivity and human conversation.
4   The search for meaning occurs through patterning; learners construct meaning through creating patterns of connections (Marshall 2000).
5   Connections mean connectivity, which cannot be achieved unless there is a genuine understanding of how the process of communications works. This means that students must participate in the creation of the learning experience. This is not only for themselves, but also for the teachers who teach them. Communication is about an exchange among equals and/or those who strive for equality.
6   An interdisciplinary or transdisciplinary approach is needed if a new paradigm of learning is to be created and the use of technologies must be factored in at all levels (Stephens 2000).

As these guidelines suggest, an engagement with processes of communication is the essential foundation for building a vision of the relationship between technology and learning. A carefully modelled and broadly interdisciplinary approach to literacy education may well provide a new foundation for learning activities within and outside institutions.

The impact of technology on learning

As I mentioned earlier, the connections between technology and learning are and have been very intimate (particularly throughout the twentieth century) and this is because educational institutions, particularly in higher education, have had to deal with increasing numbers of students and diminishing resources. There has also been an assumption that new technologies will 'improve the quality of teaching by achieving higher levels of learning, such as analysis, synthesis, problem solving and decision making' (Bates 2000: 1). Yet it is not clear how or even why new technologies can achieve something more quickly and at a higher level than that which education has been striving for over the last two centuries. Ultimately, new technologies are instruments of communication and are helping to create what might best be described as an ecology where the ways in which we interact with each other will be increasingly mediated by machines. Nevertheless, the core of Bates' argument is that increasingly information will be available in many different forms and through many different instruments.

Ironically, when television was introduced into classrooms in the 1960s, many of the same claims were made. This led to the merging of what was then a growing documentary film and video movement with *instructional* films and videotapes. (There are intimate connections between the pedagogically oriented films and newsreels of the 1930s and 1940s and the documentaries of the 1950s and 1960s.) I emphasise the term instructional, because it suggests something about the use of images and sounds that transcends, aids and sometimes bypasses teachers. Instructional television of that period was characterised by a number of major styles, but the most telling was the use of voice-over. Authority was brought to bear on images and what could be learned from them. A male voice was used to increase the pedagogical impact of the video or film. This is because during the 1960s and well into the 1970s and 1980s behavioural models were the norm in the development of instructional technology materials (McDonough 2001).

I bring up this debate about behaviourism because although there has been a strong move towards constructivism on the part of educational technologists over the last twenty years, the underlying attraction of new technologies is that they appear to make the process of communication less complex and more direct. There now seem to be many different ways in which pedagogical problems can be solved. What remains, however, irrespective of whether students are now more in charge of developing their own ideas, is the concept of information transmission. Images, whether they are on the Web or on television, are still used to structure narratives and documents as sources of information about a variety of topics and they are given a certain authority when they are used for instruction. Bates goes even further when he says, 'Well-designed multimedia learning materials can be more effective than traditional classroom methods because students can learn more easily and more quickly through illustration, animation, different structuring of materials, and increased control of and interaction with learning materials' (Bates 2000: 28). Bates' claims fit with the assumptions that have guided the introduction of new technologies in education over the last 100 years. Yet as I pointed out at the beginning of this essay, we may know far less about what happens in classrooms than what educational technologists suggest.

It is ironic that the use of technology also provokes what Leo Marx has described as 'technological pessimism' (Marx 1994: 238). The ambivalence that we feel about the use of technology comes out in the rather confused ways in which media are used in the classroom. Most of the time, film and television are used for illustrative purposes, an extension of textbooks. An entire industry has grown up with its own styles and genres designed to service the needs of teachers and learners. At the same time, there is the sense that the use of a film, for example, is just filler and learning that is more serious will only take place when the 'hard stuff' is discussed in the classroom. I will not explore this issue in greater depth here other than to suggest that there is a link between the illustrative use of media in the classroom and the use of the Web for instructional purposes. Illustration is somewhat safe and permits the use of technology without suggesting that something important has been lost in the process. Can a story, for example, be taught using illustration as the only method? How do we illustrate the meaning of a poem? How can we recognise the need to learn? Most importantly, how can learners assess what they have learned when these processes of illustration are used? How much information leads to understanding? What qualitative indicators are there to reveal the depth of what has been learned?

From a technological point of view, the response to these dilemmas has been to propose more interactive materials available over networks and through computers. It remains unclear, however, whether the Web is interactive. There is no doubt that the increasing use of simulation, both in terms of role playing and as a part of the digital environment, moves the argument about interactivity a bit closer to realisation. But, in and of itself, the use of each of e-mail, listservs, chat or hyperlinked webpages, says very little about the quality of interaction. Although efforts to observe and evaluate the use of these new instruments of communications are part of on-going research in a variety of contiguous disciplines, it will take some time to understand the nuances of interactivity in digital cultures (Barton *et al.* 2000).

The use of technology in the classroom has a long history. Language labs were among the earliest examples in the twentieth century of the mass application of technology to education. Language labs were introduced to facilitate the learning of the correct pronunciation for foreign languages and to make it easier to repeatedly practise and effectively memorise the grammar of languages like French and Spanish. The other purpose was to drill students so that they could hear the results of their efforts over and over again, based on the principle that repetition makes learning easier and the rules learned become more permanently embedded in the student. The teaching of languages using tape recorders actually appeared in the early twentieth century, with some very effective technology available in the 1930s. The widespread installation of language labs in elementary and secondary schools did not happen until the 1950s.

I present this example for two reasons. The first is that a whole host of assumptions went into the decision to use language labs and among the most important was that repetition enhanced learning. The second is that modern-day computer labs look very much like language labs. The connections here are not accidental and have to do with the ease with which a teacher can monitor the work of students and also the archival function that labs can play in tracking the progress of students from one level of learning to the next. In addition, labs are very close to classrooms in layout and orientation and are often used as substitutes for classrooms. In this example, technology does not take the place of the teacher but presumably enhances and extends the capacities of teachers to provide their students with additional sources of information and learning. The foundations for this approach are steeped in assumptions about pedagogical innovation and a general if partially understood notion that classroom experiences can be extended by the use of new technologies. Yet a lab is as much a learning environment as it is an environment of communication and interchange. The challenge is how to understand the role of communications in this example and with respect to learning as a whole. Much can be discussed here about the relationship between machines and humans and the nature of the interfaces that are used in labs of all sorts for many different disciplines. For the purposes of this essay, it is important to understand that the use of technology for learning needs to be contextualised by an awareness of the instrumentality of machine–human relations, and the communicative expectations that govern this type of interchange.

Learning and communications

It is interesting to note that the disciplines of education and communications operate quite distinctly from each other. It would be rare for a Faculty of Education to hire an expert from the field of communications and the same is true in reverse, although it is clear that both disciplinary areas invoke each other when learning and literacy are discussed. The lack of connection between these two crucial disciplines is the result not only of different paradigms and different histories, but also because of narrow definitions of the communications process and limited views of how communications, learning, pedagogy and culture interact.

What follows are three scenarios that illuminate the interconnected discourses of learning and communications.

Teacher A walks into his Grade Ten classroom and begins to talk about violence on television and how that violence influences young people. He shows a few clips from some television shows and then asks the students to comment. Some students blame the media for school shootings and other violent behaviour. Teacher A supports their comments in part because the media themselves have declared over and over again that violent images produce violent people. However, this is not the only reason. Although the research is very unclear in this area, there is a strong societal assumption that popular culture influences young people in a direct way. Many of the assumptions that guide this argument have come from a variety of disciplines, but in most cases, the studies have proved to be inconclusive. Although it is one of the tenets of communications theory to examine the origins and use of arguments about messages and meaning, this complex area cannot simply be transposed into discussions of violence. The effects of images can be as varied as the content of the narratives that use audio-visual devices to communicate their points. The question of effect is just that, a question, and needs to be approached with some sense of the history of images and the types of narratives that audiences find attractive. This goes to the heart of our expectations for learners. The debates in the discipline of communications around effects have been contentious for decades. The challenge is to work out how the information and knowledge gained can be transferred to other areas.

Teacher B walks into her classroom with some examples of popular music. She plays a few selections and then talks about the lyrics, which are angry and in some instances mention death; they also try to rally the listener to revolt against consumer society. Although the teacher valiantly tries to explain what is happening in the music and tries to connect the music to a social and political context, the lyrics have an emphasis and orientation that seems to lift them out of the context in which they were created. This makes it easier to critique the lyrics but also more difficult to understand the anger. The teacher makes use of a variety of interpretative approaches, some of which are derived from the study of literature and others which have their origins in cultural studies. The challenge is how to balance different disciplinary trajectories and come up with some explanatory models and interpretative approaches that will frame the music. The effectiveness of the analysis will depend largely on the teacher's relationship to popular culture. If she rarely listens to music and doesn't read any of the magazines that promote and comment on the performers and the industry, she will not have many critical tools at her disposal. If she has not had the opportunity to access some of the extensive material that has come out of cultural studies about rock or rap, for example, then she will miss the opportunity to enrich the students' own relationships to the music they love.

Teacher C brings examples of advertising in magazines to her class and asks the students to discuss the meaning of the ads. Most of the examples use implicit sexuality to communicate their meaning. The teacher uses a model of analysis that is derived from semiotics and the study of sign systems. However, a great deal of the information that she uses comes to her via literacy textbooks and monographs that have adapted semiotics in order to better understand the way messages are communicated. Does semiotics provide a good enough basis for analysis? How does a teacher gain a critical understanding of the debates that have suffused the field of semiotics for decades? Would that knowledge have an impact on her pedagogy? The challenge is to work out how to facilitate the students' discovery of discursive and interpretative strategies to analyse advertising.

The experiences depicted in these three scenarios are quite common. Students are among the largest group of viewers and consumers (Lund and Sanderson 1999). The premise is that they need to understand the cultural context in which they live. The pedagogical assumption is that the cultural experiences that students have can provide a base upon which to analyse and comment on popular culture. The underlying thrust here is to raise critical questions about media messages and to engage with issues like authorship, point of view, audience and representation. It is important to understand that these categories of criticism have a genealogy that reaches back into research that has been of central concern to the disciplines of communications and cultural studies as well as to literary and literacy studies. It is thus crucial to unpack this genealogy.

In the next section, I explore a number of approaches to visual cultures with an emphasis on the intellectual and historical roots of working with cultural phenomena as if they are linguistically based. It seems clear, however, that more and more self-reflexivity is required in the study of cultures. In Western societies that are dominated by decentred and dispersed forms of cultural expression, texts may well be considered as visual (Taylor and Saarinen 1994) but this does not necessarily mean that language, representation and communication are also visual. The connections between visual forms of expression and literacy need to be explored in detail before we make too many assumptions about communication and exchange.

Visual languages and literacy

One of the assumptions of visual and media literacy studies is that film and television, for example, communicate meaning using visual languages. Among the consequences of this approach is that various forms of media expression are studied as if they are texts. There would be nothing inherently wrong with this were it not for the fact that there are distinct differences between texts and images and these differences need to be theorised rather than elided. There is a general slippage in the use of the term text as a generic overlay to explain a range of representational systems. As a result, a variety of discourses and media are transformed into texts, for the purposes of study, without enough analysis of the transformative impact of the conversion (Mowitt 1992).

A further issue of some concern is that the notion of a visual language has its roots in semiotics. Although the term semiotics appears in some of the work that has been done in literacy studies, the general use tends to be derivative. This is largely because the field of semiotics is complex and connected to an even more complex area, linguistics. To further complicate matters, as I mentioned earlier, the type of linguistics that many literacy researchers use comes from the work of major cultural theorists like Roland Barthes. However, even Barthes, whose early work was dependent on the research of Ferdinand de Saussure, moved away from Saussure's structuralist approach later in his career. Barthes' original semiotic concepts were essentially canonised and have become part of the movement to analyse many different forms of visual expression. A close examination of his last book, *Camera Lucida* (Barthes 1981, see Burnett 1995), suggests that Barthes shifted from a semiotic approach to a hermeneutic strategy that all but eliminated the importance and centrality of some of his initial work on sign systems. Yet it is the case that Barthes' early work contributed to an explosion of books and articles on among other things, the *language* of film, video, painting, and so on.

In effect, this desire to use language as an overarching metaphor for representation and expression is based on a need to find structure, even to force structure into processes that are at best fluid and for the most part quite chaotic. The issue is not only whether language is a useful metaphor (which it can sometimes be) but whether it leads to simplistic notions of visualisation and communication. The tendency is to approach visual communications as if the process can be broken down into a series of constituent parts. Much like language, assumptions are made about the presence of a grammar so that some sort of relationship can be established between surface meanings and a deeper, yet not so apparent and often more important level. Barthes changed his approach in his later work because textual analysis did not seem to provide him with the analytical framework that he needed. My sense is that Barthes moved from a rationalist and sometimes reductionist strategy to a more open and hermeneutic one. His impulse to create a science of signs in *Elements of Semiology* (Barthes 1968) has remained an important influence even as other more social and political approaches have come into the foreground in the study of representational systems.

One of the characteristics of semiotics is a search for rules much like the rules which govern the use of language. For example, television images are often spoken about as if they have frames (in order to look for some coherence in that surface layer). For the most part, however, television images are continuous. It is difficult to segment a television show into its parts. In fact, from an interpretative point of view, segmenting a TV show may not deal with the complex set of devices and communicative strategies that the show uses to create meaning. One of the essential strategic values that has been proposed in analysing TV as a language is that the shows can be broken down into their constituent parts for the purposes of analysis. Television is more like the verbal than the written and our spoken languages tend to be elliptical if not fragmentary. It seems clear that it is written languages that visual processes are being compared to with the result that the linguistic metaphor has actually become a block to thinking about the complexity of modern forms of communications. Can a written text be compared to a visual form of communication? Aside from the impulse to collapse all forms of visual communications into a linguistic metaphor, there is also a sometimes explicit and often implicit assumption made that the experience of viewing is equivalent to the experience of reading.

It is clear that viewing and reading are related activities, but they are certainly not the same. Consequently, we may need to re-examine what we mean by understanding when we talk about visual images. Is the experience of watching a film more visceral than intellectual? Do we watch and understand? Alternatively, do we experience and then remember? If memory is central, then how can we locate what we know and translate our experiences into a discourse that is both comfortable and familiar? The difficulty is that viewing media is about entering a series of stages from an embodied relationship to the activities of seeing, to the more complex activities of remembering what has been seen (and what has been heard). If memory is crucial then the question of what it means to be literate must expand considerably. How do we learn from images? How do we learn from sounds? Does our participation in the activity of viewing mean that we are learning? How do we get to know whether we have learned? What prevents us from remembering what we have seen?

Conclusion

Engaging with visual cultures is a complex and sometimes daunting challenge. There is no doubt that we need many more ways of connecting what happens in classrooms with the experience of being immersed in the swirl of cultural and technology-driven activities that now surround us. We need to develop an understanding of the signposts that we are using and of the underlying cartography of the cultural landscape. In some respects, literacy educators at all levels have been in the forefront of creating the tools needed to engage with these shifting and quite complex levels of communication and exchange. The challenge is how to move outwards from classrooms into a world of cultural phenomena largely dependent on an experiential base that is fluid and often opaque. What happens when we integrate broadcast television, interactive CD-ROMs, web-based learning environments, and computer and video conferencing into the learning process? Most of these media forms are already a part of the everyday life of many students. How do we disengage those experiences or at least disassemble them to study their impact? Are the public spaces of the classroom best suited for these tasks? How can we evaluate the usage patterns and learning experiences that these technologies encourage? Do we use online and/or paper questionnaires? Do we count the number of times that students log on to gain some sense of what they are doing? I raise these questions because the analytical work of examining how technologies affect learning processes is often looped back into literacy programmes. In this case, literacy is used as an all-pervasive tool to unveil both the logic of the technologies themselves (as in courses that teach limited versions of programming and computer literacy) and the patterns of interaction.

In a similar vein, in response to the perceived power of media to influence viewers, literacy is sometimes used as a tool of demystification that is often confused with interpretation. Screen-based environments are ubiquitous. The advent of smaller and smaller digital devices means that very few of the objects that we will use will be without some connection either to each other or to the networks that we depend on. If what we are dealing with is an ecology, albeit a cultural one, how can we develop enough vantage-points to actually see what is going on? In 1993, online education was virtually non-existent. Today private investment in this area has reached over 2.2 billion dollars (Werry 2001). Does this economic argument about the convergence of private capital and education tell us something important about the role of new technologies in learning and about how we can understand their impact? Alternatively, are the implicit tools of measurement that have been used to judge the effectiveness of the education system now more visible? If the new technologies that we have available are so powerful in their effects, why are educators facing increasing demands for more universally acceptable modes of measurement of the outcomes and results of the learning experience? Why are we testing more than ever in a blatant return to the 1950s? If the effects of online learning have been so important, why are students increasingly requesting direct encounters with teachers?

Some of the answers to these questions can be found in the tropes that we use to understand the role of technology in learning. For example, 'learner-centred' is a phrase that keeps reappearing in Tony Bates' book and in other books and essays about online learning. In fact, we need only ask one question to comprehend the weakness of learner-centred approaches using digital technologies and networks. Could the learner take a bunch of webpages specifically designed to communicate in a certain way and redesign them, including their architectural and navigational structure? This is the challenge. It is not unlike what happened in the online gaming world, where a small group of hackers redesigned a game and took it over. In that instance, the creator of the game allowed the process to unfold. But would an instructor or an institution with major investments in online development permit this to happen? I doubt it. This has always been the Achilles heel of online learning, but also of any technology-driven teaching process. At the same time, in an increasingly mediated world, communications, culture and learning intersect on a daily basis. There are fewer and fewer givens in learning activities and this raises crucial issues for the future of literacy studies as well as major questions about the nature and orientation of educational institutions.

References

Barthes, R. (1968) *Elements of Semiology*, trans. A. Lavers and C. Smith, New York: Hill and Wang.
—— (1981) *Camera Lucida*, trans. R. Howard, New York: Noonday Press.

Barton, D., Hamilton, M. and Ivanic, R. (2000) (eds) *Situated Literacies: Reading and Writing in Context*, London: Routledge.

Bates, T. (2000) *Managing Technological Change: Strategies for College and University Leaders*, San Francisco: Jossey-Bass.

Bolter, J. and Grusin, R. (1999) *Remediation: Understanding New Media*, Cambridge, Mass: MIT Press.

Burnett, R. (1995) *Cultures of Vision: Images, Media and the Imaginary*, Bloomington: Indiana University Press.

Felman, S. (1982) 'Psychoanalysis and education: teaching terminable and interminable', *Yale French Studies* 63: 21–44.

Luke, C. (2000) 'New literacies in teacher education', *Journal of Adolescent and Adult Literacy* 43 (5): 425–428.

Lund, D. and Sanderson, D. (1999) '*From printed page to multimedia: evolution of a second-grade class newspaper*'. Online. Available HTTP: *http://www.readingonline.org/articles/lund/printomulti.html#theory* (4 June 2001).

Marshall, S. (2000) *The Learning Story of the Illinois Mathematics and Science Academy*. Online. Available HTTP: *http://www.learndev.org* (20 May 2001).

Marx, L. (1994) 'The idea of technology and postmodern pessimism', in *Does Technology Drive History?* M.R. Smith and L. Marx (eds) Cambridge, Mass: MIT Press, pp. 237–257.

McDonough, S. (2001) 'Way beyond drill and practice: foreign language lab activities in support of constructivist learning', *International Journal of Instructional Media* 28 (1): 73–82.

Mowitt, J. (1992) *Text: The Genealogy of an Antidisciplinary Object*, Durham: Duke University Press.

Starr, P. (1996) *Computing Our Way to Educational Reform*. Online. Available HTTP: *http://www.prospect.org/print/V7/27/starr-p.html* (20 May 2001)

Stephens, K. (2000) 'A critical discussion of the New Literacy Studies', *British Journal of Educational Studies* 48: 1: 10–23.

Taylor, M. C. and Saarinen, E. (1994) *Imagologies: Media Philosophy*, London: Routledge.

Werry, C. (2001) *The Work of Education in the Age of e-College*. Online. Available HTTP: *http://firstmonday.org/issues/issue6_5/werry/index.html* (20 May 2001).

11

TECHNOLOGICAL REVOLUTION, MULTIPLE LITERACIES, AND THE RESTRUCTURING OF EDUCATION[1]

Douglas M. Kellner

A dramatic technological revolution, centred on computer, information, communication, and multimedia technologies, is changing everything from the ways people work, to the ways they communicate with each other and spend their leisure time. This technological revolution is often interpreted as the beginnings of a knowledge or information society, and therefore ascribes education a central role in every aspect of life. It poses tremendous challenges to educators to rethink their basic tenets, to deploy the new technologies in creative and productive ways, and to restructure schooling to respond constructively and progressively to the technological and social changes that we are now experiencing. At the same time that technological revolution is under way, important demographic and socio-political changes are taking place in the United States and throughout the world. Emigration patterns have created the challenge of providing people from diverse races, classes and backgrounds with the tools and competencies to enable them to succeed and participate in an ever more complex and changing world.

In this chapter, I argue that educators need to cultivate multiple literacies for our multicultural society, that we need to develop new literacies of diverse sorts, including a more fundamental importance for print literacy, to meet the challenge of restructuring education for a high tech, multicultural society, and global culture. In a period of dramatic technological and social change, education needs to help produce a variety of new types of literacies to make education relevant to the demands of the contemporary era. As new technologies are altering every aspect of our society and culture, we need to comprehend and make use of them both to understand and to transform our worlds. By introducing new literacies to empower individuals and groups traditionally excluded, education could thus be reconstructed to make it more responsive to the challenges of a democratic and multicultural society.

Technology and the restructuring of education

To dramatise the issues at stake, we should consider the claim that we are now undergoing one of the most significant technological revolutions for education since the progression from oral to print and book-based teaching (Castells 1996, 1997, 1998; Best and Kellner forthcoming). Just as the transition to print literacy and book culture involved a dramatic transformation of education (McLuhan 1962, 1964; Ong 1988), so too does the current technological revolution demand a major restructuring of education today with new curricula, pedagogy, literacies, practices and goals. Furthermore, the technological revolution of the present era makes possible the radical reconstruction and restructuring of education and society argued for in the progressive era by John Dewey, and in the 1960s and 1970s by Ivan Illich, Paolo Freire, and others who sought radical educational and social reform.[2]

Put in historical perspective, it is now possible to see modern education as preparation for industrial civilisation and minimal citizenship in a passive representative democracy. The demands of the new global economy, culture and polity require a more informed, participatory and active citizenship, and thus increased roles and challenges for education. Modern education, in short, emphasises submission to authority, rote memorisation, and what Freire called the 'banking concept' of education in which learned teachers deposit knowledge into passive students, inculcating conformity, subordination and normalisation. These traits are becoming obsolete in a global post-industrial and networked society with its demands for new skills for the workplace, participation in new social and political environs, and interaction within novel forms of culture and everyday life.

In short, the technological revolution renders necessary the sort of thorough restructuring of education that radicals demanded during the last century, indeed back to the Enlightenment if one includes Rousseau and Wollstonecraft, who saw the progressive restructuring of education as the key to democracy. Today, however, intense pressures for change now come directly from technology and the economy and not ideology or educational reformist ideas, with a new global economy and new technologies demanding new skills, competencies, literacies and practices. While this technological revolution has highly ambiguous effects, it provides educational reformers with the challenge of whether education will be restructured to promote democracy and human needs, or whether education will be transformed primarily to serve the needs of business and the global economy.

It is therefore a burning question as to what sort of restructuring will take place, in whose interests, and for what ends. More than ever, we need philosophical reflection on the ends and purposes of education, on what we are doing and trying to achieve in our educational practices and institutions. In this situation, it may be instructive to return to Dewey and see the connections between education and democracy, the need for the reconstruction of education and society, and the value of experimental pedagogy to seek solutions to the problems of education in the present day. A progressive reconstruction of education will urge that it be done in the interests of democratisation, ensuring access to new technologies for all, helping to overcome the so-called digital divide and divisions of the haves and have nots, so that education is placed, as Dewey (1997 [1916]) and Freire (1972, 1999) propose, in the service of democracy and social justice.

Yet we should be more aware than Dewey of the obduracy of divisions of class, gender and race, and work self-consciously for multicultural democracy and education. This task suggests that we valorise difference and cultural specificity, as well as equality and shared universal Deweyean values such as freedom, equality, individualism and participation. Theorising a democratic and multicultural reconstruction of education forces us to confront the digital divide, that there are divisions between information and technology haves and have nots, just as there are class, gender and race divisions in every sphere of the existing constellations of society and culture. The latest surveys of the digital divide, however, indicate that the key indicators are class and education and not race and gender, hence the often-circulated argument that new technologies merely reinforce the hegemony of upper-class white males must be questioned.[3]

With the proper resources, policies, pedagogies and practices, we can work to reduce the (unfortunately growing) gap between haves and have nots, although technology alone will not suffice to democratise and adequately reconstruct education. That is, technology itself does not necessarily improve teaching and learning, and will certainly not of itself overcome acute socio-economic divisions. Indeed, without proper resources, pedagogy and educational practices, technology might be an obstacle or burden to genuine learning and will probably increase rather than overcome existing divisions of power, cultural capital, and wealth.

In the following reflections, I focus on the role of computers and information technology in contemporary education and the need for new pedagogies and an expanded concept of literacy to respond to the importance of new technologies in every aspect of life. I propose some ways that new technologies and new literacies can serve as efficacious learning tools which will contribute to producing a more democratic and egalitarian society, and not just providing skills and tools to privileged individuals and groups that will improve their cultural capital and social power at the expense of others. How, indeed, are we going to restructure education to provide individuals and groups with the tools, the competencies, the literacies to overcome the class, gender, and racial divides that fracture our society and at least in terms of economic indicators seem to be growing rather than diminishing?

First, however, I wish to address the technophobic argument against new technologies *per se*. I have been developing a critical theory of technology that calls attention to uses or types of technology as tools of domination, and that rejects the hype and pretensions of new technologies. A critical theory of technology sees the limitations of pedagogy and educational proposals based primarily on technology without adequate emphasis on pedagogy, and on teacher and student empowerment. It insists on developing educational reform and restructuring to promote multicultural democracy, and calls for appropriate restructuring of technology to advance democratic education and society. Yet a critical theory also sees how technology can be used, and perhaps redesigned and restructured, for positive purposes such as enhancing education and democracy, and overcoming the divide between haves and have nots, while enabling individuals to democratically and creatively participate in a new economy, society, and culture (see Feenberg 1991, 1999; Best and Kellner forthcoming).

A critical theory of technology avoids both technophobia and technophilia. It rejects technological determinism, is critical of the limitations, biases, and downsides of new technologies, but wants to use and redesign technologies for education to enhance democracy and social reconstruction in the interests of social justice. It is also, in the Deweyean spirit, pragmatic and experimental, recognising that there is no agreed upon way to deploy new technologies for enhancing education and democratisation. We must be prepared to accept that some of the attempts to use technology for education may well fail, as have no doubt many of our own attempts to use new technologies for education. A critical theory of technology is aware that technologies have unforeseen consequences and that good intentions and seemingly good projects may have results that were not desired or positive.

Consequently, the question is not whether computers are good or bad in the classroom or more broadly for education. Rather, it is a question of what to do with them: what useful purposes can computers serve, what sort of skills do students and teachers need to effectively deploy computers and information technology, what sort of effects might computers and information technology have on learning, and what new literacies, views of education, and social relations do we need to democratise and improve education today?

Media literacy: an unfulfilled challenge

Literacy involves gaining the skills and knowledge to read and interpret the text of the world and to successfully navigate and negotiate its challenges, conflicts, and crises. Literacy is thus a necessary condition to equip people to participate in the local, national, and global economy, culture, and polity. As Dewey argued (1997), education is necessary to enable people to participate in democracy, for without an educated, informed, and literate citizenry, a robust democracy is impossible. Moreover, there are crucial links between literacy, democracy, empowerment, and participation, and without developing adequate literacies differences between haves and have nots cannot be overcome and individuals and groups will be left out of the emerging economy, networked society, and culture.

In regard to reading, writing, and traditional print literacies, one could argue that in an era of technological revolution and new technologies, we need to develop new forms of media literacy, computer literacy, and multimedia literacies, thus cultivating 'multiple literacies' in the restructuring of education. New technologies and cultural forms demand novel skills and competencies and if education is to be relevant to the problems and challenges of contemporary life it must expand the concept of literacy and develop new curricula and pedagogies. I would resist, however, extreme claims that the era of the book and print literacy are over. Although there are discontinuities and novelties in the current constellation, there are also important continuities. Indeed, in the new information-communication technology environment, traditional print literacy takes on increasing importance in the computer-mediated cyberworld as people need to critically scrutinise and scroll tremendous amounts of information, putting new emphasis on developing reading and writing abilities. For instance, Internet discussion groups, chat rooms, e-mail, and various forums require writing skills in which a new emphasis on the importance of clarity and precision is emerging. In this context of information saturation, it becomes an ethical imperative not to contribute to cultural and information overload, and to concisely communicate thoughts and feelings.

In the new multimedia environment, *media literacy* is arguably more important than ever. Cultural studies and critical pedagogy have begun to teach us to recognise the ubiquity of media culture in contemporary society, the growing trends toward multicultural education, and the need for media literacy that addresses the issue of multicultural and social difference.[4] There is expanding recognition that media representations help construct our images and understanding of the world and that education must meet the dual challenges of teaching media literacy in a multicultural society and sensitising students and publics to the inequities and injustices of a society based on gender, race, and class inequalities and discrimination. Recent critical studies see the role of mainstream media in exacerbating or diminishing these inequalities and the ways that media education and the production of alternative media can help create a healthy multiculturalism of diversity and more robust democracy. They confront some of the most serious difficulties and problems that currently face us as educators and citizens.

Yet despite the ubiquity of media culture in contemporary society and everyday life, and the recognition that the media themselves are a form of pedagogy, and despite criticisms of the distorted values, ideals, and representations of the world in media culture, media education in K-12 schooling has never really been established and developed. The current technological revolution, however, brings to the fore more than ever the role of media like television, popular music, film, and advertising, as the Internet rapidly absorbs these cultural forms and creates new cyberspaces and forms of culture and pedagogy. It is highly irresponsible in the face of saturation by Internet and media culture to ignore these forms of socialisation and education; consequently a critical reconstruction of education should produce pedagogies that provide media literacy and enable students, teachers, and citizens to discern the nature and effects of media culture.

Media culture teaches proper and improper behaviour, gender roles, values, and knowledge of the world. Individuals are often not aware that they are being educated and constructed by media culture, as its pedagogy is frequently invisible and subliminal. This situation calls for critical approaches that make us aware of how media construct meanings, influence and educate audiences, and impose their messages and values. A media literate person is skilful in analysing media codes and conventions, able to criticise stereotypes, values, and ideologies, and competent to interpret the multiple meanings and messages generated by media texts. Media literacy helps people to use media intelligently, to discriminate and evaluate media content, to critically dissect media forms, and to investigate media effects and uses (see Kellner 1995a and 1995b).

Within educational circles, however, a debate persists over what constitutes the field of media pedagogy, with different agendas and programmes. A traditionalist 'protectionist' approach would attempt to 'inoculate' young people against the effects of media addiction and manipulation by cultivating a taste for book literacy, high culture, and the values of truth, beauty, and justice, and by denigrating all forms of media and computer culture. A 'media literacy' movement, by contrast, attempts to teach students to read, analyse, and decode media texts, in a fashion parallel to the advancement of print literacy. Media arts education in turn teaches students to appreciate the aesthetic qualities of media and to use various media technologies as instruments of self-expression and creation. Critical media literacy builds on these approaches, analysing media culture as products of social production and struggle, and teaching students to be critical of media representations and discourses, but also stressing the importance of learning to use the media as modes of self-expression and social activism.

Developing critical media literacy and pedagogy also involves perceiving how media such as film or video can be used positively to teach a wide range of topics, like multicultural understanding and education. If, for example, multicultural education is to champion genuine diversity and expand the curriculum, it is important both for groups excluded from mainstream education to learn about their own heritage and for dominant groups to explore the experiences and voices of minority and excluded groups. Thus, media literacy can promote multicultural literacy, conceived as understanding and engaging the heterogeneity of cultures and subcultures that constitute an increasingly global and multicultural world (Courts 1998; Weil 1998).

Critical media literacy not only teaches students to learn from media, to resist media manipulation, and to use media materials in constructive ways, but is also concerned with developing skills that will help create good citizens and that will make them more motivated and competent participants in social life. Critical media literacy is tied to the project of radical democracy and concerned to develop skills that will enhance democratisation and participation. Critical media literacy takes a comprehensive approach that would teach critical skills and how to use media as instruments of social communication and change. The technologies of communication are becoming more and more accessible to young people and ordinary citizens, and can be used to promote education, democratic self-expression, and social progress. Technologies that could help produce the end of participatory democracy, by transforming politics into media spectacles and the battle of images, and by turning spectators into cultural zombies, could also be used to help invigorate democratic debate and participation (Kellner 1990, 1998).

Indeed, teaching critical media literacy could be a participatory, collaborative project. Watching television shows or films together could promote productive discussions between teachers and students (or parents and children), with emphasis on eliciting student views, producing a variety of interpretations of media texts and teaching basic principles of hermeneutics and criticism. Students and youth are often more media savvy, knowledgeable, and immersed in media culture than their teachers, and can contribute to the educational process through sharing their ideas, perceptions, and insights. On the other hand, critical discussion, debate, and analysis ought to be encouraged with teachers bringing to bear their critical perspectives on student readings of media material. Since media culture is often part and parcel of students' identity and most powerful cultural experience, teachers must be sensitive in criticising artefacts and perceptions that students hold dear, yet an atmosphere of critical respect for difference *and* inquiry into the nature and effects of media culture should be promoted.

A major challenge in developing critical media literacy, however, results from the fact that it is not a pedagogy in the traditional sense with firmly established principles, a canon of texts, and tried-and-true teaching procedures. Critical media pedagogy is in its infancy; it is just beginning to produce results, and is more open and experimental than established print-oriented pedagogy. Moreover, the material of media culture is so polymorphous, multivalent, and polysemic, that it necessitates sensitivity to different readings, interpretations, perceptions of the complex images, scenes, narratives, meanings, and messages of media culture which in its own ways is as complex and challenging to critically decipher as book culture.

Teaching critical media literacy involves occupation of a site above the dichotomy of fandom and censor. One can teach how media culture provides significant statements or insights about the social world, empowering visions of gender, race, and class, or complex aesthetic structures and practices, thereby putting a positive spin on how it can provide significant contributions to education. Yet we ought to indicate also how media culture can advance sexism, racism, ethnocentrism, homophobia, and other forms of prejudice, as well as misinformation, problematic ideologies, and questionable values, and in this way we can promote a dialectical approach to the media.

Computer literacy: an expanded concept

In this section, I argue that students should learn new forms of computer literacy and propose a conception of it that goes beyond standard technical notions.

Critical computer literacy involves learning how to use computer technologies to do research and gather information, as well as to perceive computer culture as a terrain containing texts, spectacles, games, and interactive multimedia which call for cultivating new literacies. Further, computer culture is a discursive and political location in which students, teachers, and citizens can all intervene, engaging in discussion groups and collaborative research projects, creating websites, producing innovative multimedia for cultural dissemination, and engaging in novel modes of social interaction and learning. Computer culture enables individuals to actively participate in the production of culture, ranging from discussion of public issues to creation of their own cultural forms. However, to take part in this culture requires not only accelerated skills of print literacy, which are often restricted to the growing elite of students who are privileged to attend adequate and superior public and private schools, but also demands new forms of literacy.

To respond intelligently to the dramatic technological revolution of our time, we need to begin teaching computer literacy from an early age. Computer literacy, however, itself needs to be theorised. Often the term is synonymous with technical ability to use computers, to become proficient in the use of existing programs, and maybe undertake some programming. I suggest expanding the conception of computer literacy from using computer programs and hardware to a broader concept of information and multimedia literacy. This necessitates promoting more sophisticated abilities in traditional reading and writing, as well as the capability to critically dissect cultural forms taught as part of critical media literacy and multimedia pedagogy.

In my expanded conception, computer literacy involves learning how to use computers, access information and educational material, use e-mail and listserves, and construct websites. Computer literacy comprises the accessing and processing of diverse sorts of information proliferating in the so-called 'information society'. It encompasses learning to find sources of information ranging from traditional sites like libraries and print media to new Internet websites and search engines. Computer-information literacy involves learning where information is found, how to access it, and how to organise, interpret, and evaluate the information that one seeks.

One exciting development in the current technological revolution is that library materials and information are accessible from the entire world. To some extent, the Internet is potentially the all-encompassing library, imperfectly constructed in Alexandria, Egypt, that would contain the great books of the world. Yet while a mind-boggling number of the classics are found on the Internet, we still need the local library to access and collect books, journals, and print material not found on the Internet, as well as the essential texts of various disciplines and the culture as a whole. Information literacy, however, and the new tasks for librarians, also involve knowing what one can and cannot find on the Internet, how to access it, and where the most reliable and useful information is at hand for specific tasks and projects.

Computer and information literacies also involve learning how to read hypertexts, traverse the ever-changing fields of cyberculture, and to participate in a digital and interactive multimedia culture that encompasses work, education, politics, culture and everyday life. Hypertext was initially seen as an innovative and exciting new mode of writing which increased potentials for writers to explore novel modes of textuality and expression (Joyce 1995; Landow 1997). As multimedia hypertext developed on the Internet, it was soon theorised as a multisemiotic and multimodal form of culture. This mode is now increasingly seen as the dominant form of a new hyperlinked, interactive, and multimedia cyberculture (see Burbules and Callister 1996, 2000; Snyder 1996, 1997).

Genuine computer literacy involves not just technical knowledge and skills, but refined reading, writing, research, and communicating ability. It involves heightened capacities for critically accessing, analysing, interpreting, processing, and storing both print-based and multimedia material. In a new information/entertainment society, immersed in transformative multimedia technology, knowledge and information come not merely in the form of print and words, but through images, sounds, and multimedia material as well. Computer literacy thus also involves the ability to discover and access information and intensified abilities to read, to scan texts and computer databases and websites, and to access information and images in a variety of forms, ranging from graphics, to visual images, to audio and video materials, to good old print media. The creation of new multimedia websites, databases, and texts requires accessing, downloading, and organising digitised verbal, imagistic, and audio and video material that are the new building blocks of multimedia culture.

Within multimedia computerised culture, visual literacy takes on increased importance. On the whole, computer screens are more graphic, visual, and interactive than conventional print fields that disconcerted many of us when first confronted with the new environments. Icons, windows, mouses, and the various clicking, linking, and interaction involved in computer-mediated hypertext dictate new competencies and a dramatic expansion of literacy. Visuality is obviously crucial, compelling users to quickly scan visual fields, perceive and interact with icons and graphics, and use technical devices like a mouse to access the desired material and field. But tactility is also important, as individuals must learn navigational skills of how to proceed from one field and screen to another, how to negotiate hypertexts and links, and how to move from one program to another if one operates, as most now do, in a windows-based computer environment.

In my expanded conception, computer literacy involves technical abilities concerning developing basic typing skills, learning computer programs, accessing information, and using computer technologies for a variety of purposes ranging from interpersonal communication to artistic expression to political debate. There are ever more hybrid implosions between media and computer culture as audio and video material becomes part of the Internet, as CD-ROM and multimedia develop, and as new technologies become integral to the home, school, and workplace. Therefore, the skills of decoding images, sounds, and spectacle learned in critical media literacy training can also be valuable as part of computer literacy.

Multimedia and multiple literacies: the new frontier

The new multimedia environments necessitate a diversity of types of multisemiotic and multimodal interaction, involving interfacing with words and print material and often with images, graphics, and audio and video material. As technological convergence develops apace, individuals need to combine the skills of critical media literacy with traditional print literacy and new forms of multiple literacies to access and navigate the new multimedia environments. Literacy in this conception involves the abilities to engage effectively in socially constructed forms of communication and representation. Reading and interpreting print was the appropriate mode of literacy for books, while critical media literacy entails reading and interpreting discourse, images, spectacle, narratives, and the forms and genres of media culture. Forms of multimedia communication involve print, speech, visuality, and audio, in a hybrid field which combines these forms, all of which involve skills of interpreting and critique.

The term 'multiple literacies' points to the many different kinds of literacies needed to access, interpret, criticise, and participate in the emergent new forms of culture and society.[5] The key root here is the multiple, the proliferation of media and forms that demand a multiplicity of competencies and skills and abilities to access, interact, and help construct a new semiotic terrain. Multiple literacies involve reading across varied and hybrid semiotic fields and being able to critically and hermeneutically process print, graphics, moving images, and sounds. The term 'hybridity' suggests the combination and interaction of diverse media and the need to synthesise the various forms in an active process of the construction of meaning. Reading a music video, for instance, involves processing images, music, spectacle, and sometimes narrative in a multisemiotic activity that simultaneously draws on diverse aesthetic forms. Interacting with a website or CD-ROM often involves scanning text, graphics, moving images, and clicking onto the fields that one seeks to peruse and explore, looking for appropriate material. This might lead individuals to draw upon a multiplicity of materials in new interactive learning or entertainment environments, whereby they must simultaneously read and interpret images, graphics, animation, and text.

While traditional literacies concern practices in contexts that are governed by rules and conventions, the conventions and rules of multiliteracies are currently evolving so that their pedagogies comprise a new although bustling and competitive field. Multimedia sites are not entirely new, however. Multisemiotic textuality was first evident in newspapers (consider the difference between *The New York Times* and *U.S.A. Today* in terms of image, text, colour graphics, design, and content) and is now evident in textbooks that are much more visual, graphic, and multimodal than the previously linear and discursive texts of old. But it is CD-ROMs, websites, and new multimedia that are the most distinctively multimodal and multisemiotic forms. These sites are the new frontier of learning and literacy, the great contemporary challenge to education. Critical educators need to theorise the literacies necessary to interact in these emergent multimedia environments and to gain the skills that will enable individuals to learn, work, and create in emergent cultural spaces and domains.

Cultivating new literacies and reconstructing education for democratisation will also involve constructing new pedagogies and social relations. New multimedia technologies enable group projects for students and more of a problem-solving pedagogy in the spirit of Dewey and Freire than traditional transmission top-down teaching models. To enable students to access information, engage in cultural communication and production, and to gain the skills necessary to succeed in the new economy and culture, they need to acquire enhanced literacies, abilities to work cooperatively with others, and to navigate new cultural and social terrains. Such group activity may generate more egalitarian relations between teachers and students and more democratic and cooperative social relations. Of course, it also demands reconsideration of grading and testing procedures, rethinking the roles of teacher and student, and constructing projects and pedagogies appropriate to the new cultural and social environments.

Critical pedagogies of the future must also confront the problem of online education, of how the new cultural terrain of cyberspace produces new sites of information, education, and culture, as well as novel online forms of interaction between students and teacher. In addition, possibilities of students developing their own spaces, cultural forms, and modes of interaction and communication should be promoted. The challenge will also arise of how to balance classroom instruction with online instruction, as well as sorting out the strengths and limitations of print versus online multimedia material (see Feenberg 1999). Indeed, the new technologies and cultural spaces require us to rethink education in its entirety, ranging from the role of the teacher, teacher–student relations, classroom instruction, grading and testing, the value and limitations of books, multimedia, and other teaching material, and the goals of education itself.

Online education and virtual learning also confront us with novel problems such as copyright and ownership of educational materials; collaborations between computer programmers, artists and designers, and teachers and students in the construction of teaching material and sites; and the respective role of federal and local government, the community, corporations, and private organisations in financing education and providing the skills and tools necessary for a new world economy and global culture. Furthermore, the technological revolution forces a rethinking of philosophical problems of knowledge, truth, identity, and reality in virtual environments. Both philosophy and philosophy of education most be reconstructed to meet the challenges of democracy and a new high tech economy.

In addition, individuals should be provided with opportunities to acquire the capacities to understand, critique, and transform the social and cultural conditions in which they live; to be creative and transformative subjects and not just objects of domination and manipulation. This necessitates developing abilities for critical thinking, reflection, and for engaging in discourse, cultural creation, and political action and movements. Active and engaged subjects are produced in social interaction with others, as well as with tools and techniques, so social skills and individual capacities for communication, creativity, and action must be part of the multiple literacies that a radical reconstruction of education seeks and cultivates.

Crucially, multiliteracies and new pedagogies must become reflective and critical, aware of the educational, social, and political assumptions involved in the restructuring of education and society that we are now undergoing. In response to the excessive hype concerning new technologies and education, it is necessary to maintain the critical dimension and to reflect upon the nature and effects of new technologies and the pedagogies developed as a response to their challenge. Many advocates of new technologies, however, eschew critique for a purely affirmative agenda. For instance, after an excellent discussion of new modes of literacy and the need to rethink education, Gunther Kress argues that we must move from critique to design, beyond a negative deconstruction to more positive construction (1997). But rather than following such modern logic of either/or, we need to pursue the logic of both/and, perceiving design and critique, deconstruction and reconstruction, as complementary and supplementary rather than as antithetical choices. Certainly, we need to design alternative technologies, pedagogies, and curricula for the future, and should attempt to design new social and pedagogical relations as well, but we need to criticise misuse, inappropriate use, overinflated claims, and exclusions and oppressions involved in the introduction of new technologies into education. The critical dimension is needed more than ever as we attempt to develop improved teaching strategies and pedagogy, and design new technologies and curricula. In this process, we must be constantly critical, practising critique and self-criticism, putting in question our assumptions, discourses, and practices, as we experimentally develop novel and alternative literacies and pedagogy.

In all educational and other experiments, critique is indeed of fundamental importance. From the Deweyean perspective, progressive education involves trial and error, design and criticism. The experimental method itself comprises critique of limitations, failures, and flawed design. In discussing new technologies and multiple literacies, we also need to constantly raise the questions: Whose interests are these new technologies and pedagogies serving? Are they helping all social groups and individuals? Who is being excluded and why? We also need to raise the question both of the extent to which new technologies and literacies are preparing students and citizens for the present and future and producing conditions for a more vibrant democratic society, or simply reproducing existing inequalities and inequity.

Further, creating multiple literacies must be contextual, engaging the life-world of the students and teachers participating in the new adventures of education. Learning involves developing abilities to interact intelligently with the environment and other people, and calls for vibrant social and conversational environments. Education requires doing and can be gained from practice and social interaction. One can obviously spend too much time with technologies and fail to develop basic social skills and competencies. As Rousseau, Wollstonecraft, and Dewey argued, education involves developing proficiencies that enable individuals to successfully develop within their concrete environments, to learn from practice, and to be able to interact, work, and create in their own societies and cultures. In the dynamically evolving and turbulent global culture, multiple literacies necessitate multicultural literacies, being able to understand and work with a heterogeneity of cultural groups and forms, acquiring literacies in a multiplicity of media, and gaining the competencies to participate in a democratic culture and society (see Courts 1998; Weil 1998).

The project of transforming education will take different forms in different contexts. In the overdeveloped countries, individuals must be empowered to work and act in a high tech information economy, and must learn skills of media and computer literacy to survive in the new social environment. Traditional skills of knowledge and critique must also be enhanced, so that individuals can name the system, describe and grasp the changes occurring and the defining features of the new global order, and can learn to engage in critical and oppositional practice in the interests of democratisation and progressive transformation. This process challenges us to gain vision of how life can be, of alternatives to the present order, and of the necessity of struggle and organisation to realise progressive goals. Languages of knowledge and critique must be supplemented by the discourse of hope and praxis.

This is a time of challenge and a time for experiment. It is time to put existing pedagogies, practices, and educational philosophies in question and to construct new ones. It is a time for new pedagogical experiments to see what works and what doesn't work. It is a time to reflect on our goals and to discern what we want to achieve with education and how we can achieve it. Ironically, it is a time to return to classical philosophy of education which situates reflections on education in reflections on the good life and society at the same time that we reflect on how we can transform education to become relevant to a high tech society. It is time to return to John Dewey to rethink that intimate connection between education and democracy at the same time as we confront the multicultural challenges that Dewey in the midst of a still vital melting pot ideology and liberal progressivist optimism did not address. Most saliently, it is time to take up the Deweyean attitude of pragmatic experimentation to see what it is that the new technologies can and cannot do in order to see how they can enhance education.

In the current turbulent situation of the global restructuring of capitalism and worldwide struggles for democratisation, we have for the first time in decades a chance to reconstruct education and society. In this conjuncture, technology is a revolutionising force, whereby all political parties and candidates pay lipservice to education, to overcoming the digital divide, and to expanding literacy. The time is ripe to take up the challenge and to move to reconstruct education and society so that groups and individuals excluded from the benefits of the economy, culture, and society may more fully participate and receive opportunities not possible in earlier social constellations.

Notes

1   An earlier and different version of this study appeared in *Educational Theory* (Kellner 1998) and I am grateful to its editor Nicholas Burbules for ongoing discussion that helped develop my ideas. A later version was published in a Routledge volume on multiculturalism (Kellner 1999), edited by George Katsiaficas and Teodros Kiros and I am thankful to the editors for discussions which helped with clarification of my position on multiculturalism and education. For continuing discussions of the issues in this essay I am especially grateful to Rhonda Hammer and Allan and Carmen Luke. And, finally, thanks to Ilana Snyder for excellent editing of this text.

2   For materials pertaining to the educational reform proposed by Dewey and Freire and the broader conceptions of relating education to creation of the good life and good society advanced by Plato, Rousseau, Wollstonecraft, and others which inform this essay, see my philosophy of education website, accessible from *www.gseis.ucla.edu/ faculty/kellner/kellner.html*. See also my Education and Technology website which contains materials pertinent to this study at: *http://www.gseis.ucla.edu/courses/ed253a/ lowreskellner/index.html*

3   The 'digital divide' has emerged as the buzzword for perceived divisions between information technology haves and have nots in the current economy and society. A US Department of Commerce report released in July 1999 claimed that the digital divide in relation to race is dramatically escalating and the Clinton administration and media picked up on this theme. See the report *Americans in the Information Age: Falling Through the Net* at *http://www.ntia.doc.gov/ntiahome/digitaldivide/*. A critique of the data involved in the report emerged, claiming that it was outdated; more recent studies by Stanford University, Cheskin Research, ACNielson, and the Forester Institute claim that education and class are more significant factors than race in constructing the divide (see *http://www.cyberatlas.internet.com/big-picture/demographics* for a collection of reports and statistics on the divide). In any case, it is clear that there is a gaping division between information technology haves and have nots, that this is a major challenge to developing an egalitarian and democratic society, and that something needs to be done about the problem. My contribution involves the argument that empowering the have nots requires the dissemination of new literacies thus empowering groups and individuals previously excluded from economic opportunities and socio-political participation.

4   For an earlier and expanded discussion of media literacy, see Kellner 1998. Carson and Friedman 1995 contains studies dealing with the use of media to deal with multicultural education. Examples of teaching media literacy which I draw on include Masterman 1989; Kellner and Ryan 1988; Schwoch *et al.* 1992; Fleming 1993; Giroux 1992, 1993, 1994 and 1996; Giroux and McLaren 1994; Sholle and Denski 1994; McLaren *et al.* 1995; Kellner 1995a and 1995b; Luke 1996, 1997a and 1997b; Giroux and Shannon 1997; and Semali and Watts Pailliotet 1999. See also the work of Barry Duncan and the Canadian Association for Media Literacy (website: *http://www.nald.ca/province/que/litcent/media.htm*) and the Los Angeles-based Center for Media Literacy (*www.medialit.org*). It is a scandal that there are not more efforts to promote media literacy throughout the school system from K-12 and into the university. Perhaps the ubiquity of computer and multimedia culture will awaken educators and citizens to the importance of developing media literacy to create individuals

empowered to intelligently access, read, interpret, and criticise contemporary media and cyberculture.

5   For other recent conceptions of multimedia literacy that I draw upon here, see the discussions of literacies needed for reading hypertext in Burbules and Callister 1996 and 2000; the concept of multiliteracy in the New London Group 1996 and Luke 1997b; the essays in Snyder 1997; and Semali and Watts Pailliotet 1999.

References

Best, S. and Kellner, D. (forthcoming) *The Postmodern Adventure*, New York: Guilford Press.

Burbules, N. C. and Callister, T. A., Jr. (1996) 'Knowledge at the crossroads: some alternative futures of hypertext learning environments', *Educational Theory* 46, 1: 23–50.

—— (2000) *Watch IT. The Risks and Promises of Information Technology*, Boulder, Colorado: Westview Press.

Carson, D. and Friedman, L.D. (1995) *Shared Differences, Multicultural Media and Practical Pedagogy*, Urbana and Chicago: University of Illinois Press.

Castells, M. (1996) *The Rise of the Network Society*, Malden, MA: Blackwell.

—— (1997) *The Power of Identity*, Malden, MA: Blackwell.

—— (1998) *End of Millennium*, Malden, MA: Blackwell.

Courts, P. L. (1998) *Multicultural Literacies: Dialect, Discourses, and Diversity*. New York: Peter Lang.

Dewey, J. (1997 [1916]) *Democracy and Education*, New York: Free Press.

Feenberg, A. (1991) *Critical Theory of Technology*, New York: Oxford University Press.

—— (1999) *Questioning Technology*, New York and London: Routledge.

Fleming, D. (1993) *Media Teaching*, Oxford: Blackwell.

Freire, P. (1972) *Pedagogy of the Oppressed*. New York: Herder and Herder.

—— (1999) *A Paulo Freire Reader*. New York: Herder and Herder.

Giroux, H. (1992) *Border Crossing*. New York: Routledge.

—— (1993) *Living Dangerously: Multiculturalism and the Politics of Difference*, New York: Peter Lang.

—— (1994) *Disturbing Pleasures*, New York: Routledge.

—— (1996) *Fugitive Cultures: Race, Violence, and Youth*. New York: Routledge.

Giroux, H. and McLaren, P. (1994) (eds) *Between Borders: Pedagogy and the Politics of Cultural Studies*, New York: Routledge.

Giroux, H. and Shannon, P. (1997) *Education and Cultural Studies*, London and New York: Routledge.

Joyce, M. (1995) *Of Two Minds: Hypertext Pedagogy and Politics*, Ann Arbor: University of Michigan Press.

Kellner, D. (1990) *Television and the Crisis of Democracy*, Boulder, Colorado: Westview.

—— (1995a) *Media Culture*, London and New York: Routledge.

—— (1995b) 'Cultural studies, multiculturalism, and media culture', in G. Dines and J. Humez (eds) *Gender, Race and Class in Media*, Thousand Oaks, California and London: Sage, pp. 5–17.

—— (1998) 'Multiple literacies and critical pedagogy in a multicultural society', *Educational Theory* 48, 1: 103–122.

—— (1999) 'Multiple literacies and critical pedagogy in a multicultural society' in G. Katsiaficas and T. Kiros (eds) *The Promise of Multiculturalism*, New York and London: Routledge, pp. 211–236

Kellner, D. and Ryan, M. (1988) *Camera Politica: The Politics and Ideology of Contemporary Hollywood Film*, Bloomington, Indiana: Indiana University Press.

Kress, G. (1997) 'Visual and verbal modes of representation in electronically mediated communication: the potentials of new forms of text', in I. Snyder (ed.) *Page to Screen: Taking Literacy into the Electronic Era*, Sydney: Allen & Unwin, pp. 53–79.

Landow, G. P. (1997) *Hypertext 2.0*, revised edition, Baltimore: The Johns Hopkins University Press.

Luke, C. (1996) 'Reading gender and culture in media discourses and texts', in G. Bull and M. Anstey (eds) *The Literacy Lexicon*, New York and Sydney: Prentice-Hall.

—— (1997a) *Technological Literacy*, Melbourne, National Languages and Literacy Institute: Adult Literacy Network.

—— (1997b) 'Media literacy and cultural studies', in S. Muspratt, A. Luke and P. Freebody (eds) *Constructing Critical Literacies*, Cresskill New York: Hampton Press, pp. 19–50.

Masterman, L. (1989 [1985]) *Teaching the Media*, London and New York: Routledge.

McLaren, P., Hammer, R., Sholle, D. and Reilly, S. (1995) *Rethinking Media Literacy: A Critical Pedagogy of Representation*, New York: Peter Lang.

McLuhan, M. (1962) *The Gutenberg Galaxy*, New York: Signet Books.

—— (1964) *Understanding Media: The Extensions of Man*, New York: Signet Books.

New London Group (1996) 'A pedagogy of multiliteracies: designing social futures', *Harvard Educational Review* 66: 60–92.

Ong, W. (1988) *Orality and Literacy: The Technologizing of the Word*, London and New York: Routledge.

Semali, L. and Pailliotet, A. W. (1999) *Intermediality*, Boulder, Col.: Westview.

Schwoch, J., White, M. and Reilly, S. (1992) *Media Knowledge*, Albany: State University of New York Press.

Sholle, D. and Denski, S. (1994) *Media Education and the (Re)Production of Culture*, Westport, Conn.: Bergin & Garvey.

Snyder, I. (1996) *Hypertext: The Electronic Labyrinth*, Melbourne and New York: Melbourne University Press and New York University Press.

—— (1997) (ed.) *Page to Screen: Taking Literacy into the Electronic Era*, Sydney: Allen and Unwin.

Weil, D. K. (1998) *Toward a Critical Multicultural Literacy*, New York: Peter Lang.

CONCLUSION

COMMUNICATION, IMAGINATION, CRITIQUE – LITERACY EDUCATION FOR THE ELECTRONIC AGE

Ilana Snyder

We live in a constantly changing world that continues to be shaped and mediated by the new information and communication technologies. Speed, instantaneity, flexibility, mobility, on-the-spot readjustment, perpetual experimentation, change devoid of consistent direction and incessant reincarnation are some of the hallmarks, not only of Web literacy practices, but also of real-life social and cultural practices (Bauman 2001). They represent the ubiquitous characteristics of the new communication order that provides the focus of this book.

The essays in this volume unravel the key features of the new communication order. By expanding the theoretical perspectives available to the field, the writers illuminate the multiple dimensions of the world of communication. Their aim is to present theoretical and practical understandings of silicon literacy practices that will enable the critical use of the new technologies for educational purposes.

As is always the case in education when something new comes along and challenges the ways in which things have been done for a while, we have a renewed opportunity to ask the important questions: What is education for? What do we need to ensure that our students experience and have access to? What does their education require of teachers? Of institutions? What do we change? What do we preserve? How do we alleviate the tension between continuity and change? What priorities do we need to commit to in the context of a new technological regime? Are the new media to be used for creative growth or merely as new ways of organising older human systems? These are the big questions that the essays in this volume confront. The writers are not fixed on a hard sell of information and communication technologies (ICTs). All believe that educators need to approach the technologising of literacy, the curriculum, pedagogy and sites of education with caution, understanding and wisdom. A good education is the goal and technologies need to remain in the service of that goal: they must not be allowed to drive the agenda (Lankshear and Snyder 2000).

The development of ICTs in the context of broader economic and social changes sets the stage for a major paradigm shift in notions of literacy. There is little doubt that silicon literacies are going to become increasingly prominent in the coming years. When *Page to Screen* was published in 1997 (Snyder), we were still talking about technology enthusiasts and technology demonisers – those who celebrated the new textual practices and those who deplored them. But we have since moved beyond such simplistic bifurcations. It no longer matters to which extreme position we might be more sympathetic: literacy practices in electronic environments are different. The essays focus directly on the differences. They examine particular silicon literacy practices and their bearings and influences on other kinds of cultural practices. But the writers are also interested in the whole texture. Integral to all the essays is the awareness that it is only when micro- and macro-accounts are juxtaposed and the connections between them synthesised that we begin to articulate a holistic understanding of the new communication order.

None of the writers assert that print-based literacy practices have been rendered obsolete. Indeed, it is likely that writing will remain an important medium of communication, probably culturally the most valued form, for some time yet. However, it is also likely that writing will become increasingly the medium used by and for the power elites of society. Issues of equal access to power and its use make it essential to ensure that all students have the opportunity to achieve the highest level of competence in this mode: print and writing must not be side-lined. But students require the opportunity to achieve the highest competence in *all* the varied modes of communication now available. It is not an either or: the challenge is to create pedagogical and curriculum frameworks in literacy education that are suitable for present conditions but that are also attuned to the multiple communication possibilities that an uncertain future might yield.

Literacy education in the electronic age

In the final section of the book, I take up this challenge by examining some ideas that might inform a pedagogical and curriculum framework for literacy education attuned to the changed material and cultural conditions of the electronic age and to the unpredictability of the future. A critical analysis of Baz Luhrmann's (2001) most recent film, *Moulin Rouge*, provides a useful starting point for the discussion as it illustrates some of the qualities peculiar to the contemporary world in which we do our work.

Moulin Rouge is a technically sophisticated and artistically inventive contemporary musical. It parades the trademarks of Luhrmann's earlier concoctions – *Strictly Ballroom* (1992) and *William Shakespeare's Romeo and Juliet* (1996): theatricality, most often rendered as outrageous burlesque, and a furious pace achieved via staccato MTV-style editing techniques. The result of the constant jumping, the lightning-fast cutting from one song to the next and the frenetic movements of the performers is a relentless bombardment of kaleidoscopic images and songs (Martin 2001). The film is spectacle on a grand scale.

At the centre of *Moulin Rouge*, however, is a simple story. In a digitally produced version of Paris in 1900, an aspiring writer from England, in search of true love, becomes entangled with the bohemian set surrounding Toulouse-Lautrec that includes the alluring showgirl, Satine. As with many examples in music theatre before it, the story owes much to the Manon legend: the lovable but consumptive fallen woman intermittently swoons and coughs blood before she finally dies in the arms of her grief-stricken lover.

Luhrmann is playing in the border territory between spectacle and narrative. *Moulin Rouge* entices the viewer into the film with startling immediacy, but almost instantly reveals that what the spectator has been drawn into is artifice. However, the film does not privilege spectacle over narrative. The story, though very familiar, achieves some resonance with the audience. Luhrmann wants it to work both ways with the result that the film resists easy classification.

Critique and social comment are not entirely absent in *Moulin Rouge*. Luhrmann has created a cultural text that challenges the conservative political economy: all that is evil about an unjust system is personified in the Duke of Worcester, a twitching, meddling capitalist, who gets his come-uppance. The film also valorises the radical social margins of society, represented by the beautiful but wanton Satine and her writer lover, the penniless Christian, as well as by other various minor characters. However, Luhrmann locates the film in the 'safe' region of escape in the fantasies and nostalgia of the past.

Primarily through the techniques of parody and pastiche, the film effaces the boundaries between the past and the 1980s – the closest Luhrmann gets to the actual present, although in a postmodern world, infamous for its radical fore-shortening of history, two decades is a long time. Aware of the age of his audience, in a highly commercial decision, Luhrmann uses already known song material when celebrating Paris at the beginning of the twentieth century. The songs are mainly from the early 1980s, including David Bowie and early Madonna, but the musical performance also pays homage to everything from Jean Renoir's *French Can Can* and Howard Hawk's *Gentlemen Prefer Blondes* of the 1950s to the tango movies of Carlos Saura, contemporary rap music videos and to the tradition of Hindi musicals. Further, even the dialogue in *Moulin Rouge* seizes lines from familiar pop-song lyrics and movies. Luhrmann's world of affectation and excess is a blend of the old and the almost new.

Moulin Rouge could be seen as conterminous with postmodernism. Luhrmann's pastiche is at all moments a process of ceaseless interaction between elements. At times that interaction seems random; at other times, it seems that one element comments on another. No single element occupies a primary position for any length of time – each is dislodged in the following instant (Sarup 1993). *Moulin Rouge* may not be the ultimate postmodern text as it has a strong narrative line and themes do emerge. Yet *Moulin Rouge* is postmodern in that it 'ceaselessly reshuffles the fragments of preexistent texts, the building blocks of older cultural and social production, in some new and heightened bricolage' (Jameson 1992: 96). As a pastiche of musical and generic styles, *Moulin Rouge* can be admired as an inventive and witty film about surfaces: shimmering, enticing and bewitching. But the flip side is that it has no real depth, no lingering impact. The film's discontinuous preoccupation with the past precludes any sustained efforts to understand the present.

This absence of interest in the present can be explained as symptomatic of the rise of the social practice of pastiche. According to Jameson (1992), the shift from the period of modernism to the world of the postmodern can be charac-terised as one in which the alienation of the subject is displaced by its fragmentation. The new practice of pastiche has been brought about by the disappearance of the individual subject and the unavailability of unique and personal style. As exemplified in *Moulin Rouge*, pastiche suggests we wish to be recalled to times less problematic than our own. There seems to be a refusal to engage with the present or to think historically. Random 'cannibalisation' (Jameson 1992: 96) of past styles is the film's dominant technique, which high-lights Luhrmann's unwillingness to fashion a representation of current experiences.

Without drawing too long a bow, *Moulin Rouge* illuminates several characteris-tics of the material and cultural conditions that shape our lives and those of our students: fragmentation, superficiality and a failure to engage with the present. When we enter cyberspace, we leave the lived world of the present outside. The World Wide Web admits bits and parts of that world, but in a fragmented form. Those fragments are then ready for processing to be delivered back to the 'real' world. Cyberspace, the archetypal site of postmodern textual practices, feeds on fragmentation and superficiality – actively promoting the random cannibalisa-tion intrinsic to pastiche. Most significantly, cyberspace is becoming increasingly popular as a site for communication and interaction.

Directly connected to the process of fragmentation is a new kind of superfi-ciality, of flatness or depthlessness, a form of 'surface living' (Johnson-Eilola 1997), that for many is epitomised by the textual practices and rhetorics invited by the Web. As Johndan Johnson-Eilola (1997: 185) explains: 'We experience things not at depth but on the surface; not a slow accretion but an everything-all-at-once shout. We do not pass tales linearly, but experience them multiply, simultaneously, across global communication networks.'

There is an inclination, particularly among those more comfortable in a world framed by modernist values, to deride this way of experiencing life as superficial, artificial and dehumanising. Surface seems one-dimensional, empty, showy. Value is placed on depth, reflection, time to think. Of course, as Johnson-Eilola so eloquently argues, for survival and agency, people need to be able to negotiate both. However, if students are to learn how to alternate comfortably between the two, then frameworks for literacy education need to be reconceived to take account not only of the old cultural practices, but also of the new.

In his chapter, Michael Joyce confronts the pedagogical and curriculum chal-lenge of how to find purpose in surface, of how to make meaning and sense of the world in the active piecing together of the fragments of contiguous and contingent texts. He argues for a combination of approaches, informed by the study of rhetoric, with an emphasis on self-reflexive close readings of texts that revisit notions of the new kinds of authorship and literacy practices associated with hypertextual thinking. Similarly, Catherine Beavis suggests ways in which literacy educators can not only acknowledge the new kinds of texts and the ways in which students engage with them, but actually exploit them for educational purposes. And with the implicit aim of providing a strong theoretical basis for pedagogical and curriculum development, designed to ensure that students become informed, critical users of the Web, Nicholas Burbules extends our ways of thinking about hyperlinking and hyperreading. Clearly, literacy theorists and educators are not bereft of imaginative ideas to deal with the challenge.

Both fragmentation and superficiality – integral to pastiche – are significant cultural practices relevant to literacy education. Failure to engage with the present, however, is the practice most pertinent to my concerns in this chapter. By neglecting the present, *Moulin Rouge* highlights the importance of the capacity and will to understand the forces that shape our lives: figuring out the nature of those forces represents the first step in the process of engaging in some form of action to try to change what is less than desirable around us. We may well be happy for a film to disavow this imperative, but as literacy educators, we are obliged to continuously reassess, indeed creatively reinvent, our pedagogical and curriculum frameworks in light of this understanding so that we make sure we do not short-change our students. To prepare students to be productive and literate in the various trajectories of their future lives, however unknowable those futures might be, at the very least, we need to explore and subject to critique contemporary conditions and circumstances.

Beyond nostalgia: making sense of the present

To begin to make sense of the present, the cultural analyses of Zygmunt Bauman (2001) and Pierre Bourdieu (1998) have much to offer the field of literacy and technology studies. The very purpose of their work, which starts from social systems and the ways in which social practices are structured and regulated in contemporary circumstances, is to rearticulate the changing human condition as individuals struggle to invest their lives with purpose. They offer literacy educators insight into the ways in which silicon literacy practices are located within more general social practices and processes of change, how these practices are constituted in particular social institutions and how people's sense of personal identity is shaped by them.

According to Bauman (2001), a distinctive mark of contemporary living is an overwhelming feeling of uncertainty: the world is essentially 'undecidable, uncontrollable and hence frightening' (Bauman, 2001: 83). The message conveyed by the most effective cultural media is a message about 'the essential indeterminacy and softness of the world' (87). In this world, everything yet nothing can be done; human bonds are split into successive encounters; identities are split into successively worn masks; life is compartmentalised into a series of episodes. There is nothing that can be considered solid and reliable. The site, previously held by the state, from which any intervention or action on behalf of common interests could be undertaken, does not seem to exist. Interventions do take place but they are fragmented and discontinuous.

Bauman is concerned 'that the social individual gives way to the individualised society, where increasingly individualised individuals reign and reciprococity becomes a matter of "have a nice day"' (Beilharz 2001: 29). Some will see in Bauman's response to our predicament nothing but cultural pessimism, a longing for a world we have lost. But as Beilharz (2001: 29) explains, 'Bauman's sense is different ... the world as world is revealed to us only when things go wrong. To glimpse into the chaos is not a confession of human defeat or morbidity but a symbol of the challenge. For just as we are the peculiar animals, those who know that they will die, so do we know that we could live differently.'

What is needed, believes Bauman, is a communicative process about what it is that various groups have in common to find out what they need to regulate. Some sort of coordinated and concerted action is required. Bauman calls that action 'politics': 'the promotion of new and badly needed ethics for the new age can only be approached as a *political* issue and task' (93). Politics is required to fill the void that is densely populated by individuals speaking in many voices. 'The central issue of our times is how to reforge that polyphony into harmony and prevent it from degenerating into cacophony' (93–94).

Like Bauman, Bourdieu (1998) also argues that a hold on the present must precede any intention to transform it. However, the insecurity, the uncertainly, or what Bourdieu calls the 'precariousness' of the condition of contemporary women and men makes such a hold difficult to achieve. People have no control over the mysterious forces variously dubbed 'competitiveness', 'recession', 'rationalisation', 'fall in market demand' or 'downsizing'. Everyone is vulnerable and any social position, precarious. And the fear that is generated is diffused. As Bourdieu puts it, that fear 'pervades both the conscious and the unconscious mind'. '[B]y making the whole future uncertain ... [the state of precariousness] prevents all rational anticipation and, in particular, the basic belief and hope in the future that one needs in order to rebel, especially collectively, against present conditions, even the most intolerable' (Bourdieu 1998: 82).

But it is what Bourdieu calls the TINA creed (There Is No Alternative) that represents the most insidious of contemporary forces. This response to the world – a sense of helplessness, even hopelessness – is promoted particularly by the devotees of global free markets. TINA signifies the widely held belief that there is nothing individuals can do to halt undesirable social and cultural trends: these trends are immune to challenge. It is unfortunate that complicity with such forces, despite their capacity to amplify social divisions and inequalities, seems not only easier but is even perceived to be a viable option.

Both Bauman and Bourdieu point to the overwhelming feeling of losing a hold on the present that 'leads to a wilting of political will; to disbelief that anything sensible can be done collectively or that solidary action can make any radical change in the state of human affairs' (Bauman 2001: 53). However, as educators we have to believe that there are alternatives or else there is simply no point to existence. If one of the major aims of literacy education is to equip students with the capacity to invest their lives with sense and purpose, then the TINA position is intolerable.

By contrast, Gunther Kress (2000) is more concerned with anticipating the future and preparing students for effective participation in it. However, in arguing why it is important to rethink the relation of curriculum, its purposes and shape, to the social and economic environment of the future, Kress (2000) does describe the changes in the circumstances that characterise the present period. Rather than 'uncertainty' or 'precariousness', he chooses the term 'instability' to capture its essence. In Kress's view, tomorrow is unlikely to be like today and the day after tomorrow is definitely going to be unlike yesterday – the present period is marked by 'radical instability' (Kress 2000: 134).

According to Kress, a number of factors testify to the instability of the present. We are witnessing 'the dissolution of the frames which had held state for most of the preceding 100 years' (134). These include the frames around the institution of education, the site of education, the time of education, the educational audience, and educational knowledge. It also includes the frames between education as work and education as pleasure, between state and market, and between locations of authority. There are also the changing frames of the globalisation of finance capital, of transport, of commodities, of people and of information, as well as of a society being transformed from a monocultural to a pluricultural one.

Central to all these changes is the altering of the landscape of representation and communication. We are in the midst of a shift from an era of mass communication to an era of individuated communication; from unidirectional communication from a centre to the mass, to multidirectional communication from many locations; from the 'passive' audience to the 'interactive' audience. Clearly, these changes have direct and profound implications for literacy education – not just for the future, but also for the present.

Bauman calls it 'uncertainty'; Bourdieu, 'precariousness'; Kress, 'instability'. These three attempts to capture the present with a single marker have much in common: the world has changed and is continuing to change at an increasingly rapid rate. The world for which schools were formed no longer exists. Except for our inevitable death, the future is unknowable and unpredictable. However, while Kress concludes that we need to prepare students to adapt to a future governed by these conditions, both Bauman and Bourdieu suggest that improved modes of communication and collective action may serve to alter them so that the present – the world in which we and our students find ourselves – becomes more endurable.

In a world deeply affected by significant change and uncertainty, the enhancement of communication between individuals and among people needs to become central to the education project. A number of the contributors to this volume explore various facets of this issue. On the subject of intergenerational communication, Ron Burnett, Catherine Beavis and Doug Kellner suggest that teachers need to recognise the significance of popular culture, or else miss out on some of the most important elements in students' understanding of their own lives. There needs to be a shared understanding of culture. But there needs to be more than just a shared discourse; there also needs to be a common under-standing of communication. To achieve this requires a profound shift in the ways in which teachers and students interact within learning environments – both those in which technology is embedded as well as those in which technology is not the essential characteristic.

Raymond Williams' (1975) explanation of communication offers a solid foundation upon which to build new pedagogical and curriculum frameworks for literacy education. Like Bauman and Bourdieu, Williams is concerned with the place of the individual in society. He defines communication as 'the process of making unique experience into common experience' (38). Communication is to do with having the capacity to convey to others the nature of our unique experiences. We attempt to validate our experiences that embody our attitudes, needs and interests by making them clear to others. At the same time, the descriptions of experiences we receive from others embody their attitudes, needs and interests. Indeed, 'the long process of comparison and interaction is our vital associative life' (38). Most importantly, the process of communication involves the sharing of common meanings, activities and purposes; and the offering, reception and comparison of new meanings leads to the tensions and achievements of growth and change. In a similar vein, Bauman (2001) argues that an effective communication process establishes what it is that the various groups we belong to have in common. Through effective communication, we can work out what we need to regulate or to change about our current circum-stances.

Williams' explanation of the objective of effective communication continues to be highly relevant. Although the context has changed since *The Long Revolution* was published in 1961, as have the means of communication, we may still pursue this objective with alacrity: the challenge is to understand the nature of the changed conditions and to either adapt to them or to resist them. Any form of resistance, however, can only take place if there is understanding of the nature of the contemporary conditions in which we now operate.

Most importantly, the ideas of Zygmunt Bauman, Pierre Bourdieu, Gunther Kress and Raymond Williams provide us with new language for talking about communication. They offer literacy educators fresh vocabulary for discussing changing social and cultural realities. New language offers the means to reconsti-tute the grounds on which cultural and educational debates are to be waged. For the field of literacy and technology studies, a new language that will not be like past languages or models of discourse that have become in a sense standardised and authoritative – even in a self-conscious critical mode – is required to grasp the unfolding present and the place of enhanced communication and collective action within it.

Communication, imagination, critique

A central aim of effective literacy education in the electronic age is to provide students with opportunities to learn not only how to communicate more effectively, but also how to respond in critical and informed ways to the disintegration of conventional world views, world orders and social formations, a process mediated and accelerated by the availability of increasingly sophisticated electronic technologies. Literacy educators cannot be satisfied with merely identifying, describing and making familiar to students the new multimodal text types: this represents an increasingly inadequate response to the changes to literacy practices associated with the use of new technologies. We need to develop pedagogical and curriculum frameworks that seek to endow students with a sense of their place in the new global system, but also with the capacity to view that system critically. At the very least, we can help our students to engage in local forms of cultural critique.

In the literacy curricula that we design, specifically through the study of texts, both print and electronic, we need to think deeply about the ways in which we represent the past and the future, but in particular, the present. Students need opportunities to develop a critical consciousness of the world in which we live and to develop strategies for making it a better place through the study of texts that are increasingly mediated by the use of ICTs. Along with a sharp eye for critique, we must also look for a 'language of possibility' (Aronowitz and Giroux 1993: 149). Even dampened by the realisation that progress is not guaranteed, gaining a wider, deeper understanding of the world implies a belief in a meaningful future. If we didn't believe this, the education of our students would be futile.

Students need to be equipped with the tools to engage in acts of interpretation. They have to gain the means by which to understand their material and cultural experiences. And it is literacy education that provides a context to offer individual students the language for interpreting themselves and the world around them. In our classrooms we need to provide students with opportunities to deal with their experiences and learn to understand them at a conscious critical level. The literacy classroom has an important function because it provides discourses and opportunities for dealing with experiences by discussing them: through talk, students are able to interpret their experiences.

One way to achieve these objectives is for teachers to 'become agents of a new educational imagination' (Aronowitz 2000: 101). This entails the articulation of pedagogical and curriculum frameworks that give priority to imagination. The problem with pastiche is that it deprioritises the imagination: it borrows from the past, appropriating the products of other people's creativity. Through the study of language and literature, literacy educators need to imagine and devise frameworks that welcome the new without ignoring what is important from the past. These frameworks would build on the understanding that their knowledge foundation is always incomplete, always expanding; they would understand the popular culture base from which students are coming but also ensure that they have access to the Great Tradition; they would not submit to the commodification of knowledge or require 'usefulness' as a justification for inclusion. Most significantly, they would acknowledge the changing landscapes of representation and communication: the frameworks would build on understandings of silicon literacy practices that incorporate a range of communicational modes which are in use for particular situations and particular purposes; the frameworks would not privilege any one mode of representation over another.

Literacy educators have to devise pedagogical and curriculum frameworks that are inclusive, imaginative, critical and rigorous. To prepare students for life not work, they need to read the 'great books', the aesthetically outstanding in literature. But they also need opportunities to enjoy and examine popular texts such as *Moulin Rouge* – critically and intertextually. We have to design frameworks that offer students the tools to interrogate the past and the present, and to imagine a future through the critical study of language and literature. Literacy education needs to take account of the interrelated disciplines of literature, history, philosophy and the visual arts: these areas represent interconnected domains rather than separate disciplines.

In *The Long Revolution*, Williams (1975) describes people as learning, creating and communicating beings – and identifies participatory democracy as the only social organisation that can support unique individuals learning, communicating and controlling. Arguing along similar lines, in his essay, Douglas Kellner invokes John Dewey and his emphasis on the nexus between education and democracy. But we can't just see learning and communication as the conduit to change. 'The common prescription of education as the key to change, ignores the fact that the form and content of education are affected and in some cases determined by the actual systems of politics and economics – the political economy' (Williams 1975: 119). That is why it is so important to draw students' attention to the broader political and cultural context in which pedagogical and curriculum frameworks are situated. That is why it is important to develop students' capacities to communicate and to engage in the practice of critique but through pedagogical and curriculum frameworks infused with imagination.

References

Aronowitz, S. (2000) *The Knowledge Factory: Dismantling the Corporate University and Creating True Higher Learning*, Boston: Beacon Press.

Aronowitz, S. and Giroux, H. A. (1993) *Education Still Under Siege*, Westchester, CT: Bergin & Garvey.

Beilharz, P. (2001) 'When politics shrinks, economy rules', *The Australian Higher Education*, Wednesday 6 June, p. 29.

Bauman, Z. (2001) *The Individualized Society*, Malden, MA: Polity Press.

Bourdieu, P. (1998) *Acts of Resistance*, trans. R. Nice, Cambridge: Polity Press.

Johnson-Eilola, J. (1997) 'Living on the surface: learning in the age of global communication networks', in I. Snyder (ed.) *Page to Screen: Taking Literacy into the Electronic Era*. Sydney: Allen & Unwin and London: Routledge [1998], pp. 185–210.

Jameson, F. (1992) *Postmodernism or, the Cultural Logic of Late Capitalism*, London: Verso.

Kress, G. (2000) 'A curriculum for the future', *Cambridge Journal of Education* 30 (1): 133–145.

Lankshear, C. and Snyder, I. (2000) *Teachers and Technoliteracy: Managing Literacy, Technology and Learning in Schools*, Sydney: Allen & Unwin.

Luhrmann, B. (1992) *Strictly Ballroom*, Sydney: AFFC, Beyond Films, M&A Films and London: Rank Organisation.

—— (1996) *William Shakespeare's Romeo and Juliet*, Los Angeles: Twentieth Century Fox.

—— (2001) *Moulin Rouge*, Sydney: Twentieth Century Fox.

Martin, A. (2001) 'Moulin Rouge', *The Age*, 24 May, Today. Review, p. 5.

Sarup, M. (1993) *An Introductory Guide to Post-structuralism and Postmodernism*, Second edition. London: Harvester Wheatsheaf.

Snyder, I. (ed.) (1997) *Page to Screen: Taking Literacy into the Electronic Era*, Sydney and London: Allen & Unwin and Routledge [1998].

Williams, R. (1975) [1961] *The Long Revolution*, Westport, Connecticut: Greenwood Press.

INDEX